葛德石
近代中国考察档案文献汇编

2

张　雷　主编

学苑出版社

图书在版编目（CIP）数据

葛德石近代中国考察档案文献汇编．2 ／ 张雷主编．
—北京 ：学苑出版社，2014.7
ISBN 978-7-5077-4574-0

Ⅰ．①葛… Ⅱ．①张… Ⅲ．①历史地理－档案文献－汇编－中国－近代 Ⅳ．① K928.6

中国版本图书馆 CIP 数据核字 (2014) 第 159485 号

责任编辑：杨　雷　洪文雄
装帧设计：徐道会
出版发行：学苑出版社
社　　址：北京市丰台区南方庄 2 号院 1 号楼
邮政编码：100079
网　　址：www.book001.com
电子信箱：xueyuan@public.bta.net.cn
销售电话：010-67675512　67678944　67601101（邮购）
经　　销：新华书店
印 刷 厂：北京赛文印刷厂
开本尺寸：889×1194　1/16
印　　张：17
字　　数：300 千字
版　　次：2014 年 8 月北京第 1 版
印　　次：2014 年 8 月北京第 1 次印刷
定　　价：510.00 元

“我最热爱的是中国”

（总序）

唐晓峰

北京大学 历史地理研究中心

20世纪初年，有一些外国学者凭着强烈的学术意志，来到社会激变的中国。他们宣讲西方学术，探索中国问题，艰苦调查，著书立说，在中国近代学术发展中作出重要贡献。但是由于各种原因，他们之中的许多人都被我们忘掉了。美国大地理学家葛德石（G．B．Cressey）就是其中被忘掉的一位。

1923年，葛德石自欧洲启程，取道北方戈壁荒途来到中国，赴任上海沪江大学（英文名称为Shanghai College）地质与地理系教授，旋任该系主任，组建新式地学教育。他在1926年9月20日写给美国众朋友的公开信中说：“我一个学期要上四门课，总共十一学时，差不多有一百名学生。”“过去两年来，我主要致力于组建工作和安排讲座，从现在起，我应多做些研究了。”在1923年到1929年的六年里，他多次到中国各地进行地理考察，“旅行凡三万哩，除云南、四川、西康、新疆和福建外，足迹所至达二十余省”。当时的中国，军阀混战，社会无序，葛德石的地理考察，因“匪乱和内战，屡为阻障”。例如1926年，“我本想到内蒙古多做些工作，但由于战事而未果。我又打算对滦河做地质考察，此河从蒙古高原流下，至天津北部入海。工作本进展顺利，但到7月13日（不是星期五），我突遭五六个歹徒袭击，工作遂告中断”。

1926至1928年间，葛德石三次油印了一份关于中国地理的书稿。后将书稿完善，配以图表、照片，以 *The Geography of China*《中国地理》为名，交上海商务印书馆印刷。“1932 年即将出版时，逢日本侵入上海，底版被毁，所有图幅及照片全部损失。”此时，葛德石已经返美，在雪城大学（Syracuse University）任地质地理系主任。复经重事编纂，书稿再成，于 1934 年改在纽约出版，名为 *China's Geographic Foundation：A Survey of the Land and its People*（《中国的地理基础》）。

葛德石的书在美国出版后，在中国遂有反响，因受重视，“盗版”书不久问世。据侯仁之师回忆，1936 年先生于燕京大学留校任教，须讲授中国地理学，参考书以葛德石的著作最佳，但原版难求，只能找到非正式翻印的劣版。因一直喜爱此书，先生直到留英期间（40 年代后期），才在英岛购得原版（已然是第八次印刷版），当时的订购单与发票至今与书同为珍藏。

葛德石书原为英文，非正式的中文译本早便流传，且不止一种。直到 1945 年，此书总论部分（前六章）的中译本正式出版，译者是薛贻源，书名为《中国的地理基础》，由开明书店印行。薛氏在译序中说：“总论部分，译者于肄业师大地理系时，承系主任吾师黄海平先生的鼓励课外译读和训诲，即将初稿完成；去冬原著者葛德石教授代表美国国务院访华，于来所就任本所研究员时，得机面请教益，特将译文重加整理出版。”“至于分论部分，系由吾师谌稷如先生译出”，“定名为《中国区域地理》，将另行出版”。所谓分论部分，即第七至二十一章，均为区域地理，包括十五个大区：华北平原、黄土高原、山东辽东热河山地、满洲（东北）平原、满洲东部山脉、兴安岭、中亚草原与沙漠、中央山系、长江平原、四川红壤盆地、江南丘陵、东南沿海、两广丘陵、西南台地、西藏边陲。此分论部分于 1947 年由正中书局出版。

葛德石《中国的地理基础》一书的重要贡献之一，是采用了十五个自然区（见上）的划分方法。此前关于中国的地理著述，多利用已有的政区为区域框架。政区尽管分辨明确，易于指示，但于环境与经济方面，却相当混乱。葛德石指出，“一个农夫生活在河南或在山东的事实，其在地理上的意义，远不及他的农田是在肥沃的平原或在多石的山地。农民更关心的是谷物的适当雨量，而不是省会的名称”。所以对中国景观区域的划分，宜舍弃政治的界线，而依据环境与经济的特征。葛德石的十五区分法，早先在本书的沪江大学油印初稿中便已提出，正式出版时更臻完善。

不过，应该说，舍弃政治界线而取环境特征的中国区域划分方法，并不是自葛德石始，即使在洋人中，1908 年夏之时（L. Richard）的《中国坤舆详志》（*Comprehensive Geography of the Chinese Empire*）就已经用了自然区划法。所以准确地说，葛德石的贡献在于，他的划分更为合理，而其所合之理正是地理学中很要紧的一点，即人与地的关联性。

葛德石的书，以“人类的遗产”一节开篇，他写道：“中国人民生活的根基，深入到土地里面。细心耕种的田园，徒手收获的农作，以及土筑的屋舍，在显示着人与自然的密切联系。”葛德石的地理区域划分，以人地关系特征为指标，观察人如何“渲染”了大地，这最终体现为文化景观。重视文化景观，正是美国地理学的一大特色。一方面是理论传统的引导，另一方面可能产生于同工业化的美国景观的对照。葛德石在中国感受到人与环境的和谐完美：中国“文化景观的种种方面，曾经过了一次进化调和的广泛过程，几乎在每个地方，人们在很久以前，业已尽他所有的工具，来利用自然的富源了。……中国的人生活动已与自然环境完全相适应，我们应用生态植物学的名词，可称之为最理想的‘群落’。”这里，葛德石并非是空发议论，以他在中国“三万哩”的野外观察与情景体验，上述言语应是发自内心。

同样是因为野外考察，他常常发现旧有地理“文本”上的问题。例如在蒙古高原考察时他发现：“许多蒙古地图上都画了不少并不存在的城市，好像作图的人不愿意留出一大块空白的地区。另外，他们参考旅行者的记录，在地图上标满了地名。许多地名是河谷或牧场，也有一些只是井或者不重要的寺庙。其实城市仅仅分布在沙漠的边缘。有一次笔者来到一个地方，在一类标注已成规模的城镇的地图上，这个地方总要被标出来，但那不过是一个电报亭，只住着夫妻俩和一个孩子。还有一次，我用了好几天去找一座在最好的地图上指示的城市，可那座城市早在好几个世纪之前就被成吉思汗毁掉了。”

充分的考察体验与大量的文献整理，构成了写作《中国的地理基础》的基础。在总论中对中国地理形势的宏观把握，在分论中对十五个大区的贴近描述，令一个广袤大国的复杂地理呈现在不同的视野中。科学理性，使本书对中国的优点与劣点并举，在批评方面，并无忌讳。然而，与研究对象的亲近性，又令作者对他所描述的人文大地日渐生情。这是地理学的特点，也是地理学家的特点。我们注意到葛德石在“原序”中脱口而出的一句感慨：因为本书要冷静地对待中国的各方问题，“著者对中国的真诚的友谊，或已难为人知了。”

其实，葛德石“对中国的真诚的友谊”正溢于书表。书中对中国文明的赞美与对中国现代更新的信心，在在可见。葛德石所亲历的中国，正值内乱频发、外患不止的时代，但他在“理解中国”一节中却告诉读者：“目前是不足作为批判中国的代表时期。”“今日中国历史最重要的因素，不是报纸所通常报告的战争和饥馑。经济的、社会的和智力的改进，较之过去军事的和政治的演变，重要得多。中国变动得慢，对于她正有所觉悟的世界新秩序，做完满的适应，也许还需要数十年。而她的结局之为坚忍不拔，那是无可疑的。”

在后来的生活中，葛德石对中国的热爱之情，执著未减。他在雪城的住所，本是一座典型的洋房，却在门廊旁添立了两个中国式的红漆大柱。今天故人已去，但红柱在绿色小丘之间仍十分显眼。葛德石曾说：“中国所表现的艺术和生活的优美，似乎可于北平（北京）得之……住在北平一年，乃是一种世界的最精选的经验。”不知道他选立红漆大柱是否就是受了北京建筑景观的影响。

“二战”期间，葛德石曾任美国国务院驻华文化联络代表，居重庆，与中国地理学家常有来往，并被聘为中国地理研究所兼任研究员。1944 年，中国地理学会成立十周年，美国地理学家协会通过葛德石发来贺文，中国地理学会亦经葛德石回函致谢，信中讲，“葛德石是我们真诚的朋友，他在中国的不算长的时间里，已访过许多地方。他同中国的大多地理学家均有交往，并向我们详细介绍了美国地理学界的工作。”在信上署名的理事有胡焕庸（主席）、翁文灏、竺可桢、涂长望、张印堂、黄国璋、李旭旦（秘书长）等，这都是中国地理学界的泰斗。抗战胜利后，葛德石以个人的名义写了一封热情洋溢的致中国人民的长信，祝愿中国走出战争创痍，抓住历史新机，振兴民族事业。

1949 年春，在里斯本大会上葛德石当选为世界地理学会会长。4 月 7 日应英国著名历史地理学家达比（H.C. Darby）邀请，到利物浦大学做名为“中国的前途（China’s Prospects）”的公开演讲，演讲之后曾由侯仁之先生做答辞。那几天中令侯仁之先生最不能忘怀的是，演讲的第二天，葛德石又被邀做关于苏联的报告，当时葛德石正兼任苏联大地图集顾问，此报告为内部讲座，在报告之先，葛德石特意声明：我今天虽然讲的是苏联，但是“My first love is China（我最热爱的是中国）”。侯先生常常感慨，五十多年过去，这句话依然有声。

1952 年，因为在亚洲研究上的卓越贡献，葛德石被授予美国的戴维森勋章。戴维森勋章专为太平洋地区的地理研究而设，葛德石为获此奖项的第一人。1999 年，侯仁之先生为获此奖项的第六人。

1954 年 2 月 15 日，葛德石“以一个从事了三十来年亚洲研究的地理学家的身份”上书艾森豪威尔总统，就当时的美中关系，提出三点建议：一、台湾国民党没有希望再返回大陆，美国必须与共产党打交道。长远战略是将北京与莫斯科分别对待，莫斯科政治上可以影响中国，但要支持北京在经济上独立，不依赖苏联。这是需要的，也是可行的；二、在一年或多一点的时间以后，只要北京遵守最起码的外交礼仪和条约规定，美国就可以承认北京政权。实施程序可以是，先允许日本与北京贸易，然后美国逐渐同中国大陆直接贸易，在北京加入联合国的问题上美国不动用否决权，最后正式承认北京政权。与此同时，对美国公众做宣传教育。三、台湾问题。这是个很麻烦的问题，只要台北与北京都宣称自己代表中国，就不可能有解决办法。美国将继续支持蒋介石，但美国显然也要进行一些调整。

1954 年 3 月 12 日美国国务院助理国务卿 Walter Robertson 代表总统给葛德石回信，向他申述了美国政府的立场：美国毫无选择地要制裁中国的共产党政权，限制他们同自由世界的贸易，在政治上孤立他们。美国承认台湾的中华民国是中国的合法政权，在联合国代表中国。目前对共产党中国的任何缓和，都会增强他们军备的经济基础，使他们无虑地进攻邻国。承认共产党中国，接受他们在国际社会的合法性，无疑会提高他们的声望。另外，鉴于意识形态的联系与共同的利益，美国看不出在北京与莫斯科之间有任何分歧。美国目前的政策是，逼使北京向苏联索求苏联无法提供的援助，这样就会造成两者关系的紧张。

3 月 17 日葛德石立即给 Robertson 回信，再次申诉自己的观点。他说：我不赞成任何左派或右派的专权。我之所以给总统写信，是希望国际紧张局面能有缓和的一天。只要存在中华人民共和国愿意建立基本的外交关系的可能性，美国就应当有所准备。

用一句俗话说，真不知葛德石欠了我们中国什么，他竟如此“没完没了”地为中国操心。但是，对这样一位差不多半辈子把心放在中国的世界级的大学者，我们现在的中国人倒是太冷淡、太健忘了。回想 1987 年我在雪城大学过春节。晚会规模很大，有一位美国男子，虽不会讲中国话，却对中国人分外热情，跟每个中国人都打招呼，他必讲的一句话是：“My father is Cressey（我父亲是葛德石）。”但 Cressey 是何许人？是他的儿子又如何？他对于中国有什么特别之处？在场的中国人没有一个知道的。归国后，我到上海，找到沪江大学校友会，这个校友会办得很正规，有牌子，有联络处，有专人值守，工作应是很认真的。但是，我查遍了“在校任职外国人名单”，竟没有葛德石的名字。问工作人员，也没听说过。我也查过一些一九四九年以后的中文文献，只在 50 年代的《地理学报》上找到过一篇文章《葛德石反动地理学批判》，文中说：“在旧中国葛德石曾经挂着沪江大学‘教授’的招牌，干了多年的侦察工作。……葛德石巧于将这些反动观点，包藏在虚伪的关怀、同情与慰勉等好听的言辞当中，偷偷地进行毒害的宣传”，“华尔街走卒”葛德石“‘笑里藏刀’的暗害行为，实在较之公开的进攻更为可怕，更是可恨”。20世纪50年代以后，在中国书报很难见到葛德石的名字了。

如此看起来，是我们欠葛德石先生的太多了。问题是，像葛德石这样早年在中国治学，在内心植下对中国的热爱，在 20 世纪 50 年代的风潮中被当作帝国主义政治的陪绑，最后被中国新一代完全忘弃的外国学者，还有不少呢。

不过今日，葛德石的档案有幸被张雷发掘。张雷曾在北大随我读书，后就读于葛德石生前执教终生的美国雪城大学。寒暑几载，他得以遍览该校保存的六十箱葛德石档案，因感慨葛氏的贡献，惜其被埋没，决心在文函图件中重新发现葛德石，并将罕为人知的葛氏中国档案公布于世。档案分别以书信、考察报告、影像的门类编为三册，加上张雷自己撰写的评述葛德石与中国地理学之关系的专著一册，合为四册，一同付梓。

这套书籍，小而言之，是我们对葛德石的回报，是认识葛德石与中国地理学之关系的基础文本；大而言之，是解读近代地理学史以及中美关系史的重要文献，其意义也是不言而喻的。

2014 年 4 月 23 日 于北京五道口嘉园

注：本文最早发表于《读书》2003 年第 12 期，此处为序，略有增删。

总目录

第一卷

葛德石与中国近代地理学

第二卷

葛德石书信档案

葛德石

近代中国考察档案文献汇编

2

第二卷

葛德石书信档案

张 雷 主编

目 录

前 言

葛德石1923年来华至1950年与中国失去联系，在这近三十年中，葛德石与中国学者有着广泛而深刻的交往，而书信是其重要方式。葛德石档案中存有百余封有关中国的英文书信，多数为中国各界致葛德石的书信，而葛德石的回信则因为战乱等原因能保存下来的，极为罕见，因而葛德石档案中留存的给中国各界的来函则更显珍贵。本卷主要收集了葛德石档案中与中国各界人士和有关中国事宜的通信，共分为五大部分。根据书信的内容分类，以通讯所涉及人物顺序进行命名排列，而在每位人物通信中又以时间先后顺序进行编排。

第一部分是葛德石与中国地理学界通信录。1923年至1929年，葛德石第一次来华，主要接触的是留美地理学者，如竺可桢和黄国璋。1934年，葛德石《中国的地理基础》出版后声誉日隆，而中国地理学会也正式成立。与葛德石来往的学者增加了新近欧美留学生洪思齐、张印堂、涂长望等。1943年，功成名就的葛德石再次来华，与中国地理学界的胡焕庸、张其昀、李旭旦、林超、任美锷等学者均有来往。葛德石通过同行、同门以及师生等关系网络与中国地理学者保持互动，基本囊括民国三代地理学者，这是葛德石获取中国地理学术信息的重要途径，也是葛德石影响中国地理学的一种方式。

第二部分是葛德石与中国地质学界通信录。葛德石不仅以研究中国地理著名，而且与民国的地质学也有极深的渊源。20世纪20年代的中国，专职地理学者寥寥无几。葛德石的地质学背景使得他的交流对象首先是中国地质学会的地质学者。中国地质学会1922年创立于北京，它依托中国地质调查所，是民国时期中国最具有国际水准的学会之一。1924 年葛德石即成为中国地质学会为数不多的外籍会员之一，其来往的学者主要有翁文灏、李四光和葛利普等。

第三部分是葛德石与中国其他学者的通信往来。在中国地理学和地质学之外，葛德石与中国其他学界精英也有往来。其中包括胡适、朱家骅、王云五、刘大钧及陈裕光等，涵盖了中国学术界、教育界及出版界的精英。

第四部分是葛德石与沪江大学校长的通信录。沪江大学（Shanghai College）是 1906 年由美国南浸信会和北浸礼会在上海联合创办的教会大学，是民国时期中国十三所基督教会大学之一。葛德石在沪江大学创建地质地理系，并于 1924—1929 年间担任副教授兼系主任。葛德石与沪江大学前后两任校长魏馥兰和刘湛恩书信，反映葛德石创建经营沪江大学地质地理系的过程。

第五部分是葛德石致美国总统信函。葛德石在学术之外，还积极参与中美关系的建设。1935 年 葛德石致罗斯福总统的信与 1951 年葛德石致艾森豪威尔总统的信等都反映了一个地理学者对中美关系的认知和思考。

这些信函不仅反映了中国近代地理学界与国外的交往，是研究中国近代地理学史的重要文献；而且这些与中国学者交往的信函也是中外学术交流史和中外交流史的重要材料。例如：其与王云五先生的往来信函，对于了解中国近代出版业的编辑出版工作具有很好的参考价值。而与沪江大学校长的通信，则是研究近代大学教育的很好材料。葛德石致美国总统的信函则是中外关系史，特别是中美关系史研究一个值得参考的文献材料。为了便于各界研究使用这些文献材料，最大限度地呈现档案文献的原貌，书信以影印方式出版。遇有信函附有信封以及随寄的照片资料等也一并附于信文后，原则上信函内容不做修改或全文翻译。

第一章
葛德石与中国地理学界的通信

葛德石 1923 年来华至 1950 年与中国失去联系，在这近三十年中，葛德石与中国地理学者有着广泛的交往。1923 年至 1929 年，葛德石第一次来华，主要接触的是留美地理学者，如竺可桢和黄国璋。1934 年，葛德石《中国的地理基础》出版后声誉日隆，而中国地理学会也正式成立。葛德石来往学者又加入了欧美留学生洪思齐、张印堂、涂长望等。1943 年，功成名就的葛德石再次来华之后，与中国地理学界往来更加广泛。他与胡焕庸、张其昀、李旭旦、林超、任美锷等均有联系。葛德石的来往学者基本囊括民国三代地理学者。这些学者多有西方教育背景，从一个侧面反映了西方对中国近代地理学的影响。总之，葛德石通过同行，同门以及师生等关系网络与中国地理学者保持互动。这是葛德石获取中国地理学术信息的重要途径，也是葛德石影响中国地理学的一种方式。葛德石档案中所存书信，是研究中国现代地理学的珍贵史料。

（1）同行通信

竺可桢

竺可桢（1890–1974），字藕舫，浙江绍兴人，美国哈佛大学气象学博士，中国现代地理学奠基人。竺可桢 1920–1929 年任东南大学（后为中央大学）地学系主任，1929–1936 年任中央研究院气象研究所所长，1936–1949 年任浙江大学校长，一生从事学术和教育工作。葛德石与竺可桢来往始于 20 世纪 20 年代，因为两人都研究东亚气候，只是葛德石侧重地质时期，而竺可桢注重历史时期。两人共同参加了 1926 年太平洋学会东京年会。在《中国的地理基础》气候的部分，葛德石援引了许多竺可桢的研究。因此，竺可桢也是葛德石在前言感谢的两位中国学者之一。两人的通信跨越民国，持续至 20 世纪 50 年代初期。

國立浙江大學
NATIONAL UNIVERSITY OF CHEKIANG
HANGCHOW, CNINA

March 27, 1937

My dear Prof. Cressy,

I am glad to have your nice letter of February 19, 1937. With regard to a series of weather maps, illustrating the cyclonic development in China, my Assistants in Nanking wrote me that they were sent to you a few days ago. The Chinese government appointed me to be the President of The National University of Chekiang last April, but I do not particularly like the work, and hope to get back to the Institute of Meteorology in the near future.

Your visit to the Harvard University interests me very much. We received regularly the publications of Blue Hill Observatory, and hence were informed of the recent development over there. When next you go to Cambridge, I hope you will look up the splendid dragon and tablet which the Harvard Alumni in China dugged out from a Peiping grave and sent it to their alma mater as a gift for the Tercentenary celebration, and stands now proudly by the side of the Widner Library. This dragon may remind you of days in China.

With Best Wishes

Yours sincerely,

Coching Chu

Coching Chu

竺可桢致葛德石信（1937年3月27日）

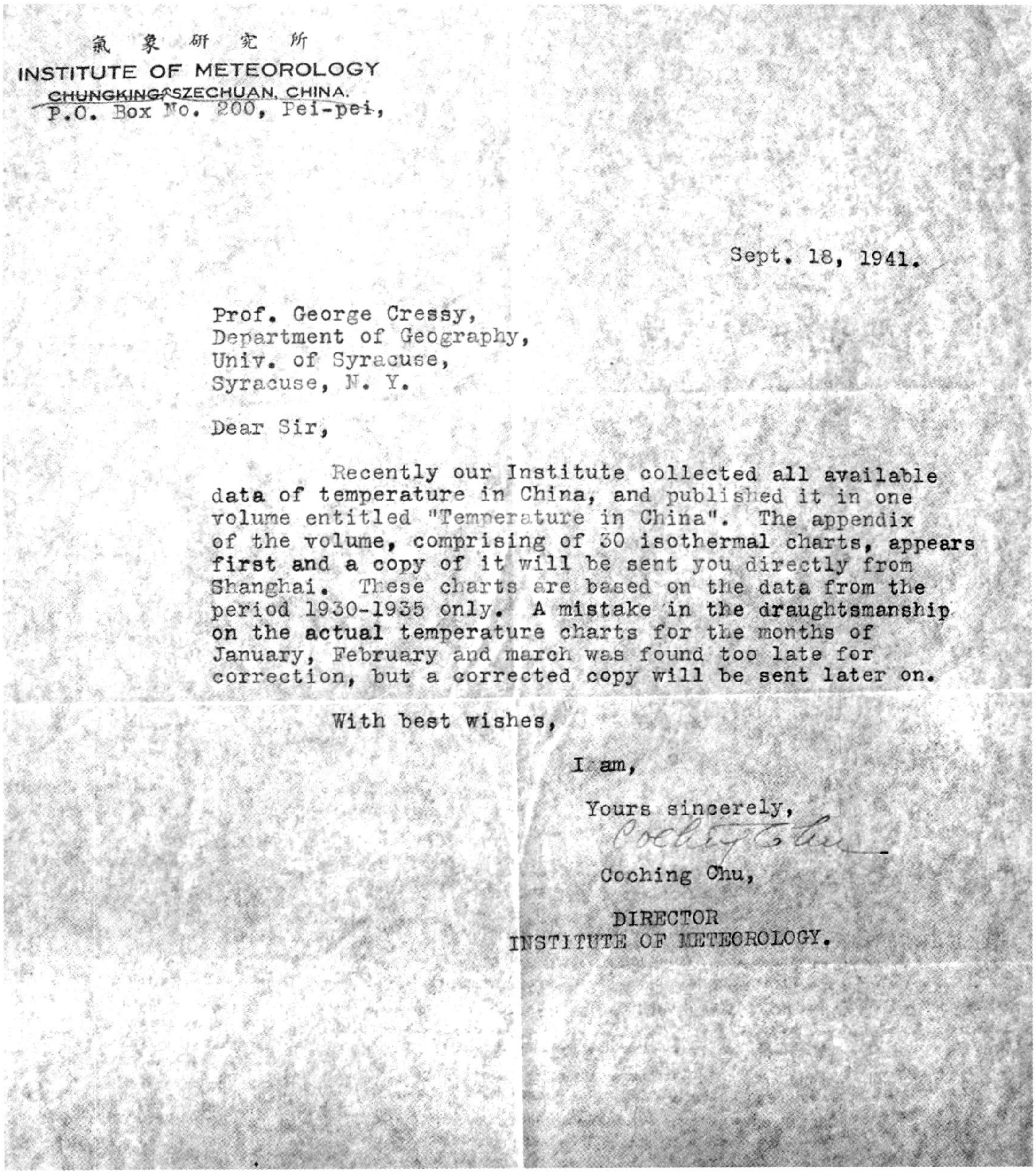

氣 象 研 究 所
INSTITUTE OF METEOROLOGY
~~CHUNGKING~~ SZECHUAN, CHINA.
P.O. Box No. 200, Pei-pei,

Sept. 18, 1941.

Prof. George Cressy,
Department of Geography,
Univ. of Syracuse,
Syracuse, N. Y.

Dear Sir,

Recently our Institute collected all available data of temperature in China, and published it in one volume entitled "Temperature in China". The appendix of the volume, comprising of 30 isothermal charts, appears first and a copy of it will be sent you directly from Shanghai. These charts are based on the data from the period 1930-1935 only. A mistake in the draughtsmanship on the actual temperature charts for the months of January, February and march was found too late for correction, but a corrected copy will be sent later on.

With best wishes,

I am,

Yours sincerely,

Coching Chu,

DIRECTOR
INSTITUTE OF METEOROLOGY.

竺可桢致葛德石信（1941 年 9 月 18 日）

NATIONAL CHEKIANG UNIVERSITY
HANGCHOW. CHINA

OFFICE OF THE PRESIDENT

April 2, 1948.

Prof. George B. Cressey,
Department of Georgraphy,
Syracuse University, N. Y. , U. S. A.

Dear Profdessor Cressey,

I am glad to have your airmail of March 22, asking my opinion about the effective way of handling American aid to China, and how can China best help herself. As you know I am a climatologist by profession, I am not very well versed on political questions. So you are really "enquiring a blind for the way-about" as we would say in Chinese. However, I will tell you frankly how I looked at these questions.

First of all, it seems to me that General George Marshall 's Mission to China two years ago was bound to be a failure, for the simple reason that when he was endeavoring to make the Chinese communist cooperate with K. M. T or the Central Government Party, U. S. and U. S. S. R were drifting further and further apart in the UNO. If your country can come to some kind of accord with the Soviet Russia in the international dealings, it will certainly have a tremendously effect on the possibility of the rapprochement between K.M.T. and the Communist in China.

We Chinese are looking toward U.S. for assistance, not only for such materials as food and ammunition, which you have supplied us in abundance in the past, but also for moral and intellectual leadership. The Chinese have a natural abhorrence for the doctrine of class warfare preached by Marx, or war among nations promoted by Hegel which latter theory will encourage power politics and eventually will lead to the World War Third. It is, therefore, to our great disappointment that events in the international field for the last year and half

竺可桢致葛德石信（1948 年 4 月 2 日）

NATIONAL CHEKIANG UNIVERSITY
HANGCHOW, CHINA

OFFICE OF THE PRESIDENT

and half have made the ~~curtain~~ iron curtain drawn tighter between the democ acy on the one hand,andthe communism on the other. Besides,the wavering of your foreign policy,as is made evident in your dealing with the Pa-lestine Partition, raise doubts in our mind. "Love Thy Enemy" has been a Christian creed. But it takes a Hindu, Mahatna Gandhi, to practise it. We all hope that you will have another Abraham Lincoln to be your next president in order to ride over this great crisis, and to save the world from destruction.

I am afraid I am not answering your questions. But in a long view, whether you give to China one million or ten billions in aid matter little. We need peace more urgently than anything, and we cannot have world peace if we play power politics as the big powerful nations playing now.

Yours Sincerely,

Coching Chu.

May 23, 1950

Dear Dr. Chu:

For some time I have been planning on coming to Asia next winter. I fortunately have a leave of absence from Syracuse, and a travel grant from the Social Science Research Council. At the same time, I recognize that this is a difficult time in which to visit China. I wish to be of any possible service to Chinese geographers and to learn what they have done in recent years. I should also like to reexamine the basis for geographic regions. It is possible that I may write a new book on Chinese geography.

I have research and writing which will keep me in Syracuse until December. I then plan to spend several months in Eastern Asia. If China is not open, I can at least learn a great deal in Hong Kong, but I hope that I may visit several University centers. I shall appreciate your advice as to how I may secure permission to travel in China.

You may be interested to know about the International Geographical Union, to which China was admitted at the Lisbon Congress in April 1949. Sessions of the Congress date back to 1870, and the XVII Congress is to be held in Washington in August 1952. Three dozen countries are now members. Last fall I visited several of the National Committees in Europe and in January and February of this year I flew to thirteen countries in Latin America. I shall again be in Europe in August when the Executive Committee meets in London. One purpose of my trip next winter will be to confer with geographers in Asia.

Part of the work of the Union between sessions of the Congress concerns our thirteen Commissions. We also publish two bibliographies and a Newsletter. Copies have been sent to the Institute of Geography in Nanking as the adhering body for China, but I have not heard whether they have been distributed. I have extra copies which I shall be glad to send you directly if necessary.

Sincerely yours,

George B. Cressey

Dr. Co-ching Chu
Chekiang National University
Hangchow
Chekiang
China

gbc:srb

葛德石致竺可桢信（1950 年 5 月 23 日）

September 28, 1950

Dear Dr. Chu:

The most interesting news in your letter of August 11 is that the Academia Sinica has taken over the Institute of Geography. I am sure that this is a wise change for it gives geography the same professional standing which is enjoyed by other sciences. Unless you indicate otherwise, we shall therefore list Academia Sinica as the official adhering agency for the International Geographical Union. In each country there is a formal adhering body, usually the chief Academy of Science. The Academy, in turn, appoints a representative National Committee of geographers with whom the Union carries on most of its work. Until I hear from you as to the Chairman of this Committee, I shall see that the correspondence is sent to you.

I regret that you have not seen the two Newsletters. I am sending copies by first class mail; please let me know when they arrive. We shall be happy to send you or the National Committee additional copies for all of the geographers in China without charge. Is there some address in Hong Kong through which they may be forwarded?

The International Geographical Union now includes 35 countries. The first Congress was held in 1870 and we all hope that China will be well represented in Washington in August 1952. I need not tell you that the Union is entirely without political connections. We are therefore free from the diplomatic problems which so unfortunately disturb the peace of the world.

As you have probably heard, the Congress in Lisbon fixed the dues for each country at $100.00 per unit. Our membership is divided into eight categories and each country is free to select the category under which it wishes to adhere. Those with a large number of geographers obviously choose the higher categories. I would hope that China would select category two or three, but the initiative is yours.

I still plan to spend several months in Hong Kong early in 1951, but will write you later as my plans develop.

Sincerely yours,

Dr. Coching Chu
3 Wen Ching Chieh
Peking
China

George B. Cressey

gbc:erb
cc: Dr. George H. T. Kimble

葛德石致竺可桢信（1950 年 9 月 28 日）

CABLE, SINACADEMY
ADD. 3 WEN CHING
CHIEH, PEKING
CHINA

中國科學院
АКАДЕМИЯ НАУК КИТАЯ
ACADEMIA SINICA
ACADÉMIE DES SCIENCES DE CHINE

電報掛號 2233
地址：北京文津街三號

30 December 1950

Prof. George B. Cressey
Department of Geography,
Syrocuse University, Syrocuse 10,
N.Y., U.S.A.

Dear Prof. Cressey,

I am glad to have your letter of September 28, 1950, and two newsletters of the International Geographical -Union, which reached me about a week ago. Owing to the present discordant international situation, it would be hard to say whether China can send any delegate to the 17th International Geographical Congress to be held in Washington in August 1952. However, we are seriously considering of sending a delegation to the forthcoming International Astronomical Congfess the coming August in Leningrad under the auspices of International Astronomical Union.

The world seems to be drifting farther and farther apart. It is the habit of a man of science to see things objectively and to report it in its truw light. I hope your prospective visit to Hongkong will make the Chinese Peoples' Republic better understood in America.

Yours sincerely

Coching Chu

P.S. This is the duplicate copy, the original was sent to Syracuse on 30 Dec. 1950 C.C.C.

Received 2/21/51

竺可桢致葛德石信（1950年12月30日）

Syracuse University

George B. Cressey
Maxwell Professor of Geography

Department of Geography
Syracuse 10, New York

August 31, 1956

Dear Dr. Chu:

I have recently returned from the XVIII International Geographical Congress held in Rio de Janeiro. Perhaps you know that I was President of the International Geographical Union at the Congress in Washington in 1952, and that I continued as a Vice President until the end of the Rio Congress. I am no longer a member of the Executive Committee so that this is purely a personal letter, written because of our long professional friendship.

Let me first explain the small difference between the Union and the Congress. The Union is the continuing organization, while the Congress meets every four years. Both are entirely professional and non-political. The International Geographical Union is made up of nearly fifty Academies or National Research Councils, and is administered by the General Assembly of the Union which meets during the Congress, and by an Executive Committee. The Congress is open to any geographer, without invitation, and is arranged by the National Committee (appointed by the adhering Academy) in the host country.

The Congress at Rio had 1006 geographers present. This included about 100 from the United States, some 40 from France, 11 from the Soviet Union, geographers from both East and West Germany, a good group from the countries of Eastern Europe, and so on. The next Congress will meet in Sweden in 1960. The new President of the Union is Dr. Hans Ahlman of Stockholm, and the new Secretary-Treasurer is Prof. Hans Boesch of the University of Zurich in Switzerland. May I repeat that both the Congress and the Union are open to all, regardless of political relations. We do not recognize countries as countries; the membership in the Union resides in the Academy or Research Council rather than the government. The Statutes provide no specifications for membership other than that the application come from a properly qualified body, and there is no way to exclude a member except for non payment of dues.

Since the Union desires to be of service to all geographers everywhere, I personally hope that the Academia Sinica of the People's Republic of China will wish to apply for membership. While only the General Assembly can formally admit a new member, it might be that the Executive Committee could take preliminary steps, such as supplying you with copies of the Newsletter and Commission reports.

You will remember that China was admitted to the Union at the Lisbon Congress in 1949. With the division of China and the emergence of two Academia Sinicas, the Union informed each that we had no political concern and that both were eligible to continue. No answer arrived from Peking, but Taipeh continued to pay dues and is still in good standing. Since Peking has not paid its dues, it has been regarded as dropped. If you apply for membership, it will in a sense be asking for reinstatement.

葛德石致竺可桢信（1956年8月31日）

-2-

As a preliminary step to joining the International Geographical Union, may I suggest that your Academia Sinica apply for membership in the International Council of Scientific Unions. I.C.S.U. is a federation of over a dozen International Unions, and is the top body in the field of international science. It is the sponsoring body for the International Geophysical Year and, like the I.G.U., is non political. The admission of the People's Republic of China into the International Geographical Union might be more logical if you were first admitted to the Council. The President of the Council is Dr. Lloyd Berkner, Associated Universities, Inc., 350 Fifth Avenue, New York 1; and the new Secretary is Sir Harold Spencer Jones, I.C.S.U., 29 Tavistock Square, London W.C.1, United Kingdom.

I enclose a copy of the Rio program, the latest Newsletter with the statutes, and the report of our Secretary-Treasurer.

Sincerely yours,

George B. Cressey

Dr. Coching Chu
Academia Sinica
3 Wen Ching Chieh
Peking
People's Republic of China

gbc:jf
enc.

胡焕庸

胡焕庸（1901—1998），字肖堂，江苏宜兴人，著名地理学家，竺可桢的高足之一。中央大学地理系教授兼系主任，著名“胡焕庸人口线”的提出者。1946 年，应美国马里兰大学地理系之聘，访学一年。现存与葛德石的通信一封，正是在此时期所写。

INTERNATIONAL HOUSE
1414 EAST FIFTY-NINTH STREET
CHICAGO

August 2, 1946

My dear Dr. Cressey:

I am grateful in receiving your letter of July 31. Thank you also for sending me the pamphlet of your Department.

Relating to the redivision of the Chinese provinces I have published several articles in Chinese. The reason why we want our provinces a little smaller is to make our administration much more efficient.

As most of our provinces are too large in area and also too populous we have an intermediate administrative level between the provincial government and the hsien government, which is called district or chu. We want to eliminate that chu government so we have to make the present provinces a little smaller.

When I was at Washington I prepared the Climatic Atlas of China which will be published in near future with the joint name of Unversity of Maryland and the Central University of Nanking. Herewith I send you a copy of the list of that atlases.

I may stay in the States for another year and I will be back next spring or next summer.

Yours very sincerely

Huangyong Hu

胡焕庸致葛德石信（1946 年 8 月 2 日）

张其昀

张其昀（1901–1985），字晓峰，浙江鄞县人，著名地理学家，竺可桢的高足之一。1927 年起执教中央大学地理系，1936 年受聘浙江大学史地系教授兼主任，1943 年受美国国务院之邀，在哈佛大学访学一年。张其昀与葛德石通信现存两封，但其中一封并不是专门写给葛德石的，而是类似于群发。

Dr. Cressey- Could you reply please? LWB

NATIONAL CHEKIANG UNIVERSITY
HANGCHOW, CHINA

Geographical Institute
Faculty of Arts
Nov. 6, 1947

Dear Mr. President;

The Geographical Research Institute of the Faculty of Arts, National Chekiang University, was founded recently by the instruction of the Ministry of Education with two specified purposes: to provide facilities of advanced study for postgraduate students; and to edit geographical publications in which our emphasis is laid on the promotion of real international understanding. We shall be much obliged if your University will aid and facilitate our work by supplying us, now and then, with books, magazines, maps, and other publications relating to our work. We know that a good deal of the valuable reference sources must be obtained through official channels, instead of from the ordinary publishing firms, by the ordinary means of pecuniary exchange. We are therefore applying to you in the hope that you will give us sympathy and assistance.

Our receipt of the aforesaid source materials, the staff and students of our Institure will utilize them to undertake research work along the following lines:

(1) The compilation, at regular intervals, of index, glossary and bibliography, based on the materials received. Copies of these will be distributed to different universities, educational and research institutions in China.
(2) The holding of exhibition of pictures, photographs, pamphlets magazines books, etc. illustrative of the life and the manners of the people of the United Nations.
(3) The writing of book reviews, comments, the translation either complete of in excerpts for inclusion in learned journals or for publication, in a serial form, in magazines and newspapers, for the purpose of arousing public interest in the Unites Nations.

We sincerely hope that this project will call forth an enthusiastic response and active cooperation on your part, and shall appreciate very much if you will furnish us with maps, charts, atlas, photographs, films, models, specimens, books, magazines, year-books or other relevant source materials which you can spare and which in your opinion will be serviceable to us. In appreciation of your kindness we shall send to you our publications at frequent intervals. Hoping that this cooperation between us will lead to substatial contribution and beneficial results.

I am,

Yours very sincerely

Chi-yun Chang

Chi-yun Chang
(Chairman of the Geographical Research Institute, Dean of the Faculty of Arts)

RECEIVED
DEC 5 1947
CHANCELLOR'S OFFICE

张其昀致雪城大学转葛德石信（1947 年 11 月 6 日）

卅

Prof. Chang Chi-yun
11 Chung Shan Rd. South
Taipeh, Taiwan (Formosa)
China, Feb. 15, 1951

Prof. George B. Cressey
C/O Department of Geography
University of Hong Kong
Hong Kong

Dear Prof. Cressey:—

It really makes me regretful to have left your letter unanswered for several days owing to the labouring of present work. I am very happy to know that you have come back to the East for a more penetrating and wider study of your subject and you are working out a plan for attaining the purpose.

As you are going to continue your studies on Chinese geography, I think it will be useful and necessary to make a fact-finding tour to this island. To my knowledge, there will be little difficulties in travelling to Tainan if you get the visa for your passport through formal diplomatic channel. Formosa is now, as it was, as stabilised as any part of the world which keeps the Communist aggression far from it. If you decide to make arragement for travelling to Taiwan, I will, of course, do what I can for you.

Since the Nationalist Party made a sweeping change for its organisation last autumn, the Central Executive Committee, the supreme policy-making body of Kuomintang, was replaced by the Central Reform Committee of which I was nominated as the Secretary-General. This position, naturally, makes hardly free to do my personal affairs. My son is now studing at Clark University, Worcester. As to Mr. Lin Yu-tang's address, I am not sure to know exactly. It is better if you will an inquiry to the Institute of Pacific Relations, 1 East 54th Street, New York, N.Y.

Very faithfully yours,

Chang Chi-yun

张其昀致葛德石信（1951 年 2 月 15 日）

张印堂

张印堂（1903–1991），山东泰安人，1929 年毕业于英国利物浦大学地理系，师从罗士培，获得地理学硕士。1933 年执教清华大学地学系，1938 年张印堂出任西南联合大学地质地理气象学系教授兼地理组组长。他在人口地理与边疆地理都有较深研究，与葛德石在三十年代初结识。抗战期间主持葛德石《亚洲地与人》一书的中文翻译。

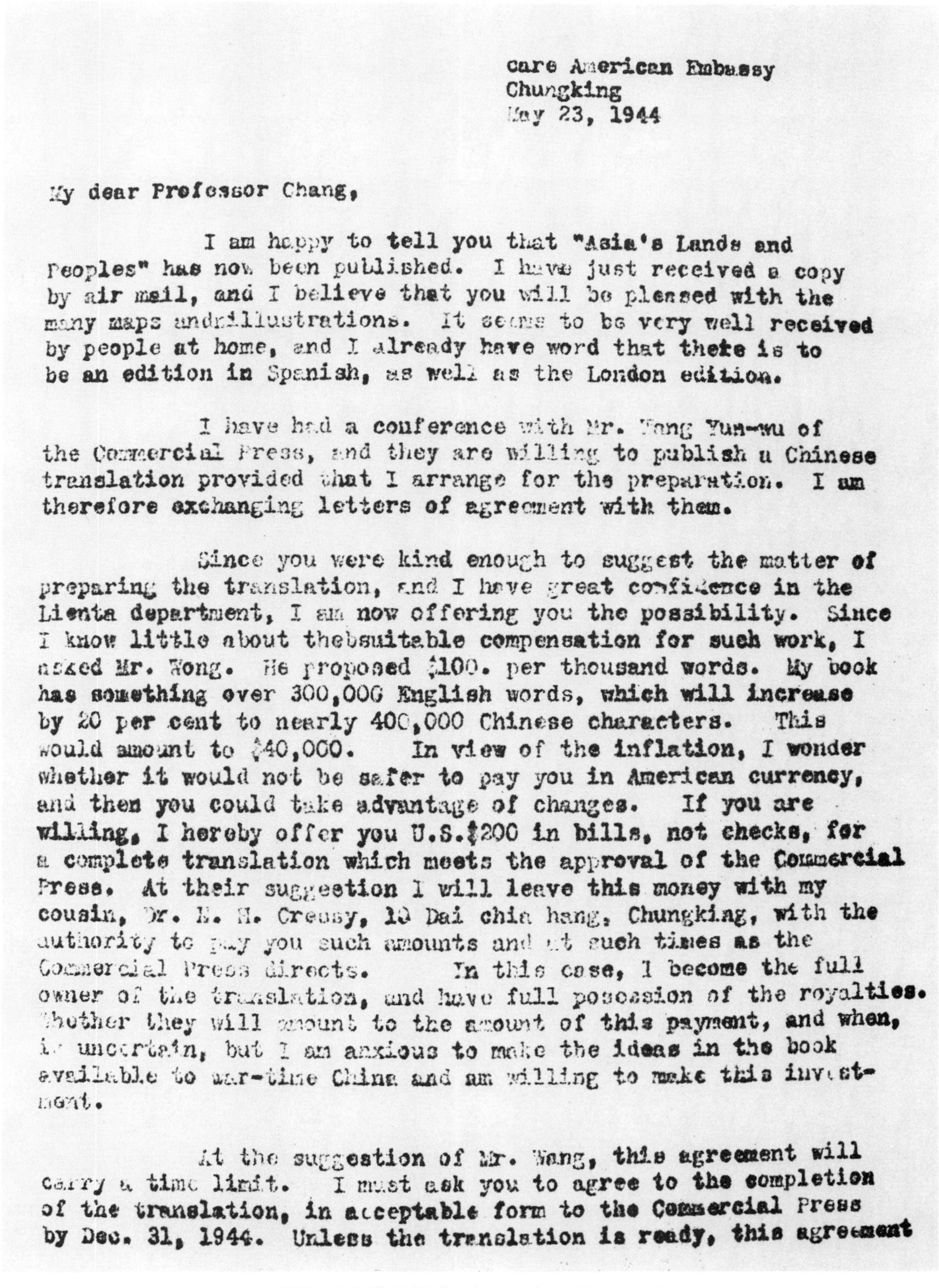

care American Embassy
Chungking
May 23, 1944

My dear Professor Chang,

I am happy to tell you that "Asia's Lands and Peoples" has now been published. I have just received a copy by air mail, and I believe that you will be pleased with the many maps and illustrations. It seems to be very well received by people at home, and I already have word that there is to be an edition in Spanish, as well as the London edition.

I have had a conference with Mr. Wang Yun-wu of the Commercial Press, and they are willing to publish a Chinese translation provided that I arrange for the preparation. I am therefore exchanging letters of agreement with them.

Since you were kind enough to suggest the matter of preparing the translation, and I have great confidence in the Lienta department, I am now offering you the possibility. Since I know little about the suitable compensation for such work, I asked Mr. Wong. He proposed $100. per thousand words. My book has something over 300,000 English words, which will increase by 20 per cent to nearly 400,000 Chinese characters. This would amount to $40,000. In view of the inflation, I wonder whether it would not be safer to pay you in American currency, and then you could take advantage of changes. If you are willing, I hereby offer you U.S.$200 in bills, not checks, for a complete translation which meets the approval of the Commercial Press. At their suggestion I will leave this money with my cousin, Dr. E. H. Cressy, 10 Dai chia hang, Chungking, with the authority to pay you such amounts and at such times as the Commercial Press directs. In this case, I become the full owner of the translation, and have full possession of the royalties. Whether they will amount to the amount of this payment, and when, is uncertain, but I am anxious to make the ideas in the book available to war-time China and am willing to make this investment.

At the suggestion of Mr. Wang, this agreement will carry a time limit. I must ask you to agree to the completion of the translation, in acceptable form to the Commercial Press by Dec. 31, 1944. Unless the translation is ready, this agreement

葛德石致张印堂信（1944 年 5 月 23 日）

becomes void. It must also be agreed that copy will be submitted monthly, in approximately equal installments. The Commercial Press will then authorize Dr. Earl Cressy, as my agent, to advance such payments as they believe suitable. It is also understood that the copy for this book, like all others, must pass the Chinese censor, and this contract is conditioned upon their approval of publication.

Because of war-time conditions, the Commercial Press will be unable to include the half tones, but they will reproduce the maps. I will supply an preface, so that this will be the authorized translation. I also understand from Mr. Wang that they will be able to actually publish the book within a reasonably short time after the manuscript is ready. Since the material is of interest for reconstruction, I hope that your copy may be ready much earlier than next winter.

Asia's Lands and Peoples represents five years of concentrated writing on my part, plus two decades of travel and research. It thus represents a sizeable part of my life. A very large amount of money has gone into it, but I have been glad to do so as a contribution to geography and to Asia. This is not the kind of a book that makes money, it is a "labor of love". I hope therefore that you will also undertake the translation with equal devotion. You may feel free to say so if you feel that U.S.$200 is not enough for the work, but this kind of work can not be a money making job for either of us.

I shall be returning to America within a few weeks, so I hope that you will reply immediately by air mail in order that we may clear up any details. When I send you a copy of the book, I must ask you to agree that it will not be used for any other translation that this one.

Give my kind regards to all of your associates.

Sincerely yours,

George B. Cressey

Professor Chang Yin-tang
Department of Geography
Lienta University, Kunming

carbon copies to
Mr. Y. W. Wang and Dr. E. H. Cressy

Dept. of Geography,
Lianta. Kunming.
May 28th 1944.

Dear Prof. Cressey,

Thanks for the nice letter of the 23rd. instant, I am very much pleased in hearing that your long-expected book on "Asia's Land and Peoples" has been published and sent to you now. I am sure we geographers are all proud of your two decades hard work on it. It represents not only the result of your labor of love of research, it is also a great contribution in the field of contemporary geographical work especially towards the rebuilding up of post-war Asia. I will be more deeply interested in reading the book with all your carefully selected maps and illustrations than my last mere glance of the proof of it, while you were with us in Kunming.

As to the general arrangement of the work of translating the book into Chinese and submit it for publication by the Commercial Press in Chungking, I do agree with it. However, I still have few points which I would like to draw your attention to and wait for your approval.

1. To safeguard your royalty of the copyright of the translation you arranged directly with us or anybody else, you must either notify the Chinese censor Committee to not allow any other's for publication or strictly limit the distribution of the book in English verse in China within the period of translation; otherwise no body can stop other people to translate and get it published by other printing press and the pirated translation maybe even to catch an earlier market.

2. The translation work will be chiefly done by the assistants under my supervision.

3. If you object the assistants name to appear on the outface, you must say so, but I do suggest to mention all the names helping the work in a commentary preface which I will add in for you.

4. The amount of compensation for the work suggested by Mr. Wang is fair enough for the mere translation

张印堂致葛德石信（1944 年 5 月 28 日）

2.

of the words - considered in Chungking, but if locked from the cost of living in Kunming, it does not mean much, for as you know, the purchasing power of $40,000 N.C. in Kunming now is equivalent only to $40. the value before the war. As you said, neither the Author nor the translator can make any money out of the work of a book as such, we accept Mr. Wang's suggestion and your thoughtful consideration to pay in term of American notes, so to avoid any further inflation in Chinese currency, but as you know the exchange rate of one American dollar is only $160. N.C. on the black market now in Kunming. Therefore the $40,000 N.C. would mean $250.00 in American notes instead of $200.00, that will be just enough for the translation of 400,000 words at $100 per 1,000 words.

5. Besides mere translation, as you know for reproducing the illustrations, tables and maps even without the half tones from English into Chinese it is not only a tedious work, but quite a costly one too, especially at the present moment. So I would suggest you to add another $100.00 Am. for drawings and to cover the expenses of tracing paper, etc.

6. Provided the above modifications are acceptable the translation manuscript will be mailed to Mr. Wang of the commercial Press, in three lots, at the end of August, October and December of this year. Your cousin Dr. E. Cressey will remit us the payment in three allotments at $150.00 $100.00 $100.00 after being informed by Mr. Wang in the receipt of each lot of manuscript respectively.

7- If the above terms do not suit you, I would suggest you to arrange the work of translation with Mr. K.C. Huang to get it done by the Chinese Geographical Institute, under his supervision it may be a little cheaper, for the cost of living in Szechuan is not so high as in Kunming.

3.

8- If you want to save money and bother you need not care about the matter of translation and the royalties of it - it will be translated somehow by somebody, and printed by some publishers - for some firms and somebody live upon such work!

I am sorry to hear that you are leaving China so soon. I hope you have enjoyed your visit of Kunming, if not all your tour in China this time. My book on the Eco. Geog. of Western Yunnan has been just published too. It is in Chinese with 100.000 words. In this publication only sketches and tables are inserted, while all the other details' maps and snaps are left out on account of the war and the difficulty of printing. I intend to rewrite it out in English as a Geography of Yunnan and get it published either in the U.S. or England, if the war does not finish within two years time

Herein I send you a copy of the reprint of a summary of it which appeared in the "Geography" 1942.

With All best regards from the Family

Yours Sincerely

Chang Yin-Tang

Chang Yin T'ang.

To Dr. George B. Cressey
C/O American Embassy
CHUNGKING.

AIR MAIL

care American Embassy
Chungking
June 3, 1944

My dear Chang,

I greatly appreciate your letter of May 28th with its willingness to translate "Asia's Lands and Peoples". I will take up your items one by one.

Six copies of the book are on the way, and I will put a note in each one that I have arranged for a translation to be published by the Commercial Press, and also ask them not to permit any translation from their copy for a year. It is obviously important for you to have your translation ready as soon as possible, otherwise I have no protection.

I recognize that most of the translating work will be done by your assistants, under your direction. Since I have taken great pains to write in good English, I am anxious to have a polished Chinese version.

I should be gladcto have the names of all translators appear, in whatever way you wish. Since, however, I am the author it is only proper that my name be in a different category. I believe that you know my Chinese name.

In view of the greater expense in Kunming, I shall be glad to increase the compensation to U. S. $250. I am leaving the bills with Mr. E. H. Cressy, 10 Dai chia hang, and he will pay you the money at such times and in such amounts as The Commercial Press may direct. I am sure you will recognize that at this price it is doubtful whether I will get my money back, much less make a profit for some years. I shall therefore expect both a superior job and early completion.

Mr. Wang of the Commercial Press has agreed to repro.uce a few of the maps, but none of the photographs. Since the ma.s have very few English words on them, they will not need to be redrawn.

I am sending you at once the galley proof, and ~~within~~ as soon as the bound volumes arrive, you will have a copy of that also. I will likewise supply the Commercial Press with a copy.

If you need to reply to this letter, it will either reach me here or be forwarded. It is possible that the American Consulate in Kunming, or A.P.O., will be able to send letters to me for you during the summer while I am still a Department of State employee. After that my address will be Syracuse

葛德石致张印堂信（1944 年 6 月 3 日）

Prof. Chang Yin-tang 2 June 3, 1944

University, Syracuse, New York

So much for the translation business, and I want you to know that I greatly appreciate your willingness to cooperate. Several others have asked for the opportunity, but I am confident that you and the people at Lienta will do a superior job. Do not hesitate to write me about any details. I assume that you will also have to fead proof. I should also add that the bibliography will be omitted from the Chinese edition. There should of course be mention of the original book in English, with its illustrations etc.

I am today sending you two packages of magazines for the departmental library. Perhaps you have them already, if so I will let ypu decide on their best use.

It now looks as though I shall go home via Tihwa, for I have secured a Soviet vise for Alma Ata, Tashkent and Baku. It will be a great trip, but the only catch is that I am not sure about air passge from here to Tihwa. I rather expect to get away in a week or two; if not I shall travel through India.

Best wishes, and my regards to all the others in the department.

Sincerely yours,

George B. Cressey

Prof. Chang Yin-tang
Lienta
Kunming

copy to The Commercial Press
E. H. Cressey

國立清華大學
NATIONAL TSING HUA UNIVERSITY
PEIPING, CHINA.

April 22, 1948.

Dear Dr. Creasey,

I am glad to have your letter of the 20th. of March and interested to hear that you are deeply concerned that the United States act wisely in our present world. Judging from the recent world political development, I must say that the determined attitude of the United States and Britain towards the U.S.S.R. regarding the Berlin issue and the proposed return of Trieste to Italy certainly has put up a check to Russia's feeling around in her underhand aggression to Europe. Of course this alone can't stop the advance of Russian imperialism. However the polling result in Italy means something. It is very unfortunate that the whole world is divided so clearly everywhere and the people think so differently; it seems that the two extremes will never meet in harmony. Personally I believe in individual freedom and that liberal democracy will eventually win over totalitarianism. I simply can't tolerate the way of underhand dealings and the horrible destruction as well as the social chaos and the threatening by terrorism caused by the communists especially in our part of the world. I am glad to know that the people as a whole and the government of the U.S.A have realised the danger that the communists have cast over to humanity. Of course we want peace and order as well as freedom of thinking and from wants which are essential and precious to human progress and world civilization. The U.S.A. being the leading power of the present world, should take up the responsibility honourably and boldly in protecting world peace and order and safe guarding the security of the relatively poor and weak nations and guide them wisely on to the highway of prosperity. As to the recent development in China, I quite acknowledge that conditions are far from being satisfactory and sometimes disappointing, but I am equally convinced that a nation like China with such old traditions, a country so vast in area with such a multitude of peoples of whom most are still in a primitive state of life and with no education whatever, progress of any kind especially in the sense of western liberal democracy will take time and need patience and sympathy. Any drastic change will be in favour of totalitarianism, a turn from bad to worse. The trouble in China just like Italy, Greece and Korea, is not merely an internal strife, it is the prelude of an open global war between the two blocks, communistic totalitarianism and liberal democracy, which are opposing each other in every respect all over the world. As you have mentioned in your Asia's Land and Peoples, China will have her share and geographically she is a consolidating factor especially over the so-called Far East. Certainly she bears some weight in the balance of the two worlds. Surely your government has seen the importance of this nature. We appreciate your sympathy and help and the co-operation between our two nations won't be in vain. This is only a friendly personal talk, I would like to have your opinions.

Mr. Shen-en Hu was one of our students, he graduated from the Geography section of our department in 1937 at Kunming. Then he took his post graduate work in Chekiang University at Kuei-yang. He went to the States on his own during the war. I believe he has been studying at Berkeley under Dr. Sauer all the time. He may have been handicapped in a way by his not very good English. From the point of the need of Geography teaching in China at present, I would like to see them back to do some service to their own country. I don't know much of his recent work in California. He was a mediocre when he was with us. However if you have vacancies you can try him. As I mentioned before we have some more brilliant graduates who have served for some years in teaching but simply haven't got the chance of going abroad for advanced studies. If you can give one or two scholarships to.

pto.

张印堂致葛德石信（1948 年 4 月 22 日）

for me to introduce one or two really qualified ones to you, I shall be much obliged and it will be a great help to the development of Geography in China. Here I am sending you the past records of one of them for your approval. You may like to hear that Prof. Trewartha of Wisconsin has expressed his willingness to come to us as a visiting Professor under the Fulbright Act, next year provided political conditions over north China permits him. He may have to delay for another year, I haven't got his last word yet. I am glad to hear that you hope to visit China again within 2 or 3 years. I hope you will be able to come to Tsing Hua under the Fulbright Act some day after Prof. Trewartha. Our present government pay does not allow us to extend our wish to invite any foreign professor to come to teach unless there is some other subsidies. However let us hope that things will become better soon in China.

With best wishes from the family,

Yours very sincerely,

Y. T. Chang

Chang Yin T'ang,

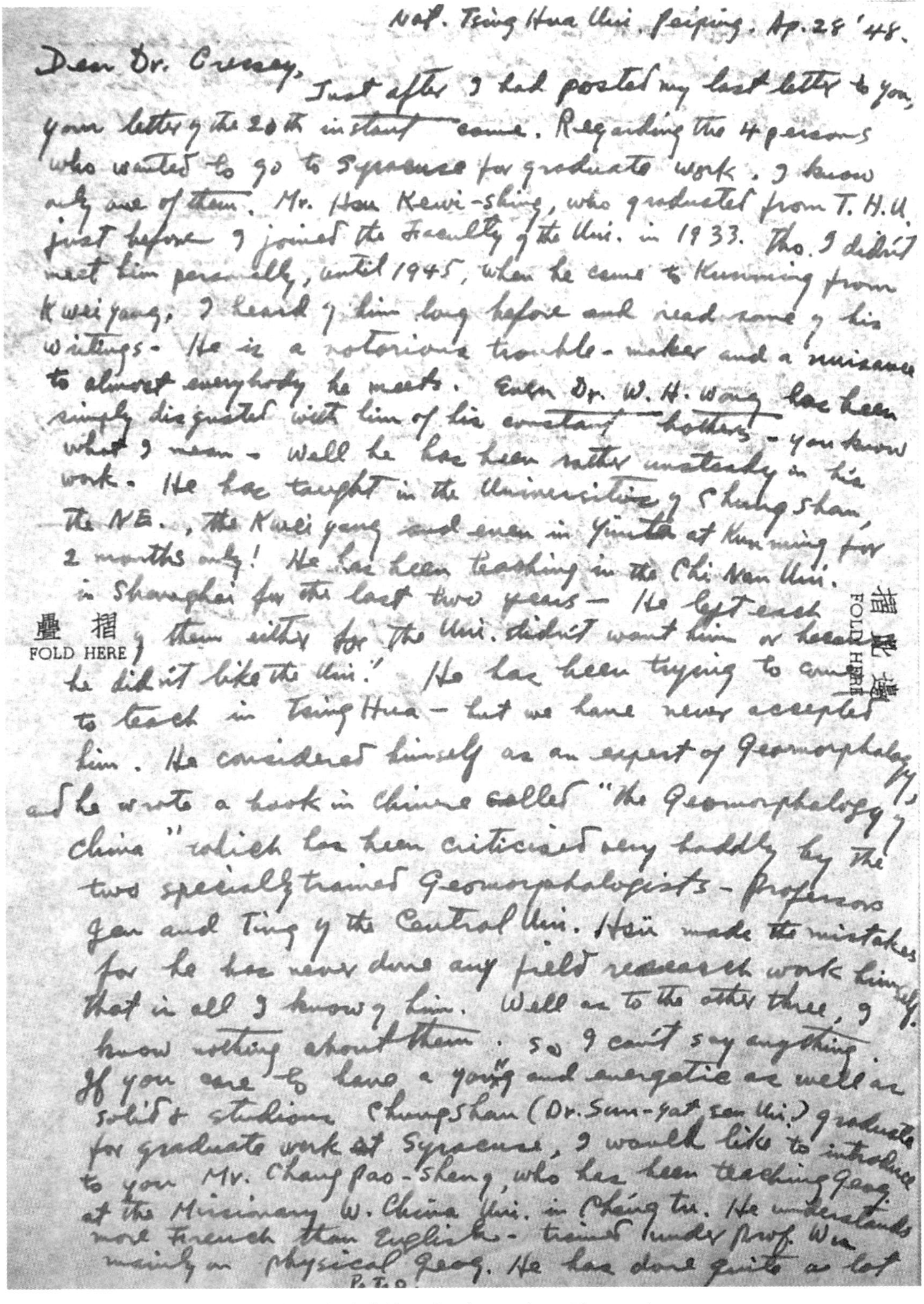

Nat. Tsing Hua Uni. Peiping. Ap. 28 '48.

Dear Dr. Cressey,

Just after I had posted my last letter to you, your letter of the 20th instant came. Regarding the 4 persons who wanted to go to Syracuse for graduate work, I know only one of them. Mr. Hsu Kewi-shing, who graduated from T. H. U just before I joined the Faculty of the Uni. in 1933. Tho. I didn't meet him personally, until 1945, when he came to Kunming from Kweiyang, I heard of him long before and read some of his writings. He is a notorious trouble-maker and a nuisance to almost everybody he meets. Even Dr. W. H. Wong has been simply disgusted with him of his constant bothers - you know what I mean. Well he has been rather unsteady in his work. He has taught in the Universities of Chungshan, the NE., the Kweiyang and even in Yunta at Kunming for 2 months only! He has been teaching in the Chi Nan Uni. in Shanghai for the last two years. He left each of them either for the Uni. didn't want him or because he didn't like the Uni.! He has been trying to come to teach in Tsing Hua - but we have never accepted him. He considered himself as an expert of Geomorphology and he wrote a book in Chinese called "the Geomorphology of China" which has been criticised very baddly by the two specially trained Geomorphologists - professors Jen and Ting of the Central Uni. Hsü made the mistakes for he has never done any field research work himself. That is all I know of him. Well as to the other three, I know nothing about them. So I can't say anything.

If you care to have a young and energetic as well as solid & studious Chungshan (Dr. Sun-yat sen Uni.) graduate for graduate work at Syracuse, I would like to introduce to you Mr. Chang Pao-sheng, who has been teaching Geog. at the Missionary W. China Uni. in Cheng tu. He understands more French than English - trained under Prof. Wu mainly in physical Geog. He has done quite a lot

P. T. O.

摺 疊
FOLD HERE

摺 疊
FOLD HERE

张印堂致葛德石信（1948 年 4 月 28 日）

of field work in N. Kwangtung and Szechuan — especially on the Chengtu plain and the region near the Kwan Hsien irrigation work. He wanted to have a chance of going abroad to do some advanced work in Geog. Besides the Mr. Tsou whom I mentioned in my last letter to you, if you can grant this Mr. Chang a scholarship, I am sure it will be a great help to the teaching of Geog. in the West China Univ. Well so much for this letter —

With kindest regards to you and your family from the Changs —

Yours very sincerely,

Gintang.

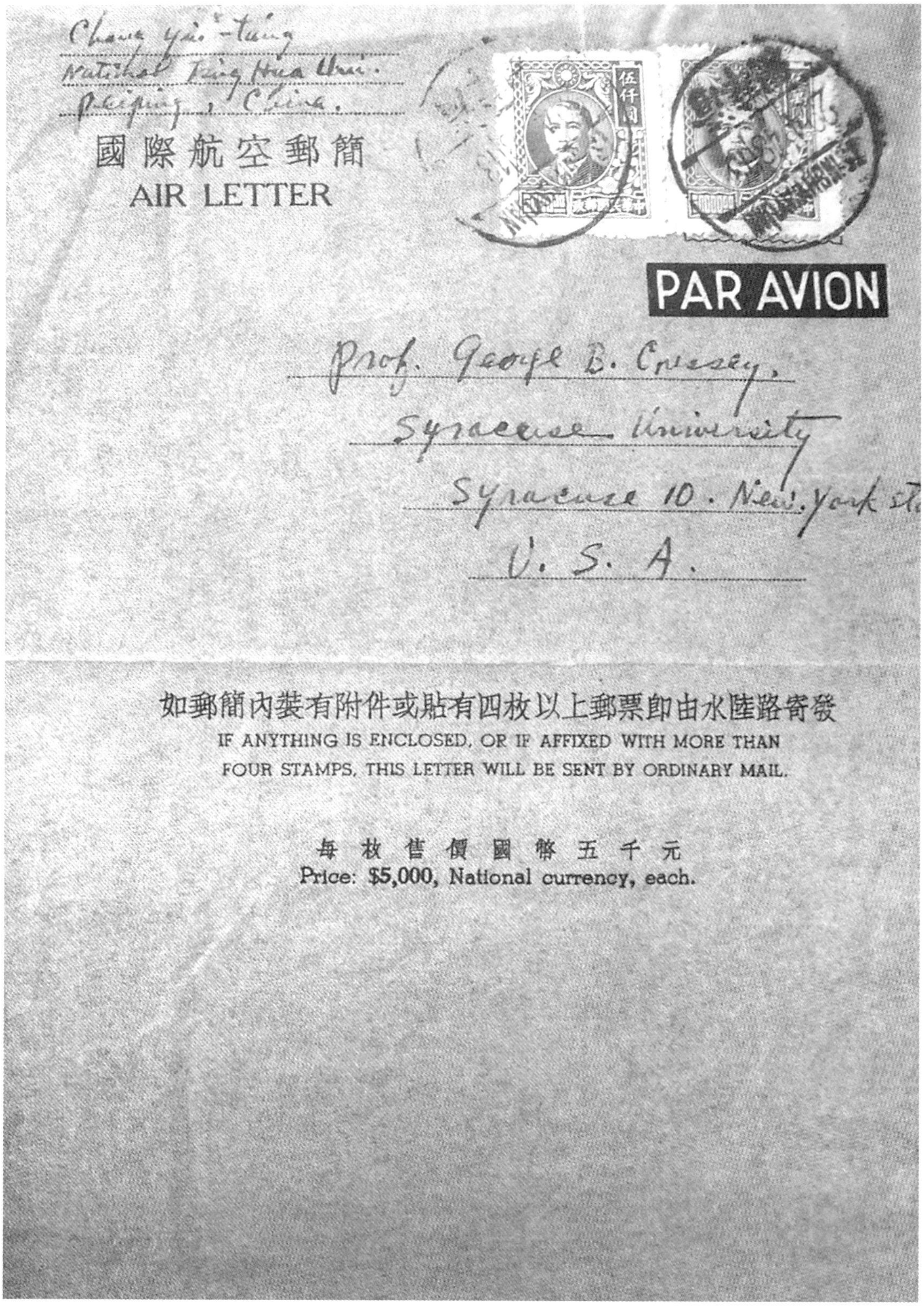
Chang yü-tung
National Tsing Hua Univ.
Peiping, China.

國際航空郵簡
AIR LETTER

PAR AVION

Prof. George B. Cressey.
Syracuse University
Syracuse 10. New. York st
U. S. A.

如郵簡內裝有附件或貼有四枚以上郵票即由水陸路寄發
IF ANYTHING IS ENCLOSED, OR IF AFFIXED WITH MORE THAN
FOUR STAMPS, THIS LETTER WILL BE SENT BY ORDINARY MAIL.

每枚售價國幣五千元
Price: $5,000, National currency, each.

洪思齐

洪思齐（1906–1984），又名洪绂，1932年法国里昂大学地理学博士，清华大学地学系教授，他曾师从著名地理学家德马东（E . de Martone），擅长法语和英语。他的博士论文《茶叶地理》被列入里昂大学地理学院丛书，在法国尼罗研究所出版。他曾在中国推介葛德石之书，1949年移居台湾之后，与葛德石未断往来。

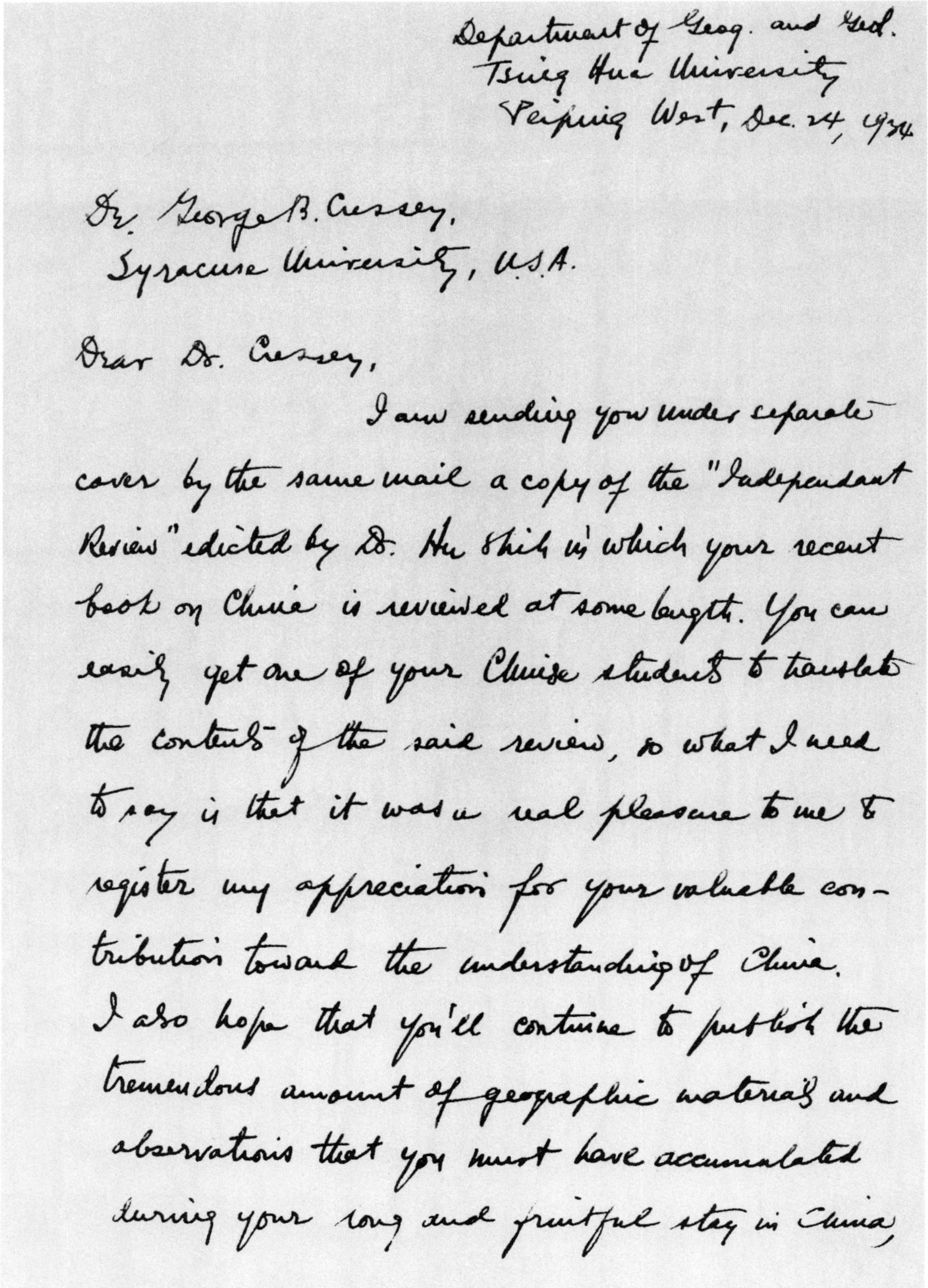

Department of Geog. and Geol.
Tsing Hua University
Peiping West, Dec. 24, 1934

Dr. George B. Cressey,
Syracuse University, U.S.A.

Dear Dr. Cressey,

I am sending you under separate cover by the same mail a copy of the "Independant Review" edicted by Dr. Hu Shih in which your recent book on China is reviewed at some length. You can easily get one of your Chinese students to translate the contents of the said review, so what I need to say is that it was a real pleasure to me to register my appreciation for your valuable contribution toward the understanding of China. I also hope that you'll continue to publish the tremendous amount of geographic materials and observations that you must have accumulated during your long and fruitful stay in China,

洪思齐致葛德石信（1934 年 12 月 24 日）

which I have no doubt will be greatly appreciated by all Chinese geographers.

Taking this opportunity to renew my pleasant memory of your kind visit to the Hung family,

Very Cordially yours,

Frederick Hung

洪思齊

House 4, Lane 44, Sub-Lane 16
Sin Yi Lu Section II
Taipeh, Taiwan, China

Professor George B. Cressey
President, International Geographic
Union.

Dear Professor Cressey,

Prof. Sha, my colleague at the Taiwan Teachers' College, has transmitted to me your enquiries about me, which I appreciate very much. I came to this Island in May, 1949, joined the College the same year, and have been engaged in writing a complete series of junior middle school text-books of geography, including 3 books on China, 2 books on the World, 1 suppl. vol. on Taiwan, all of which excepting the last part on the World has been finished. Your volumes on China and Asia have been a valuable source to me and I wish to express my thanks. In 1947 I have worked out a detailed plan for the redivision of Chinese provinces which has been accepted by the Chinese National Government as a basis for study. I believe I have sent a copy of the plan to Syracuse University, Department of Geology and Geography. I have also revised and improved on my Detailed Division of the Geographic Regions of China in 1945, which study was first published in 1937 and which you had so kindly and indulgently reviewed in the Geographical Review. I do hope to be able to continue my regional studies, if circumstances permit, as a basis for planning the economic and cultural reconstruction of China in line with modern scientific and technological development while keeping the best of Chinese culture and way of life.

I have read with much interest the accounts of your lectures in Hongkong from the British paper which I received regularly. Prof. Sha has asked me to invite you to speak to the students of Taiwan Teachers' College on any subject of your choice. We also wish to be hosts together with other geographers in Taiwan to a launch or dinner party in your honour. Will you please let me know when you are coming and where you stay. If you need a travelling companion around the Island I may be available although I am a poor mountain climber.

洪思齐致葛德石信（1951 年 2 月 24 日）

-2-

When I was in Shanghai I served concurrently in the National Christian Council and had the privilege of meeting your cousin Dr. Earl Cressey, and we have often talked about you. I have long thought of writing him but I have always been such a poor correspondant! I know he had a project of writing a symposium on Christian culture in China, and inviting Chinese Christian scholars to collaborate with him, i.e., before the Great Crisis which we have not foreseen. Please give my best regards to him when you next see him.

Sincerely yours,

Frederick Hung

Frederick Hung (Hung Fu)

House 4, Lane 44 Sub-lane 10
Sin Yi Lu Section II, Taipei
30 March, 1951

Dear Professor Cressey,

I have your letter of 21 March. It was indeed a great pleasure for old friends to see you again, and for Chinese colleagues to meet with a distinquished geographer who has contributed so much towards a deeper understanding of China and the Chinese people. I am especially happy to tell you that your visit has served as a timely stimulus to Chinese colleagues in the Island. We have decided to revive the Chinese Geographical Society which will hold its second post-War annual meeting in Taiwan sometime this coming summer. The group has also named Professor Sha and myself to approach the Academia Sinica for the necessary steps to set up a China Committee of IGU. Dr. Chu Chia-Hua, the president of the Academy, has been very receptive of the idea, and has already named the Committee members. When the organizational and financial arrangements are completed, he will no doubt communicate directly with you which will formalize adherence to the IGU. I have also discussed with Prof. Sha about the mailing list of IGU Newsletter which is hereinwith enclosed. I do hope to be able to attend the 1952 IGU Congress in Washington, and to present a paper on the "Systematic Division of the Geographical Regions of China" (with map). My presence will depend upon financial aid of the travelling expenses which I may or may not obtain next year. If I am unable to attend I shall arrange to have the paper read for me.

I was informed that there is a world-wide exchange programme of professorship sponsored by the U. S. Department of State through the U. S. Information Service. I have accordingly submitted an application to Mr. W. Henry Lawrence, Jr., the director of USIS in Free China and a former student of yours, for an apportunity. I believe if you could recommend me to the State Department as to my qualifications, academic attainment and linguistic capacity, your words will carry weight.

Sincerely yours,

Frederick Hung

Frederick ~~Hung~~ (Hung Fu)

Prof. George B. Cressey
University of Hongkong
Hongkong

Enclosure

洪思齐致葛德石信（1951 年 3 月 30 日）

李旭旦

李旭旦（1911–1985），江苏江阴人，英国剑桥大学地理学硕士，人文地理学家，中央大学地理系教授兼系主任，《地理学报》主编。1946–1947 年在马里兰大学访学一年，与葛德石过往频繁，现存书信三封均为 1946 年之后。

June 20, 1947
Prof. Shu Tan Lee
University of Maryland,
College Park, Md.

Prof. George B. Cressey,
Department of Geography,
Syracuse University,
Syracuse, New York.

Dear Prof. Cressey:

I am very grateful for your kindness of sending me a word of greeting on hearing my planned departure. Yes, I am going back to China this September. But what a different China is now since your last visit. Tortured by poverty and civil war, China seems to be sinking into the rock bottom with little hope of recovery. I really do not know what I am going to do after I go back to China. As always a true friend of my country, you will, I trust, share with me the distress over those dark pictures.

I am now working on the China Atlas on the part of agricultural resources, but progress is extremely slow owing to the lack of draftsmen here in this department.

Since I am planning to stop off in Syracuse and other places on my way back to San Francisco, I shall be looking forward to seeing you then probably in the middle of September.

The other day I received a letter from the councellors of the Geographical Society of China appointing me as the editor of the "Journal". I am hesitating to accept that work which I do not think I am really fit for. However, in case I shall not be free to escape, may I rely on your direction and help?

It is certainly a great thing to hear that your great book on Asia has been translated into Chinese.

Yours sincerely,
Shu-Tan Lee
Shu Tan Lee

李旭旦致葛德石信（1947 年 6 月 20 日）

THE GEOGRAPHICAL SOCIETY OF CHINA
C/O NATIONAL CENTRAL UNIVERSITY
NANKING, CHINA

May 4, 1948

Prof. G. B. Cressey
Dept. of Geography
Syracuse University
Syracuse, New York
U. S. A.

Dear Prof. Cressey,

I take it as a great honour to have you asking my comment on the current Sino-American relations. Since my return to this country, I have had various opportunities to meet many peoples especially professors and students, and have also attended several meetings discussing the current problems of China. There are popular voices of discontent and even angry protests against the present regime and also urgent calling for action toward the possible changing of status to a better and more efficient government. Immediate progressive actions are desired by every liberal citizen.

The final election of General Lee Chun-Jen as the vice-president shows the disintegration of the "Party" power and the popular desire for having a progressive leader. I believe, however, that the national government might, at this last moment, still be able to win over the support of people, if she could take immediate and drastic progressive reformation.

As to the American Aid, I am sure that most Chinese welcome it. But it should be used only for relief measures and, if necessary, political conditions should be attached. That money should be made sure that they really go the pockects of the need.

There is no way out, if there is no peace. My personal view is that peace should come first of all. Fighting is no solution; for as the present situation stands, neither side could hope for immediate victory.

The dilemma is that no body dares to talk for peace in spite that every body wishes it. Will Lee Chun-Jen do something? We believe he is a daring man.

李旭旦致葛德石信（1948 年 5 月 4 日）

THE GEOGRAPHICAL SOCIETY OF CHINA
C/O NATIONAL CENTRAL UNIVERSITY
NANKING, CHINA

I am sorry I could not tell you very much about the evaluation of the four young geographers who are looking for graduate work at your department. I could only tell you what I know. Mr. Hsu chi-Kang was my student. He is a serious worker and is lately paying much time on English language study. Mr. Hsu Kwei-Shing is now teaching at Chi-Nan University at Shanghai. He is the eldest of all and is interested especially on the study of physical geography. I know nothing about Mr. Chen and Mr. Yu, the two Sun Yat-Sen University graduates. But Mr. Lin Chao told me that the former is a more competent worker.

I wish to inform you that the Jour. Of Geog. Soc. of China is issuing four numbers a year since 1947. As the editor in chief of this journal, I am looking for your collaboration in submitting from time to time articles on Chinese geographic research. We also welcome those articles which you may feel worthy to recommend. First hand research and reports are most desirable. We will do the Chinese translation.

Finally, I am very glad to hear the continuing prosperity of your institution. Please extend my best regards to your faculty menbers and research students.

Yours sincerely,

Shu-Tan Lee

Shu-Tan Lee

National Central Univ.
Nanking, China
Oct. 30, 1948

Dear Prof. Cressey:

I am glad to know that you are planning to apply for the Fulbright fund of 1950 and that you might come again to China with all your family. It is a great news to all of us.

We only hope that China will be in a better shape than ~~that~~ she is now, and that your staying here will not be troubled by disorder and war. Right now everything seems to be dim and hopeless.

I have not had chance to talk with Dr. Lin Chao yet. He is now the director of the China Geographical Research Institute and is ~~quite~~ in Canton attending his father's funeral. The institute is quite roomy and I think he will be glad to offer you rooms. It is also possibbe that the National Central Universitycould supply you one unit of faculty dormitry. But these new built units are rather small, most of them consisting of only two rooms apartment. However, the department of Geog. has just moved into the new quarters which is considerably larger than ~~that~~ the old places. We will be glad to offer you one research room, with all the facilities of using our library and map room. I might wish to resign the post of chairmanship the next year, but I am sure this ~~is~~ can be definitly arranged.

As you call China you "second home," so welcome Home. Please give all my regards to your wife and all your children.

Yours sincerely,
Shu-Tan Lee

李旭旦致葛德石信（1948 年 10 月 30 日）

任美锷

任美锷（1913–2008），浙江宁波人，英国格拉斯哥大学地理博士，自然地理学家，复旦大学教授兼史地系主任，中央大学地理系教授。现存与葛德石的书信两封。

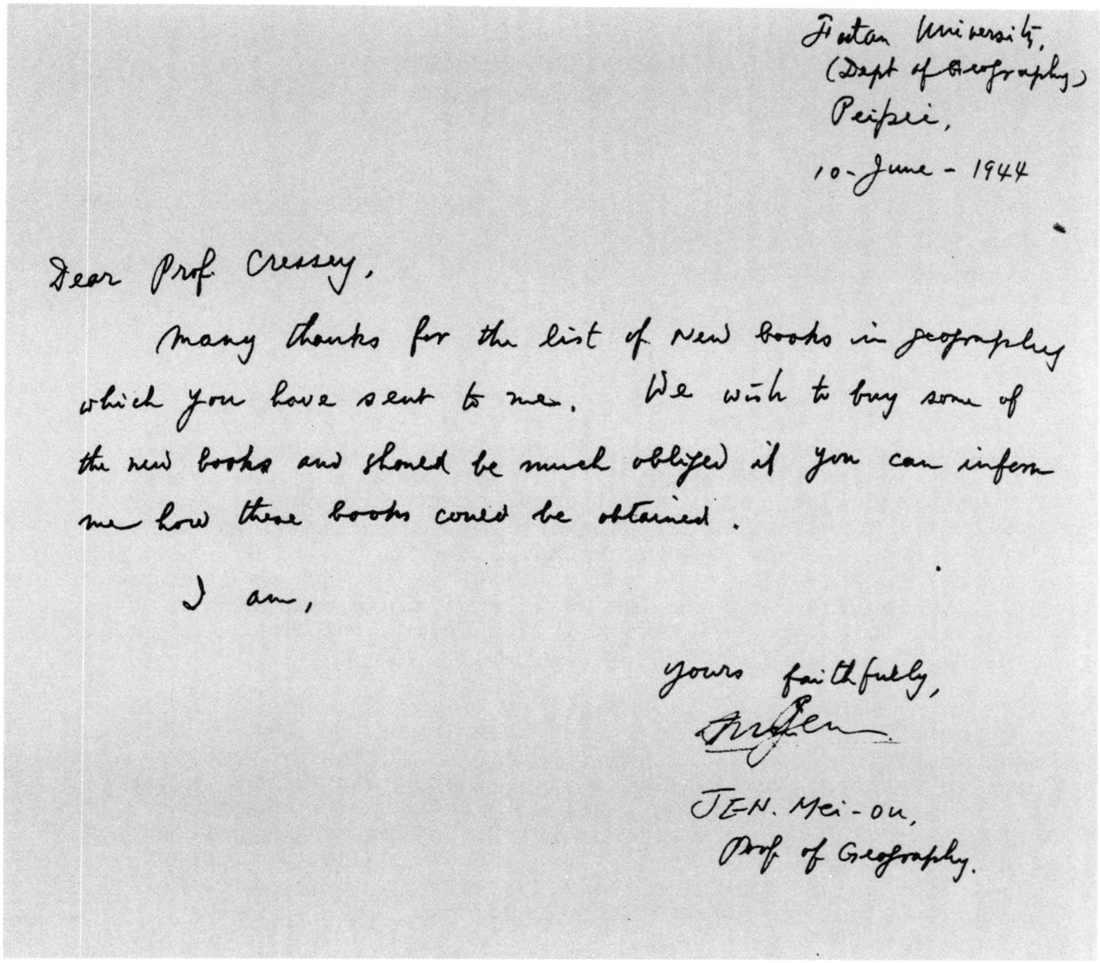

Futan University,
(Dept of Geography)
Peipei,
10-June-1944

Dear Prof. Cressey,

Many thanks for the list of new books in geography which you have sent to me. We wish to buy some of the new books and should be much obliged if you can inform me how these books could be obtained.

I am,

Yours faithfully,

JEN. Mei-ou,
Prof of Geography.

任美锷致葛德石信（1944年6月10日）

THE DEPARTMENT OF GEOGRAPHY
NATIONAL CENTRAL UNIVERSITY
NANKING, CHINA

June 28, 1947.

Professor George B. Cressey,
Geography Department,
Syracuse University,
Syracuse 10, New York, U.S.A.

Dear Prof. Cressey,

Thank you for your letter of May 19. It is my long-cherished hope that a number of type localities can be chosen for detailed land use study so that the whole picture of the Chinese landscape could be bettered known. I am happy to tell you that a number of detailed study like mine have been completed for the Kunming Lake Region, Yunnan, Chengtu Plain, Szechuan and I myself am directing some senior students to work on land use study in eastern Nanking. The results of these studies will be published in subsequent issues of the Journal of the Geographical Society of China.

During your last visit in China, I recall I had the pleasure of meeting you in Peipei when I was the head of Department of History and Geography in National Fu-Tan University. I came to National Central University on 1944 and am now in charge of the Geography Department. Recently I have been elected as delegate of the Geographical Society of China to the International Geological Congress to be held on 1948 in London. I am eager to visit America and should be very grateful for any opportunity which you might be able to arrange for me.

Sincerely yours,

Mei-Ngo Jen.

任美锷致葛德石信（1947 年 6 月 28 日）

林超

林超（1909–1991），字伯超，广东揭阳人，英国利物浦大学地理学博士，地理学家，中国地理研究所所长。1949 年代表中国加入国际地理学联合会。现存林超致葛德石书信两封，葛德石的回信两封。

中國地理研究所
CHINA INSTITUTE OF GEOGRAPHY
78 SHANSI ROAD
NANKING

TELEPHONE:32314

TELEGRAM:0098 NANGKING

Nov. 23, 1948

Prof. George B. Cressey
Chairman, Department of Geography
Syracuse University
Syracuse 10, New York

Dear Dr. Cressey:

Your letter of Sept 29 reached me in due time concerning your visit to China in the academic year 1950-51. I wish to take this opportunity to extend, on behalf of this Institute, our hearty welcome to your visit.

Your association with this Institute as a Correspondent is fresh in the mind of the members here, who are all looking forward to your revisit. The Institute has its own building and is gradually building up its library. We shall all be glad to offer you office facilities, while you are in Nanking. We have at present inadequate housing accommodations for our staff and are afraid that we cannot arrange a furnished home in the near future.

Hoping this will help you in making your decision, I remain,

Yours sincerely,

Lin Chao

Lin Chao
The Director

lc:sth

林超致葛德石信（1948 年 11 月 23 日）

Syracuse, New York
July 20, 1949

Dear Professor Chao:

I am anxious that the International Geographical Union be of maximum service to the geographers of the world and in particular to the various National Committees. Much of the routine business will be handled through the office of the secretary, but I hope that you will feel free to let me know whenever problems arise where I can be of service. I am sure you will agree with me in feeling that there are many ways in which geographers of different nationalities may cooperate professionally, and that our science has significant contributions to the problems of our world today. Plans are already under way for the XVII Congress, to be held in Washington in July 1952.

At its meeting at Lisbon the Executive Committee discussed a number of ways in which we might make the Union of greater service. One of these is through the establishment of a newsletter about which Professor Kimble will be writing you later. We are also anxious to assist the new Commissions in every way possible. If you have suggestions as to additional Commissions or other activities, I trust that you will write to us.

The Executive Committee has expressed the hope that it may be possible for either Professor Kimble or me to visit each of the National Committees during the next year or so, but these arrangements will depend upon the availability of travel funds from UNESCO. We have already received a grant which will enable me to travel in Latin America during January and February of 1950. I also expect to visit the National Committees in Norway, Sweden, Denmark and Britain this coming September in connection with the meetings of the International Council of Scientific Unions. If UNESCO approves our request for travel funds in 1950, it may be that Professor Kimble will be able to visit Europe next year.

Sincerely yours,

George B. Cressey

Professor Lin Chao
National Institute of Geography
Canton
China

gbc:srb

cc: Professor George T. Kimble

葛德石致林超信（1949 年 7 月 20 日）

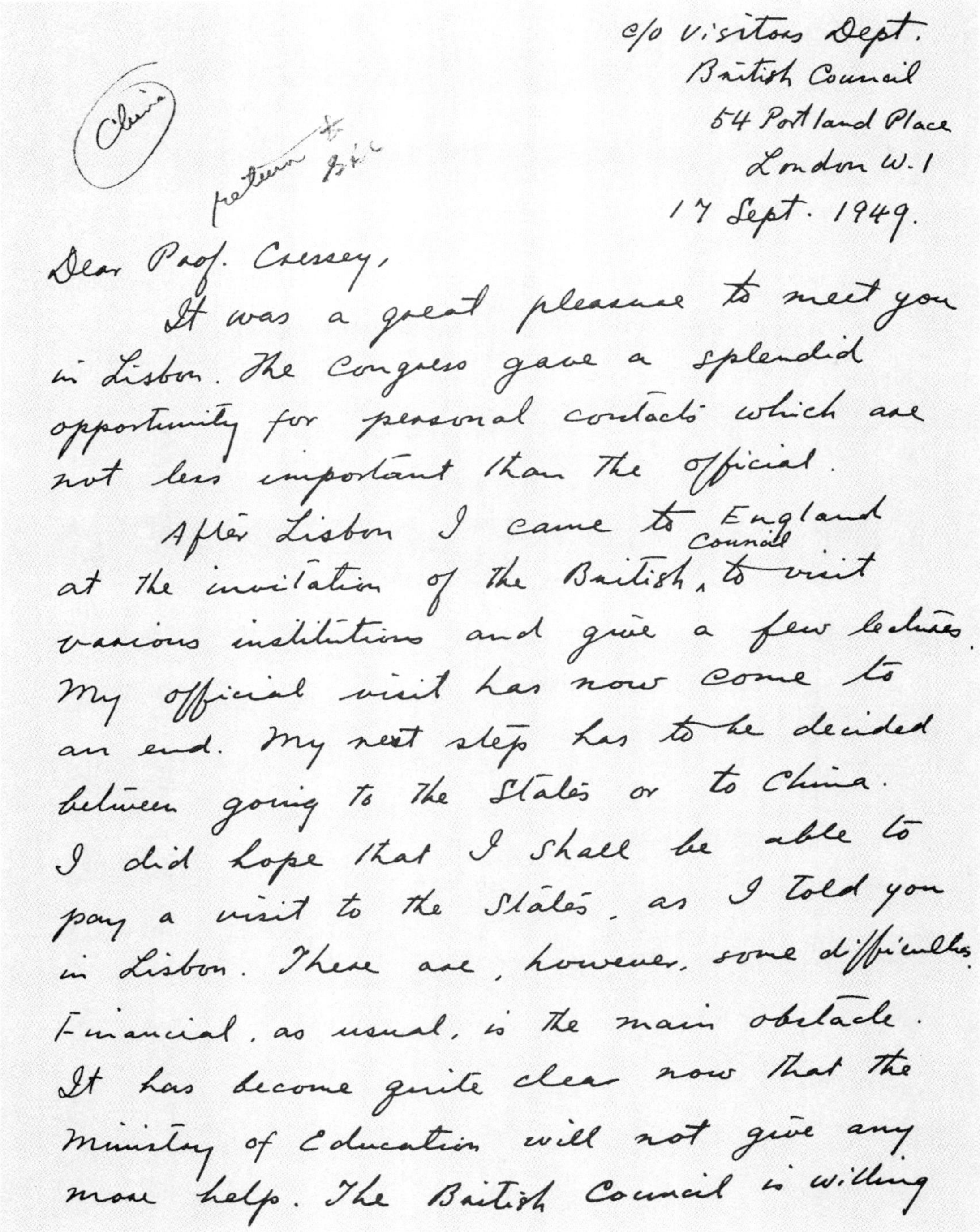

China

return to

c/o Visitors Dept.
British Council
54 Portland Place
London W.1
17 Sept. 1949.

Dear Prof. Cressey,

It was a great pleasure to meet you in Lisbon. The Congress gave a splendid opportunity for personal contacts which are not less important than the official.

After Lisbon I came to England at the invitation of the British Council to visit various institutions and give a few lectures. My official visit has now come to an end. My next step has to be decided between going to the States or to China. I did hope that I shall be able to pay a visit to the States, as I told you in Lisbon. There are, however, some difficulties. Financial, as usual, is the main obstacle. It has become quite clear now that the Ministry of Education will not give any more help. The British Council is willing

林超致葛德石信（1949 年 9 月 17 日）

to book my passage to the States, but not the passage from the States to China. So that I shall have to find some help for my passage back. There is also the problem of maintenance. I could manage to keep myself for sometimes, but would not be enough. Thirdly I shall have to get some sort of invitation from certain institution in order to get the necessary visa. In fact, I found that the difficulties are rather enormous. However, I am writing to a few friends to ask for their help and advice. I should certainly like to have yours before I give it up.

I had some news from our institute in Canton. Our books & equipments have been sent to Taiwan for safe, but our staff are still in Canton. There seems to be great difficulty for them to move to Taiwan. If Canton falls, they will probably go to Szechwan again or to Hainan Island.

During the last few years, Asiatic geographical research has suffered great setback in Europe, not only by the loss of such persons as Roxby, Credner & Sion but also in spirit. There is not much hope of its revival. I can not help looking across the new continent for new leadership. We in China, if we are allow to carry on, hope to play our full part. In this new effort, Syracuse and our institute have a common purpose and I wish cooperation be closer in the future.

Let me conclude this letter, by expressing once more, my congratulation and satisfaction of the selection of New York as the place for the next Congress and upon your election as its new president.

With best wishes

yours sincerely

Lui Chao.

Syracuse, New York
September 27, 1949

Dear Mr. Lin:

Your letter of the 17th was waiting for me when I returned from a brief flight to Europe last week. I am sorry that I did not know your address while I was in London for it would have been a great pleasure to have visited with you again. I naturally hope that you will be able to visit the United States on your way back to China, and if so, we shall look forward to seeing you here at Syracuse. I recognize the financial problem which you face, but much to my regret I have no immediate solution to offer. All of us in this country are eager to be of service to our foreign friends but the number of those who are currently knocking at our door seems to be beyond our immediate resources.

You will be glad to know that Professor Chang Yin-tang has secured a position at the University of Buffalo for the present year. I have just heard from him that he and his family have arrived and are comfortably settled. My own plans for coming to China a year hence are still uncertain, again largely for financial reasons, but I shall plan to keep you informed of any developments.

Shortly after my return from Lisbon I wrote to the Chairmen of all the National Committees of the International Geographical Union pointing out that we were anxious to be of the greatest possible service and inviting suggestions and comments. I did not write to you at that time as I was uncertain as to your address, but I want you to know of our desire to make the Union of maximum service. Do not hesitate to write to me or to Professor Kimble as ideas occur to you.

Sincerely yours,

George B. Cressey

Mr. Chao Lin
c/o Visitors Department
British Council
54 Portland Place
London, W. 1
England

gbc:srb

葛德石致林超信（1949 年 9 月 27 日）

丁骕

丁骕，生卒年不详，云南曲靖人。1928 年转入燕京大学地学系，毕业之后入中央研究院地质研究所工作。1937 年获英国格拉斯哥大学地质系博士，归国执教中央大学地理系。现存丁骕 1944 年致葛德石的书信两封。

丁骕用笺

June 1st., 1944

Dear Professor Cressey,

Enclosed please find a type-copy of one of my manuscripts to be published in the Bulletin of the Geological Society of China. It may perhaps interest you for it appears though unaimousmy, to be my opininn regarding the Symposium arranged by the Association of American Geographers. It seems to me that I have made an effort to elobarate Davisian by emphasis laying on Penck, and ended with a geographical conception!

Yours sincerely,

S. Ting

丁骕致葛德石信（1944 年 6 月 1 日）

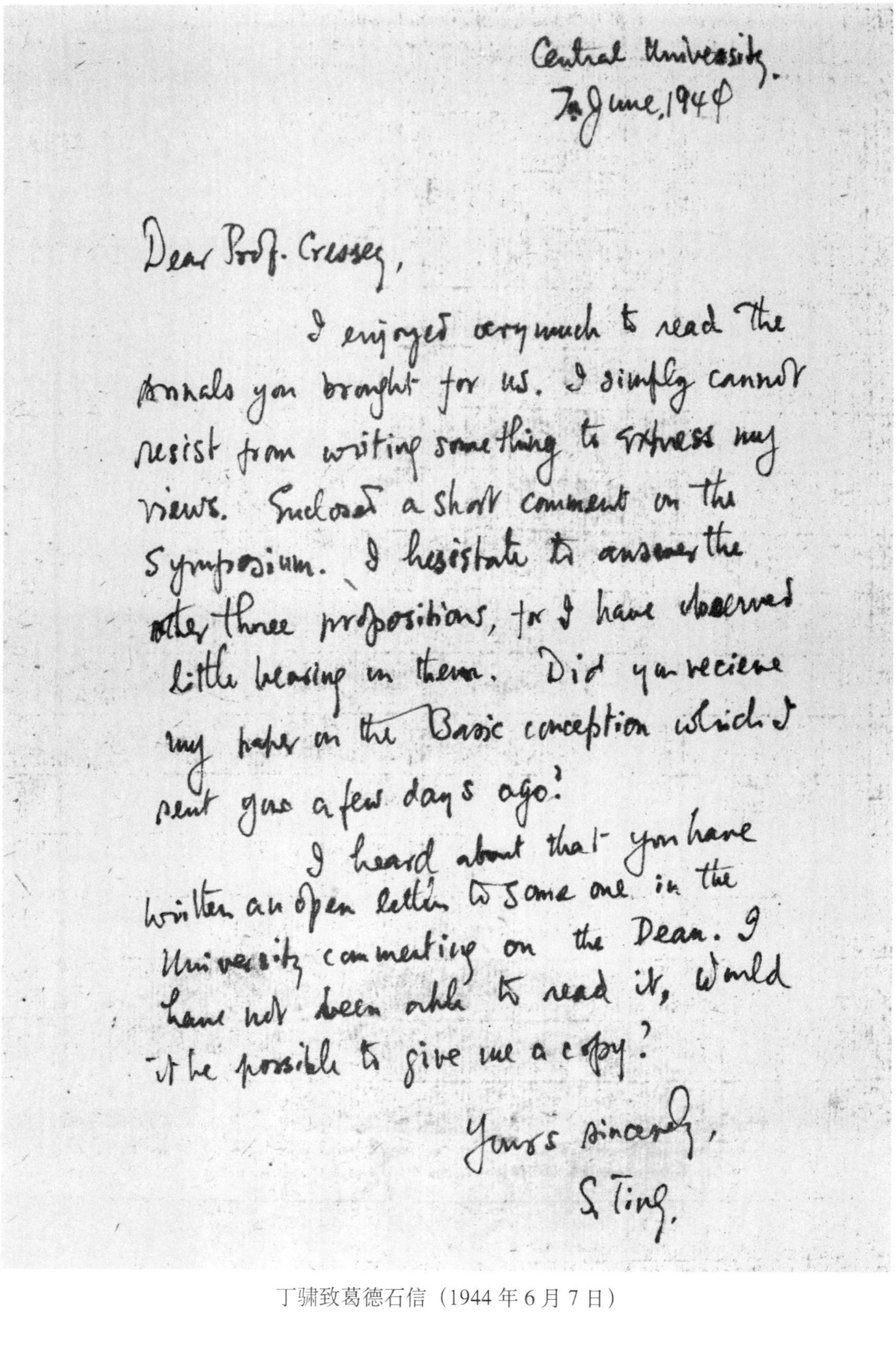

Central University.
7 June, 1944

Dear Prof. Cressey,

I enjoyed very much to read the Annals you brought for us. I simply cannot resist from writing something to express my views. Enclosed a short comment on the Symposium. I hesitate to answer the other three propositions, for I have observed little bearing in them. Did you recieve my paper on the Basic conception which I sent you a few days ago?

I heard about that you have written an open letter to some one in the University commenting on the Dean. I have not been able to read it, would it be possible to give me a copy?

Yours sincerely,
S Ting.

丁骕致葛德石信（1944 年 6 月 7 日）

徐近之

徐近之（1908–1981），重庆江津人。1940 年获得英国爱丁堡大学地形学博士。因战时回国受阻遂绕道美国，在哈佛大学和哥伦比亚大学等地游学六年，得以结交葛德石。现存书信两封。

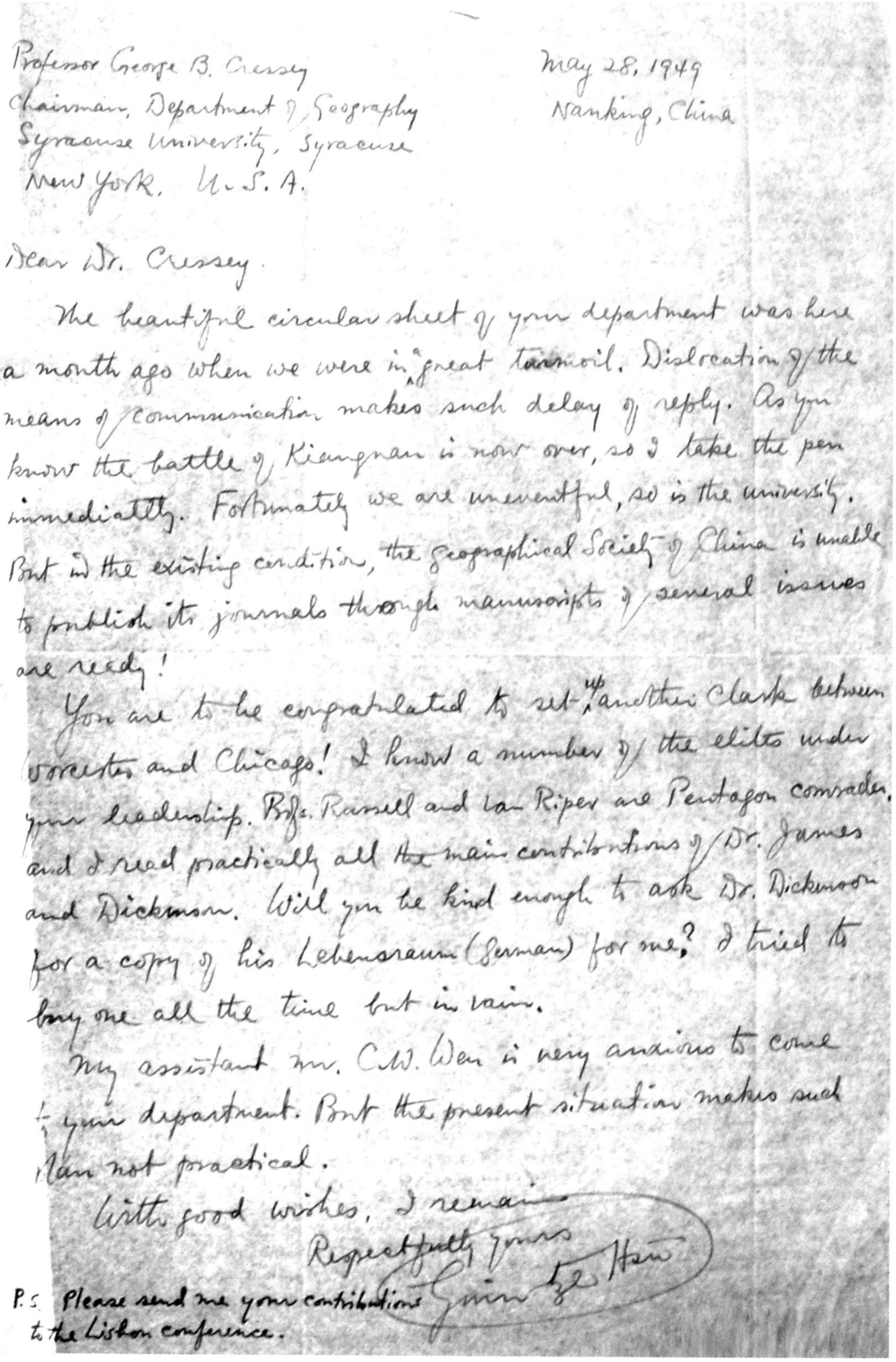

Professor George B. Cressey
Chairman, Department of Geography
Syracuse University, Syracuse
New York, U.S.A.

May 28, 1949
Nanking, China

Dear Dr. Cressey,

The beautiful circular sheet of your department was here a month ago when we were in great turmoil. Dislocation of the means of communication makes such delay of reply. As you know the battle of Kiangnan is now over, so I take the pen immediately. Fortunately we are uneventful, so is the university. But in the existing condition, the Geographical Society of China is unable to publish its journals though manuscripts of several issues are ready!

You are to be congratulated to set up another Clark between Worcester and Chicago! I know a number of the elites under your leadership. Profs. Russell and Van Riper are Pentagon comrades, and I read practically all the main contributions of Dr. James and Dickinson. Will you be kind enough to ask Dr. Dickinson for a copy of his Lebensraum (German) for me? I tried to buy one all the time but in vain.

My assistant Mr. C.W. Wen is very anxious to come to your department. But the present situation makes such plan not practical.

With good wishes, I remain

Respectfully yours
Gin-tze Hsu

P.S. Please send me your contributions to the Lisbon conference.

徐近之致葛德石信（1949 年 5 月 28 日）

rec'd 2/21/51

Professor George B. Cressey
c/o Department of Geography
Hongkong University
Hongkong

Feb. 10, 1951
Nanking, China

Dear Professor Cressey:

Your letter is here. It is nice to know that you
are touring round the world on behalf of the International
Geographical Union. Since the return of Mr. Lin Chao from
Lisbon, we know very little about your activities. I am
glad the next Congress is going to be held in the District
of Columbia.

Now Mr. Lin teaches in Tsin Hwa University. And Dr. Chu
is always in Peking. Whereas David Lao is still in Canton.
the Institute of Geography is a part of the Academica Sinica,
whose headquarter is in the former Fan Memorial Institute of Biology.
So far as I know official connections must go through the
administrative office.

Personally I have published a note on the International
Geographical Congresses in the vol. 16, of the Journal of the Geographical
Society of China P. 111-129. Unfortunately I have no extra reprint to
send you. Included please find a rewritten manuscript on the
Burma Road. As there is practically no necessity to publish
here. Perhaps you are interested in such historical events.

Very Sincerely yours
Gnin-tze Hsu

徐近之致葛德石信（1951 年 2 月 10 日）

罗开富

罗开富（1913–1992），湖南长沙人，美国克拉克大学地理学博士，地理学家。罗开富与葛德石虽同出于克拉克大学地理系，但是罗氏 1944 年方获得博士，晚葛德石十余年，因此两人交往不多，仅存 1950 年的书信一通。

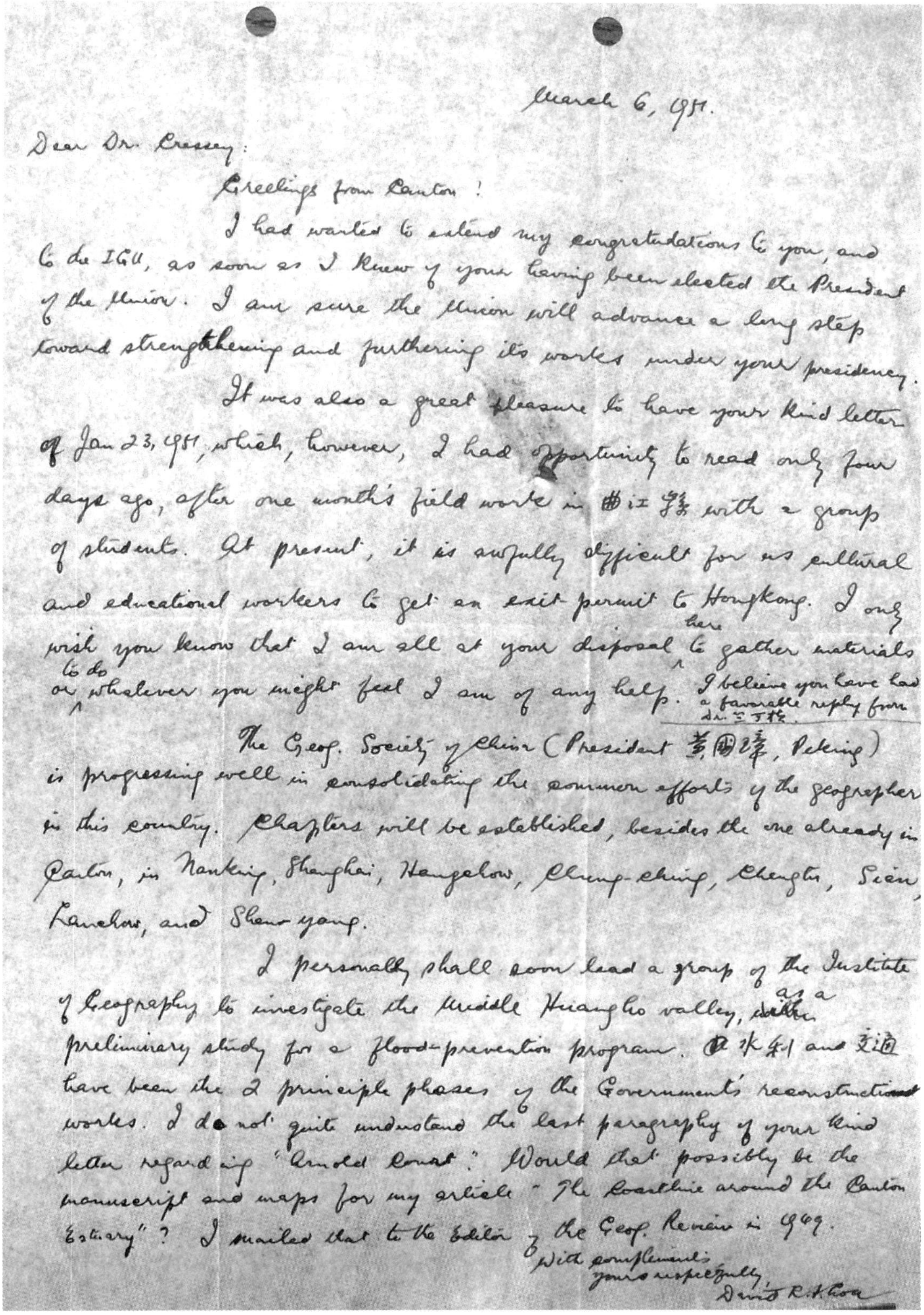

March 6, 1951.

Dear Dr. Cressey:

Greetings from Canton!

I had wanted to extend my congratulations to you, and to the IGU, as soon as I knew of your having been elected the President of the Union. I am sure the Union will advance a long step toward strengthening and furthering its works under your presidency.

It was also a great pleasure to have your kind letter of Jan 23, 1951, which, however, I had opportunity to read only four days ago, after one month's field work in 曲江县 with a group of students. At present, it is awfully difficult for us cultural and educational workers to get an exit permit to Hongkong. I only wish you know that I am all at your disposal here to gather materials or to do whatever you might feel I am of any help. I believe you have had a favorable reply from Dr. 竺可桢.

The Geog. Society of China (President 黄国璋, Peking) is progressing well in consolidating the common efforts of the geographer in this country. Chapters will be established, besides the one already in Canton, in Nanking, Shanghai, Hangchow, Chung-ching, Chengtu, Sian, Lanchow, and Shen-yang.

I personally shall soon lead a group of the Institute of Geography to investigate the Middle Huangho valley, as a preliminary study for a flood-prevention program. 水利 and 交通 have been the 2 principle phases of the Government's reconstruction works. I do not quite understand the last paragraphy of your kind letter regarding "Arnold Lomat". Would that possibly be the manuscript and maps for my article "The Coastline around the Canton Estuary"? I mailed that to the Editor of the Geog. Review in 1949.

With compliments,
yours respectfully,
David K.F. Lo

罗开富致葛德石信（1951 年 3 月 6 日）

谌亚达

谌亚达，生卒年不详，江西南昌人，北平师范大学地理系教授，葛德石《中国的地理基础》一书前半部的中文译者。

June 5, 1940

My dear Mr. Shen:

I am glad to receive your letter of March 14 together with the note from my good friend Professor Huang. May I ask you to give him my very kind regards. I am sure that you find many problems with the removal of the University to Shensi, but it is splendid to know that you are carrying on nevertheless. I hope to revisit China as soon as the war ends.

In view of your work on "China's Geographic Foundations" you will be interested to know that the English edition is now in the third printing, and that a year ago a French edition was published by Payot and Co. in Paris, under the title of "Geographie Humaine et Economique de la Chine."

Ever since my visit to China in 1934, I have hoped that it might be possible to arrange for a Chinese edition in order to make the book more widely useful to Chinese students, as it was for them that the material was originally written. I thus greatly appreciate your willingness to assist in this translation. While I was in China in 1934, I made arrangements with Mr. Y. W. Wong, Managing Director of the Commercial Press in Shanghai, whereby they agreed to publish the Chinese edition providing that I could secure a translator. I am therefore sending a copy of this letter by airmail to Mr. Wong, so that he will know of my correspondence with you. I have his letter of December 26, 1935, concerning royalty and Chinese copyright.

To help with the publication of the authorized Chinese edition, I should be glad to prepare a new preface, bringing some of the material up to date and giving a word of greeting to my friends in China. I can also send you several pages of corrections for mistakes which crept into the first English edition. I shall also be willing to forward to the Commercial Press in Shanghai the original drawings and photographs for all of the illustrations. This will make it possible for them to prepare very much better cuts.

葛德石致谌亚达信（1940 年 6 月 5 日）

Professor Y. T. Shen -2- June 5, 1940

When the French edition was published, I received a special payment of fifty dollars for the use of these original illustrations, but in view of the unfavorable condition of Chinese exchange, I shall be willing to waive this fee.

In my arrangements with the Commercial Press, they agreed to offer me a royalty of fifteen per cent. They also suggested either that I provide $800, Chinese currency, for the translator and retain all royalties myself, or that the translator receive one-third of the royalties up to a total payment of a thousand dollars, Chinese currency. In either case, the Commercial Press agreed that the Chinese copyright will be held in my name. Since your letter arrived, I have been in correspondence with the McGraw-Hill Book Company of New York City, who hold the original copyright, and now have their permission to have the text translated into Chinese.

In view of the large amount of work which you have put on the translation, as well as the responsibilities of proof reading and seeing the book through the press, I shall be glad to pay you either one thousand dollars, Chinese currency, on publication or one-half of all royalties as received from the Commercial Press. This is considerably more liberal than I have previously felt justified in offering. As a matter of fact, the preparation of the book involved an expenditure of some $4000, United States currency, on my own part, so that I have a large investment in the book.

Since I am anxious to make certain that the Chinese edition will be edited with particular care and represent an outstanding piece of geographic translation, I must ask for two reservations concerning your manuscript. In the first place, it must be entirely acceptable to the Editorial Board of the Commercial Press both as to Chinese style and geographic quality. Throughout my work I have had close contact with the China Council of the Institute of Pacific Relations, especially with the Secretary, Mr. Liu Yu-wan. In order to provide an objective evaluation of your work, I will ask them to examine and approve it also. I am therefore sending Mr. Liu a copy of this letter also.

If these arrangements are satisfactory with you, I should be glad to have your acceptance, whereupon I will forward the corrections and preface to you, and the illustrations to the Commercial Press in Shanghai.

Sincerely yours,

George B. Cressey

Professor Y. T. Shen
National Northwestern University
Cheng-ku
Shensi, China

Carbon copy to: Mr. Y. W. Wong, The Commercial Press, Ltd., 211 Honan Road, Shanghai, China
Mr. Liu Yu-wan, 10 Peking Road, Kowloon, [illegible]

Commission of Civil Service
Examination,
Goh-lo Hill, Chungking,
China,
Feb. 17, 1941.

My Dear Mr. Cressey:

Your letter of June 5, last year was duly received, when I was still in Chengku. Since then, I left for Chungking in July and returned to Chengku in October. Not very long ago, I came again to Chungking at the request of the Examination Yuan to participate in the work for the impending Higher Examination. I had asked leave of absence from the University, and would stay at Chungking until July. For all this, I failed to send you a reply in time. Hence I must offer you my very humble apology.

Three years and a half have elapsed since the outbreak of the Sino-Japanese War. The Japanese have certainly fallen into dire straits. In a year or two, we would probably win the day. We will heartily welcome you to come to China again at that time. To be sure, after the war, China, especially her Western part will well worthy visiting.

This is always my utmost pride that I translated your great work "China's Geographic Foundations" into our own language. With the consent of you and the McGraw-Hill book Company, I have asked Mr. Y. W. Wang, Managing Director of the Commercial Press in Hongkong to publish the translation. I appreciated very much all that you pointed out for me for revision. But, allow me to tell you my own ideas. To meet the general demand of the Chinese students, I laid special stress on the study of geographic regions of China. A scientific writing such as yours is greatly needed in China, and hence I concentrated my attention in translating the fifteen geographical regions, and entitled my translation "The Geographical Regions of China" "中國區域地理".

To the translation I wrote a preface, in which I intended to tell the readers how I translated the book; in which I expressed my respect to you on the division of the fifteen geographic regions of China, uniquely well-done as it was. Although there are some preliminary studies on the geographic or natural regions of China, your method is, nevertheless, the most rational and scientific. In the near future, the new political divisions of China will be regulated, based on these geographic units, for I am quite sure that the political division of China after the war must be decided from the geographic point of view. This will be the fundamental problem for the reconstruction of China.

If you would kindly permit me to publish the translation, I hope you will to the following for me as I was promised:

First, please write a preface. Better write it with pen and ink in order to put it in type. My translation of the preface will be appended. This will be an honour to me.

谌亚达致葛德石信（1941 年 2 月 17 日）

- 2 -

Second, please send me a copy of the third edition of your book for reference.

Third, please send me several pages of corrections for mistakes which crept into the first English edition.

Lastly, instead of taking any tax on edition, I should like to receive from you a thousand dollars, Chinese currency once for all.

Besides, pray give the sum of money in advance, soon after your receipt of Mr. Liu's letter.

Meanwhile, please urge the Press to have the book published as soon as possible -- I will, of course, do the same -- after a delay of over four years, I hope for the earliest publication of my translation which was completed at Peiping before the war.

I firmly believe that your great work is not only requisite to the students of geography, but equally helpful to the intellectual class in China as a whole

I was fortunate enough to use your original illustrations gratis. Herewith I express my deep thanks to you.

In publishing the book, I will do what the Press will ask me to, and revise it when necessary.

Hoping for an immdiate rply.

Sincerely Yours,

Y. T. Shen

Y. T. Shen.

Professor Dr. George B. Cressey,
Department of Geology and Geography,
Syracuse, N. Y.,
U. S. A.

cc copy to: Mr. Liu Yu-wan, 10 Peking Road Kowloon, Hongkong

I have also received your air-mail of 25th, March

Goh-lo Hill, Chungking,
China

First, Nov, 1941

My Dear Mr. Cressey:

Your airmail of Sep, 12th is to hand. I have learned that you ask me to deliver your great writing "China's Geographic Foundation" which I have already translated, to the Commercial Press for printing. I wish to express my sincere appreciations to you.

Receiving your valuable preface for Chinese edition, I wish to express more thanks to you. I will send it to the Commercial Press as soon as I finish my translation.

With regard to my present address, Mr Y. W. Wang has written you formerly. I hope you will remitt a sum of thousand dollars in Chinese Currency for writing fee at your early convenience. Mr. K. C. Hwang is now in Chungking. We welcome you to make a visit to Chinese again China

Sincerely yours
Y. T. Shen

my address →
Mr. Y. T. Shen (Shen Ya-Ta)
Examination Commission,
Goh-lo Hill, Chungking,
China

谌亚达致葛德石信（1941 年 11 月 1 日）

1943—1944 年中国地理学会与美国地理学会互致信函

1943 年，葛德石作为美国国务院访问教授来华，带来美国地理学会致中国地理学会的慰问信函，作为回应，中国地理学会请葛德石带回致美国地理学会信函一封。

The Association of American Geographers

September 25, 1943.

To our colleagues in China -

The Association of American Geographers is glad to send its greetings to the Geographical Society of China through Professor George B. Cressey. This action was taken by the Association during its Fortieth Annual Meeting in the City of Washington on September 15.

Geography has been called upon by our government to play a large role in the war, and more than 200 geographers are working for different agencies in Washington. These include Military Intelligence, the Army Map Series, the State Department, the Office of Strategic Services, the Office of Economic Warfare, and many others. Some of these studies relate to America's part in the post-war world. In addition to services in Washington, many geographers are doing geographical work with the armed forces in meteorology, aerial photography, and map making. Serveral hundred thousand soldiers have been assigned to our universities fr further training, and most of these programs call for intensive work in geography. Such studies involve the technical aspects of cartography and meteorology, as well as world-wide regional investigations.

While geography is greatly stimulated by government services, it remains an independent and virile discipline with a vigorous exchange of ideas. Professor Cressey will be able to tell you in detail of the current status of geographic thought in the United States, and we hope that you may be able to follow some of the current articles through microfilm.

Geography is inevitably global in its interests. It increasingly has its practical aspects in land planning, economic reconstruction, and strategy, but it also remains of fundamental importance in all cultural and physical disciplines. We earnestly hope that geography in both the United States and in China may contribute to the complete victory of the United Nations, and to the development of a secure and peaceful world.

In common with all Americans, we send our deep appreciation for China's valiant part in the war and assure you of our earnest determination to achieve complete victory. We shall be glad to have you inform us of the development of geography in China.

Sincerely yours,

Ralph H. Brown.

1943 年美国地理学会致中国地理学会函

THE GEOGRAPHICAL SOCIETY OF CHINA
Chungking, China

President, Huan-Yuan Hu

Councilors -
Wen-Hao Wong
Joseph Lee
Co-Ching Chu
Manod Jen
Chang-Wang Tu
Yin-Tan Chang
Kuo-Chang Wang
John Lee

Secretary, Shu-Tan Lee
National Central University, Chungking

Treasurer, Pin-Hai Chu

Editor, G. Yun Chang
National Chekiang University, Tsunyi, Kweichow

June 5, 1944

To our fellow workers in the United States -

The Geographical Society of China is honoured with the message of greetings from the Association of American Geographers through Prof. George B. Cressey, and is glad to reciprocate its congratulation to you for the useful service to our common cause and the valuable contribution to the progress of the science.

Geography is everywhere a modern science. It has a even shorter development in China. Only in the year 1929 the first department of geography was inaugurated in National Central University in Nanking (now in Chungking). Before this, geography was only a branch attached to the geological department in universitis. During the years 1929-37 geography made good and sound progress both in education and research. Departments of geography were established in Sun Yat-Sen University, the Peiping Normal College, the Nanking Woman College, etc. Books and equipments were brought in, professors from Europe and America were engaged, and expeditions were sent to the frontier provinces. Official and popular interests in geography were aroused. In the year 1934 the Society was organized in Nanking. Since 1935 it has published its quarterly 'Journal' until the outbreak of war. The war has hindered our path of progress, but the increasing importance of the science is vastly acknowledged. More people show their interests in geography. The member of the society increases, up to now, to a number of three hundreds. We are still far from sufficient for the work of studying the regional geography and geographical problems of our vast territory. Only during the last three years, geography has been partly called upon by our government. A small number of geographers are

1944 年中国地理学会致美国地理学会函

THE GEOGRAPHICAL SOCIETY OF CHINA

now working for the agencies relating to communication, regional planning, and economic problems.

We believe that China must have her own geography and that the Chinese geographers must take the full responsibility of studying their land and their problems. To this, we feel that we are seriously out-numbered. We need far more and better geographers to take part in the great task of the nation-wide postwar reconstruction. They are to be trained. That is why most mature geographers in China are now engaged in the work of university teaching. We trust that you will guide us and cooperate with us in the years to come.

Prof. G. B. Cressey has been a sincere friend of us, he travelled many places during his short visit to China and kept contact with almost every geographers here in this country. He gave us detailed account of the work in your counrty and in turn, he knows many things among us. We ask Prof. Cressey to return our admiration and deep appreciation for your success of war in the both oceans and pray that an early but complete victory will soon be achieved.

Lastly, we wish to express our thankfulness for your valuable 'Annals' complete to the end of 1942.

Yours sincerely,

Secretary of the Society

（2）同门通信

黄国璋

黄国璋（1896–1966），湖南湘乡人，北京师范大学地理系教授兼系主任，中国地理研究所首任所长，在民国地理学界与胡焕庸并称“南胡北黄”。1926年，黄国璋在耶鲁大学地理系师从地理名家亨廷顿，1927年转入芝加哥大学地理系，并于次年获硕士。葛德石曾在1921至1922年在耶鲁大学受教于亨廷顿，因此与黄国璋有同门之谊；而黄国璋最终从芝加哥大学毕业，这与葛德石又有同校之谊，因此，二人定交甚早，始终保持深厚的友谊与频繁的互动，现存通信数封。

國立中央大學
National Central University
Nanking, China

September 17, 1935

Dr. George B. Cressey, Chairman
Department of Geography and Geology
Syracuse University
Syracuse, N.Y., U.S.A.

My dear George:

At first I have to acknowledge the receipt of your letter of June the 18th and to apologize for my delay in writing you this letter. I got back from Yunnan in the middle of July and, two days after my arrival at Nanking, I had to teach in the University Summer School for Secondary School Teachers. This kept me busy through the whole summer.

We left Nanking last year at the end of September. It took us one month to get to Yunnanfu by the way of Liang-Kwang and two and one-half days' travel on the Indo-China-Yunnanfu Railroad. The expedition started from Yunnanfu on the 17th of November. Making our way directly southward without long stops on the way, we reached Szemao in the middle of December. From there another six days' travel took us to the region of the Tai Culture where our intensive field studies were concentrated. This region including six districts, touches the borders of both Burma and Indo-China. The native tribes are diversified but conspicuously dominated by the culture of the Tai people. In other words, the Tai people form the ruling tribe of the region. Of course, they are under the administration of the Chinese Magistrates, now. The whole population are purely agricultural in occupation. Both basin agriculture and mountain agriculture are very well developed there. Intensive sample studies were made together with extensive surveys. We started back from there near the end of April, fearing the coming of the rainy season which usually interrupts the communication between the south and Yunanfu. We made comparative field studies on the way back. Two villages were carefuuly surveyed in the Yunanfu Basin. We left Yunnan for home on the first of July and arrived at Nanking on the 13th. Happily to say, all of us were healthy and cheerful during the whole expedition; no one of the four Chinese members having been ill for a second. How lucky we were! Now I am hard at work on a scientific report, and, besides, I wish also to write a travel book for public reading.

黄国璋致葛德石信（1935 年 9 月 17 日）

學大央中立國

National Central University

Nanking, China

The Geographic Society of China is getting along very well. I have told the society secretary to send you as a gift the first volume of the magazine which, I hope, will reach you in the near future. The communication with the society is better through this department.

Before I close, I wish to thank you for the geographic bulletin which you sent to me and which I enjoyed reading very much.

With best wishes and success

Sincerely yours,

Kuo-chang Huang

Kuo-chang Huang

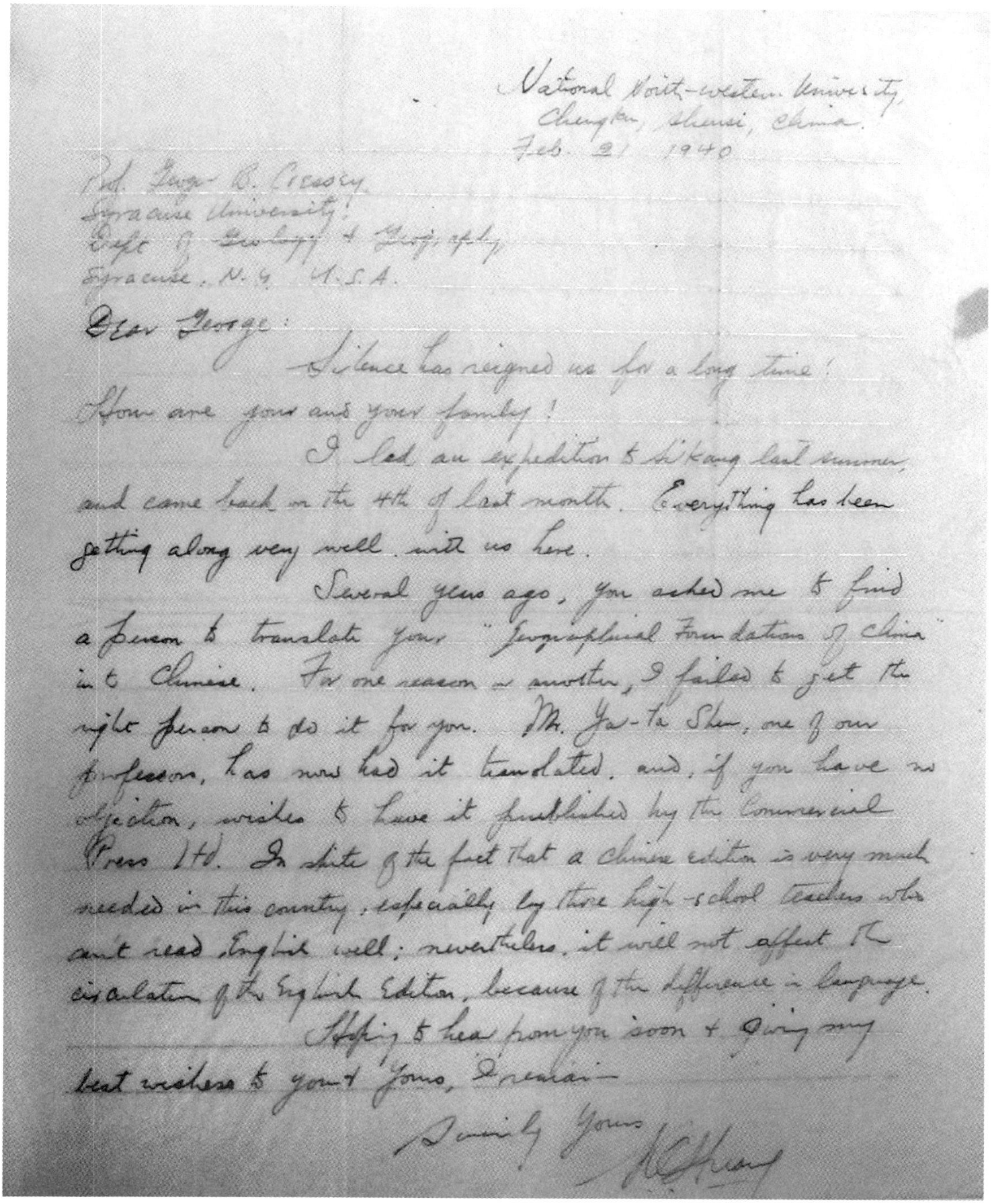

National North-western University,
Chengku, Shensi, China.
Feb. 21 1940

Prof. George B. Cressey
Syracuse University
Dept of Geology & Geography
Syracuse, N.Y. U.S.A.

Dear George:

Silence has reigned us for a long time! How are yours and your family!

I led an expedition to Sikang last summer, and came back on the 4th of last month. Everything has been getting along very well with us here.

Several years ago, you asked me to find a person to translate your "Geographical Foundations of China" into Chinese. For one reason or another, I failed to get the right person to do it for you. Mr. Yu-ta Shen, one of our professors, has now had it translated, and, if you have no objection, wishes to have it published by the Commercial Press Ltd. In spite of the fact that a Chinese edition is very much needed in this country, especially by those high-school teachers who can't read English well; nevertheless, it will not affect the circulation of the English Edition, because of the difference in language.

Hoping to hear from you soon & giving my best wishes to you & yours, I remain

Sincerely Yours
K. C. Huang

黄国璋致葛德石信（1940 年 2 月 27 日）

Chungking
Jan. 10, 1944

PERSONAL

My dear K. C., Huang

I am indeed interested in your proposal to have the China Institute of Geography study the problems of borderland geography. As a geographer I have long been interested in these regions, and it has seemed to me that China has not given adequate attention to them. Heretofore, the essential part of the country has been in the east while the western and northern areas have been "outer territories". Post war planning and development must consider the country as a whole, and as a basis for this there must be a sound understanding of the physical and cultural foundations. I personally doubt whether some of the very optimistic hopes of agricultural settlement are sound, but no one is entitled to any opinions until we make much more careful studies of soil, climate, minerals, grasslands, transportation, people, and all the rest of geography. Localized mining and industry may be more important than widespread agriculture. The political aspects are also obvious.

The first step in such a program is to find out what is already known. This means collecting the thousands of articles which have been written by Russian, French, British, American and other explorers, as well as the proper Chinese records. Many of these publications are in obscure sources, and not easily found. I would suggest that you employ a book agent such as Stechert in New York or someone in London to secure material as listed in Owen Lattimore's bibliography. And where it is impossible to buy the originals, the Library of Congress can easily microfilm them. I do not know how much this may cost, but I should imagine that the available material might run to U.S.$5000.

In view of the economic and diplomatic importance of China's borderlands, I consider this a sound proposal.

Sincerely yours,

George B. Cressey

Dr. K. C. Huang
China Institute of Geography

葛德石致黄国璋信（1944 年 1 月 10 日）

CHINA INSTITUTE OF GEOGRAPHY
PEIPEI, SZECHUAN
CHINA

August 22, 1945.

Professor George B. Cressey,
Department of Geology and Geography,
Syracuse University,
Syracuse 10, New York,
U. S. A.

Dear George:

I am very glad to have your letter of February 7, 1945 and know that you had an interesting trip on your way back home. To leave Africa one day and reach America the next certainly makes the world small and distance insignificant.

I have just about enough to keep me busy. Owing to inflation the work of our Institute is somewhat handicapped at present. Now that the war is over, we hope conditions will become better and financial matters will be less oppressing. We do not expect normalcy at once but we do hope to have a longer period of steady prices than what we are having now.

We feel very grateful for what your country and people have done and are doing for us. Without your participation the war could not have been ended so soon and victoriously. By your unselfish efforts you have attained the leadership of the world and it is now up to you to establish peace permanently on the earth. Our post-war problems are tremendous and our success or failure to solve them will determine our future destiny.

I quite agree with you on the problems of Chinese geography. Just as you said, it is fortunate that Chinese geographers have received their training in different countries of the world and thus have had a chance to come in contact with various schools of thought and background. But owing to transportation difficulties, especially during the last few years, they have had no opportunity to come together and exchange ideas. I hope this defect can be remedied when conditions become normal. Each geographer may have his own ideas and methods of attack but together all work for a common objective and unified philosophy.

As soon as communication permits the Chinese Government plans to return to Nanking. Our Institute may follow the government organizations though we have not yet reached any decision.

Yours sincerely,

Huang Kuo-chang

黄国璋致葛德石信（1945 年 8 月 22 日）

刘恩兰

刘恩兰（1904–1986），山东安丘人，英国牛津大学地理学博士，金陵女子大学地理系教授。1929 至 1931 年，刘恩兰曾在美国克拉克大学地理系攻读硕士，此时葛德石在此攻读博士，两人是名副其实的同窗，在学术上经常互通有无。特别是刘恩兰 1946 年访美之后，两人时有长信往来。

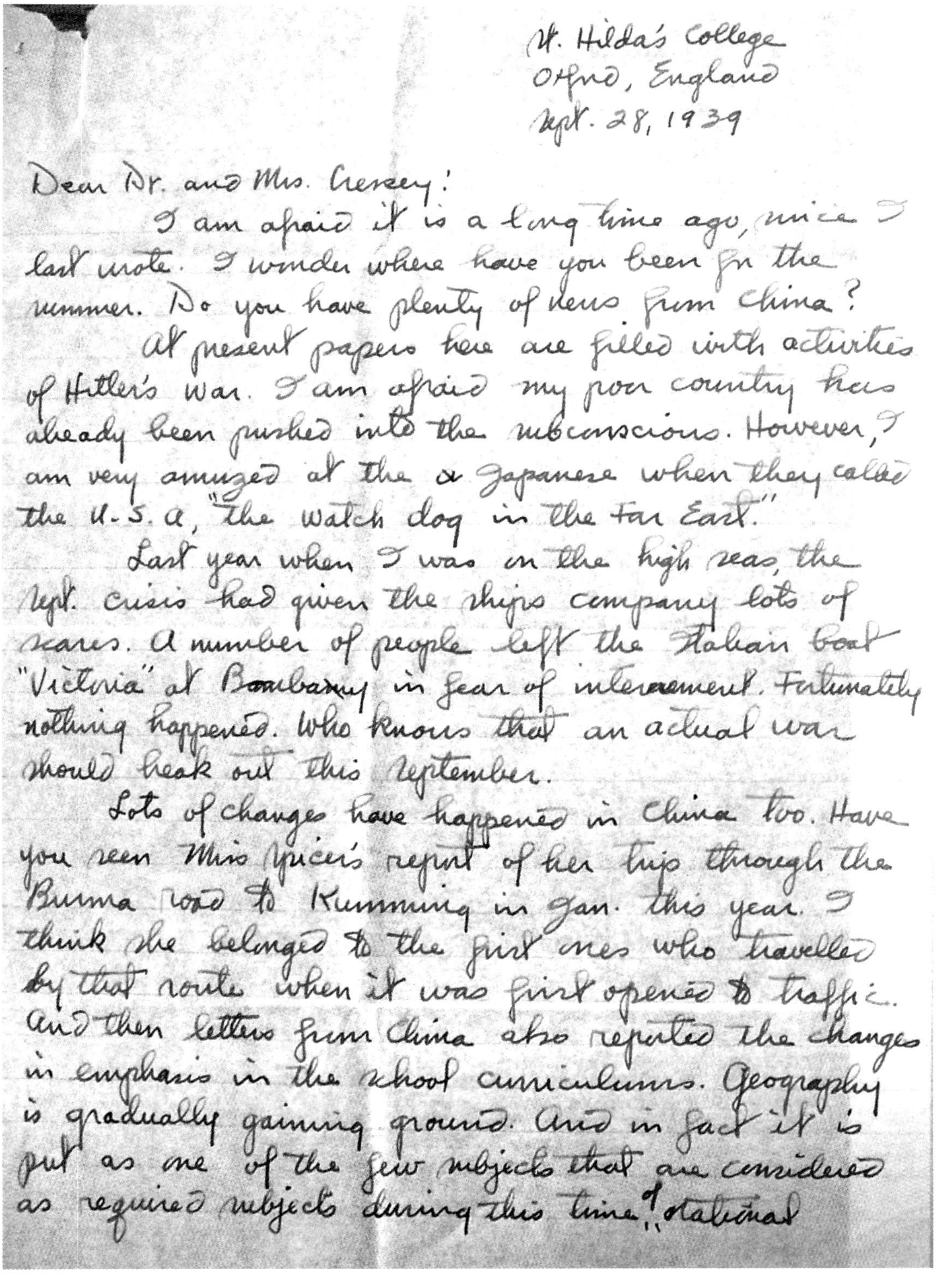

St. Hilda's College
Oxford, England
Sept. 28, 1939

Dear Dr. and Mrs. Cressey:

I am afraid it is a long time ago, since I last wrote. I wonder where have you been for the summer. Do you have plenty of news from China?

At present papers here are filled with activities of Hitler's war. I am afraid my poor country has already been pushed into the subconscious. However, I am very amused at the ~~a~~ Japanese when they called the U.S.A. "the watch dog in the far East."

Last year when I was on the high seas, the Sept. crisis had given the ships company lots of scares. A number of people left the Italian boat "Victoria" at Bombay in fear of internment. Fortunately nothing happened. Who knows that an actual war should break out this September.

Lots of changes have happened in China too. Have you seen Miss Spicer's report of her trip through the Burma road to Kunming in Jan. this year. I think she belonged to the first ones who travelled by that route when it was first opened to traffic. And then letters from China also reported the changes in emphasis in the school curriculums. Geography is gradually gaining ground. And in fact it is put as one of the few subjects that are considered as required subjects during this time of national

刘恩兰致葛德石夫妇信（1939 年 9 月 28 日）

emergency. I am rather anxious to get back to work. I heard many untrained people are sent to the southwest to do investigation work and exploration. There are so few trained leaders in the field of Geography in China.

I wonder if you happen to know Dr. H. Weissmann who has been ~~in~~ professor of Geomorphology at Central University in Nanking for years. Not long ago I heard from him that he is teaching in Tübingen University, Germany. In June he wrote me that he has been doing some field work in Arabia for some months and he was expecting to come to London. Then I heard nothing from him and I wonder what is happening to him now.

Dr. Y. F. Wu also wrote me that the ministry of education is very anxious to develop Geography as a subject in all the schools. But at present they have to depend almost entirely upon Mr. H. Y. Hu of Central University for suggestion and plans. The field of Geography is so great and there are so many branches in it. It really requires much thought to work out a suitable program to meet the various needs. I am sure, you, from your various experiences must have a good many bright ideas to offer.

Your trips and some of your papers I read in the geographical magazines are most interesting. I wonder what is the latest development in your work.

When I first came to Oxford, Dr. Buxton was my supervisor. After his death, Prof. Roxby is now my supervisor. I am expecting to complete n to finish my work by next June, if everything goes well. I do not know by which route I am going back now, as I have to wait and see about the general conditions in international developments. If circumstances permit, I'll go across India by rail and then from Madras to Rangoon and via the Burma Road to Kunming. But that I have to wait and see.

How are you and your family? Would you be going out to China someday in the future?

With best wishes

sincerely yours

En-lan Liu

Ginling College
Nanking, China
6 April, 1948

Dear Dr. Cressey:

It is very kind of you to be so sincerely concerned with China that you are willing to know China from all points of view. It has always been my feeling that the general U.S. understanding of China is terribly one-sided. Some sypports the national government. Some think the best of the communists. Some only see the picture of the unbalanced and over-emotional youth, and some only see China from the point of view of Chinese corruptions. China is a vast country and has many variations and many complicated problems. Naturally it is difficult to see a clear picture of anything in an upheaval of chaos, especially when everything is changing so exceedingly fast. Things change so fast that now every day actually brings new surprises-both pleasant and unpleasant, encouraging and discouraging, of hope and of dismay. Each morning one looks to the new day with great suspense as to what the new day might bring some have more courage inspite of the choas to make plans in faith and hope and steer ahead as long as circumstances permit. Some do not have too much faith to make plans and get restless and drifting and they got more and more despondent by worrying so they themselves become problems to increase the complications of the situation. I can see why under such situation it is difficult for others to render a hand. You give me great comfort in wanting to know what is actually going on here.

A brief definition of the present chaotic mass is insecurity backed by suspicion and economical insecurity is above all other insecurities. The farming class for centuries has been the most stable foundation of the Chinese national structure. Dynasty came and dynasty went, the farmers worked on and held on. The country on the whole, in spite of all changes and upsets, was fundamentally unshaken. But at present the stability of the farming association is broken down. They are refugeering in the cities. There are over 100,000 refugees in Nanking. Chinkiang and Shanghai have no less. Letters and peoples who came from Peiping and Tsingtau give the same report. From my own visits

刘恩兰致葛德石信（1948 年 4 月 6 日）

to the refugees living in the earth holes in the hills around Ginling, I learned that some of them are really small landlords. One family living in a tomb cave said they have more than one hundred mow of land but they were driven away by communists. The great majority of the refugees are refugeeing for the same reason. Others are refugeeing due to flood. Lots of young men are drifting because of conscription. The result is that the land is laid idle and people are starving. My father has over a hundred mow of land but he has not got a cent from his land for ten years. First he let the tenant families have the returns. At present even the tenant families can not even cultivate the land. My father has been relying on his children who are working outside. But what do the tenant families live on besides begging. When people can not see their way for living, desperation will drive them to do all kinds of things otherwise they would not think of doing.

The train that carries coal from Hwai-an to Pu-ko is always literarily covered with refugees throwing off coal from the trains. The guarding police can do nothing. Besides the fact that some were crushed by the train and others were punished with death and their heads were hanging on the trains to frighten the rest. But no one was scared off because they are dying anyhow they choose to get hold of things that might offer a chance to live. Not only coal, they do the same to the trains that carried beans. They are really desperate.

At present the People's Assembly is in session, naturally the military police are specially on guard. Some pistols were found on refugees-disquised trouble-makers. This caused the removal of refugees to the north of the river by police force. This means that some of the refugees who could manage to live with short periods of work in the city are now forced to cross the river too-to intensify the misery north of the Yangtze.

I studied a village during the winter vacation, you can well see how they farmers can not help themselves and their entire economic structure is collapsing. People who stay in cities and claim to work on rural problems and intend to help the farmers are really dealing with problems of by-gone days. They must change their technique. There are good ones, but they are working under tremendous difficulties.

Business people are rushing and working to make some money. At the present

2.

rate of inflation, they are too busy involved with their own calculations to entertain any public thinking. Students, now-a-days, have less financial means than before but have a larger ambition. For some of them in reaching some special ends of theirs they recieve ~~liberty~~ bribery of money from certain people for fermenting certain difficulties for particular groups. For some of them financial insecurity cause them to worry and they got restless and excitable, so they are always on strikes of one kind or another. Fortunately there are some good ones, But they are quiet and too much withdrawn from the current affairs or they are too weak to make a lead in matters more constructive. The professors are so badly paid that those with large families must do extra part time work here and there. They are so burdened with extra loads and extra worries, Naturally they can not do good work and they can not really give the time to guide the students in their thinking. Others have less financial responsibilities are having too much mental worries as to what one should do under the present situation. I was told many times by College professors in Nanking: "The communists are surely to win, the Kwoh-min-tang is sure to fail and we must die." I used to protest "no", we are not to die. We must look for a solution", "You do not understand " or "you are too optimistic." is their response. I mention this to show the general mood of the professors.

About a year ago Hu Shih started a movement among professors somewhat similar to the municipal League in the United States. The group in Peiping has helped the election of delegates to the present National Assembly. The Nanking professors have had three meetings in organizing themselves into a League. The aim is really very good and it is a piece of political constructional work. But somehow it got stuck.

Suddenly it appeared in the papers on March 25 an article signed by 47 professors, I read the names over. They are all univdrsity of Nanking professors, but some are part time only). The article impressed me as very sincere and with deep feeling asking for certain improvements from the present government. To me it appears as a straight foreward opinion of present conditions. Two days later another article appeared in the papers signed by one hundred professors of the Political University and Central University. The style of the articles are more or less alike with only little variations on emphasis. University of Nanking Profs pointed at the four general defects of the government, namely: 1. Uneven distribution of land property. 2. Poor treatment of soldiers so they do not

2

fight well. 3. Only imitate the western form of democracy but actually practicing autocrac . 4. Too much party ways in the training of the citizenship. The government University Profs emphasize more on the economic weakness. To my great surprise the comment on the Shanghai Evening Post is " Profs Rape the Govt". and called the article "Bill of wrongs ". Who is mis-interpreting whom?

I do not know what has happened that I am elected to be a delegate on the present People's Assembly and to elect the president in about two week's time. Some say I am used by others. I do not know by whom. Up to the present minute, no one has claimed credit for nominating me. And no one has made any special approach to ask me to do anything special for them. Most of the delegates have spent a great deal of money for tickets. But I spent not a cent because I wished no one would vote for me. Since I am elected I am going to the meetings. Though I have not spend all my time at the meeting, because I am still carrying my teaching load. (I have not missed a single lecture yet) yet I have got certain impressions of the meetings. The delegates of the Youth Party are too childish, excitable and rude. They certainly have shown a great deal of lack of training, of experience and lack of deep thinking. Delegates of the Social-Democrats are too "oilly". They do not appear to be constructive either and their thoughts appear to be too one-sided. Another group, myself included, do not belong to any party are only watching and listening with great interest and is, at present, very quiet. The Kwoh-min-tang members show more experience. On the whole the delegates are enjoying much freedom of speech. They shout at the chairman and being very impolite. The people who are managing the business of the assembly are certainly constantly being abused. They greatly impressed me with their patience and dignity and fortitude. To lead a country is certainly no easy job.

I will write you my impressions of the assembly later, but now I must stop. I am badly pressed by time. I went to the meeting this morning and stayed in for classes this afternoon. I refused the invitation from general Li Tsung-Ren to dinner to-night because I must write some letters. He is working for the vice-presidency. I meant to get Dr. Wu's opinion first before I write you. Since I could not get hold of her when I can, I decided to write you now, I will write you her ideas after I talked with her.

I have a kind of feeling what happens in Nanking gives a fair indication of political changes in China. The ordinary people are driven into chaos by poverty.

4.

Students turned into communists not because they know what communists are, but they want to try if they can have an easier time. Farmers join communists, not because of ideas and not even for a ~~better~~ outter living, But for a bit at a time. They know they must die, but they hold on because they still hope to live. Lots of communists are not communists by the western definition. They are simply starving people making their last struggles. Without external military help, economic aid would stop the civil war in China. If the educational class could lead the educational facilities educationally and not as an instrument of any ~~kind~~ other sort, the citizens with real qualities of citizenship could naturally stand their own ~~grow~~ ground. I have a feeling U. S, could help a great deal in many ways than military. At particular moments may be military help is necessary, but in the long run is economic~~ally~~ important and education in an educational way-not to turn China American but to aid China to be China in her own way.

As an illustration, after 1927, I have always been feeling that private institutions especially Mission Inst were being treated like step-children. Teachers are paid less than those in government institutions and they have less privileges. Government faculty activities seldomly asked faculty members of Mission institutions to join. The Natural Science Society of China has been a monopoly of National Central University for years. During the war years in West China, due to connections with Prof. Needham of the British Science Cooperation, it was opened to Mission institutions and a number of University of Nanking men became members. But, at present, they not only want people from Mission institutions to join but they also let them be officers. This is only one instance but from many other instances too, the educational pessonnels seem to be drawn closer because they realized if they work closer together they could get help easier.

Of course many people would like to have straight forward military help to get ride of the Communists. But " communists" at present involve such a wide range of different ideas and peoples. A sense of economic security would solve a great portion of the difficulties. And it is a surer way too. The question is how to get the economic security on the right path by the right force behind it.

Sincerely Yours

Liu En-~~lan~~ En-lan

P.S.

a great deal is written in the papers in connection with the U.S. aid to China in the last few days, I will try to make a summary as soon as I can. E.L. Best wishes to Mrs. Cressey

Ginling College
Nanking, China
13 May, 1948

Dear Dr. and Mrs. Cressey:

Since the beginning of March 1948, I seldom found moments of leisure, packed as each day was with ceaseless activity and emotional strain. It was rarely that, as the long anxious days were flickering away, I found time to be myself. Even when I have a few minutes to myself, the events in my surroundings are so momentous and my mind so unconsciously preoccupied with them, that to think of anything else is out of the question. I found it difficult to be detached in the face of the tempo of everyday events to analyze my thoughts, to reach conclusions, besides my daily teaching.

Letters came from different directions, all carrying news of student unrests and poor war conditions. There are nice comforting ones too. I did not write. I did not answer any of them with my sincere apologies. My mind soared and wandered over reports and experiences printed indelibly in my mind-to North China, to the never ending column of refugees. I saw them everyday, some are living in earth caves in the clay cliff a few yards outside of my window. The clay hills back of the College are full of them. They have left hundreds of mows of cultivated land and their property behind but living on pathetic little bundles and threatened with starvation. I wondered what is happening to my own family whom I have not seen for ten years.

On March 9th when I have just finished my eight oclock lecture, my brother suddenly appeared at the door of my office door. He is a medical student in Shantung Christian University at Tsinan. Nearly the whole medical school was evacuated because the city gates of Tsinan were closed and Tsinan was threatened. Nearly the whole of Cheeloo was packed like sardines at the Drum Tower hospital. Ginling was also ready to take care of some women students when the necessity arise inspite of the existing crowdedness.

The future is always unknown. Since Tsinan still holds its own and the railway is still running while there are many difficulties in re-establishing themselves in a new environment the Cheeloo refugees after three weeks of refugee life, returned to their original position at Tsinan.

For the first time in history China is electing a president by the people via their delegates according to a constitution. I missed the beginning of the preparation for the election of delegates, when I was in the hospital in New York, I did not have any Chinese papers. My first knowledge of this whole affair of election came to me on S.S. Marine Swallow where several passengers on board were coming back home to run for their elections to be regional delegates. Then in Nanking I met different old friends who came to Nanking to have their name "circled" for election because each party is to have so many nominees, and they wanted to be O.Ked first by their own party headquarters. I watched all with interest as an event but indifferently. On November 17th to my great surprise, several people came to tell me that my name appeared as a nominee to be elected as a women representative of women professors. After consultation with friends in Ginling all agreed the best way to decline the job was to keep quiet. Few people would look at such small prints. When no one would notice my name, I surely will escape. Nothing was said at the time of voting in Feburary. In March my name again appeared as elected. I have no experience in this line, I felt exceedingly unequal to the task. I waited for a formal notification then I can resign. But none came. On the day before the opening of the National Assembly I went to check in order to resign. The man in charge said I must register for the meeting instead of resigning because it was too late for them to do otherwise. I am telling you my actual experience to show that the actual way of election of delegates is not as corrupt as reports sound. I have no party friends and I am not an important person, from all ways considered, and I exerted no influence anywhere but I am elected. People thought I might be used by others. But no one has asked me to do anything special. I was and still am absolutely free in forming my own thoughts and in sharing in any activities I desire. My mind whirls when other people talking about the corruptions of election and saying evils of everyone. I can not understand.

刘恩兰致葛德石夫妇信（1948 年 5 月 13 日）

mentioned above. They are by far the minority but they are making the loudest of noises and the greatest damage to the nation. Something must be done with education, but the students are running wilder everyday. Isn't this the limit. Economic stability and a rightful channel for emotional outlet would save the situation. But how?

I am afraid my long rambling of thought ~~give~~ is offering no constructive suggestion either. I hope by knowing little facts seeing the reality of the situation you may be able to see a solution clearer at a distance than when one is right in the midst of it. I talked with many people to see what suggestions do they have, everyone seems to have their tougues tied or their minds rigid. Is not this terrible.

May 21, 1948

Dear Dr. Cressey:

Thank you for sending me the Text of proposed China Aid Bill etc via the Embassy. I had been wanting to get more people interested in this question, but the "left" force is very enthusiastic in getting the students constantly on the move for anti-U.S. activities, the faculty is tied ups with immediate duties of keeping order and peace, no mind seem to be able to work. I tried to talk with Dr. Wu many times but I have not succeeded on this question yet. It is always on immediate student troubles. There is no freedom nor democracy in "Communism" in China. I know them well now from the personal experiences of my family members. But they seem to be getting into the minds of the economic crippled youths very easily.

Sincerely

En-lan

Impressions of the National Assembly

A good deal has appeared in the press in China and probably some abroad, regarding the meetings of the National Assembly in Nanking March 29-May 1, 1948. It was the first meeting of its kind in the history of China to elect a president by the delegates elected by the people, and to begin to act by a constitution. The beginning of any enterprise is difficult, hence the National Assembly was no exception. During the session of thirty-two days it has faced many tempest and storms, chaos and upsets. At moments I felt the little craft launched on its maiden trip was to be wrecked by the ferocious poundings upon hard rocky obstacles.

March 30-April 5 was a period of six days of preparation meeting to get the presiding officers elected. The number of presiding officers was changed, from 25 as prescribed in the constitution, to 85 and reflected a great deal of emotional upsets. The atmosphere of the meeting was one of distrust and suspecion and full of outbursts of long suppressed emotions.

At the very beginning of the meeting the Assembly cancelled article 27th of the constitution which was considered to limit the power of the assembly and added the discussion of National problems. Two meetings were given to government officials to report their plans and policies for their departments of work. Seven study committees were initiated following the reports according the various suggestions in regard to National problems raised by the assembly.

	No. of suggestions raised by delegates
1, problems in connection with national economy	124
2, problems in connection with war conditions	91
3, problems in connection with educational and cultural problems	45
4, problems in connection with the revision of constitution	44
5, problems in connection with social welfare	32
6, problems in connection with border	11
7, problems in connection with foreign affairs	8
	351

The number of suggestions under each topic given by the delegates reflects the importance of the various problems on the minds of the people. Naturally problems of National economy are of prime importance and that dealing with war conditions second. It is very noticeable that problems of foreign affairs seem to be rather remote. Out of the eight problems 5 is concerning relations with Japan, 2 with U.S.S.R., one concerning a S.E. Asian League.

Suspecion over the constitution was strong. There seems to be a great variety of reasons among various groups. For one group they feel, the constitution in many ways is against the teaching of Sun, for others they emotionally feel no footing in political policies, so they want to enlarge the power of the assembly, still others feel the constitution is giving uneven privileges to the various parties concerned. Therefore the majority stood firmly for the revision of the constitution, to enlarge the power of the assembly, by policy forming power and to increase the number of meetings.

Unfortunately the desire for power is one thing, the ability to execute power is another. The desire for democracy is one thing, the fair play of real democracy is another.

The constituents of the assembly are delegates from 35 provinces, 12 municipalities, two outer territories: Mongolia-Tibet, Border tribes, overseas, professional groups; agricultural, fisherman, labour; business group, industrial and mining groups, educational, other professionals as medical doctors lawyers etc, women groups and people with special habits (Mohammedans). The regional delegates were elected in their own regions and the professional delegates were by people of their own professions in a nation-wide nature

1.

附刘恩兰《国民大会印象》文

When only a small proportion of the population are educated the difficulties of a general election is tremendous. The election of regional delegates was faced with the special hardships of electorates who can neither read nor write. When one can not read and can not write, naturally he has to forfiet his right of election to the will of the one who reads and writes for him. That is the loop hole where people could use money to run the election. What is democracy when people are illiterate. Therefore difficult problems in connection with the election of regional delegates were numerous and complicated, with certain cases resulted in courts and others on "hunger strikes". Furthermore not all the elected delegates have the necessary qualifications to be delegates and some know little what they are supposed to do besides their feeling of superiority that they rank as high as old day officials-they think they now belong to a specially privileged class. Unconsciously they have given democracy a different meaning-democaracy to them means no one can do anything to rule over them, but they should rule over others. That is part of the reason why a great number wanted to revise the con-stitution to enlarge the power of the assembly. Yet they never stop to think over the difference between policy-making and policy execution. They roaringly made over three hundred suggestions in connection with national problems, but they made no provision to see how these suggestions are to be taken care of.

They anxiously wanted to enlarge the power of the assembly because of their distrust of the government. Unhesitantingly they cancelled article 27 but they unconsciously given greater power to the president by adding a clause to give him emergency power. This only reflects the fact that most of the delegates know not what they are doing. Little did some of them realize that producing the leader of the country is a dignified and serious job bound by moral and intellectual principles and obligations. In the psychology of the people should be grand and honorable, but they only carried odds and ends and unsystematic business, while the atmosphere of the meeting house was constantly charged with shouts screams, curses and abuses. Parlimentary rules were discussed, passed and printed and each had a copy in hand but few used it in reality.

The assembly wanted to elect their own presiding officers from the different groups represented-"democracy". It seemed everyone wanted to be the chairman that is why the number was changed from 25 to 85. As soon as the presiding officers were elected, they were shouted at and distrusted. The assembly wanted to discuss national problems and to make suggestions. They were dying to have it; over three hundred suggestions were quickly made. After they were printed on paper few attended the discussion meetings and few seem to care what is going to happen to these suggestions. The general impression created is that the meeting was a failure. The delegates feel they did not get enough power and the people feel equally dis-satisfied with the delegates at their mentality, behavior and attitudes.

However, I came out from this experience with more optimism for China than before because I feel I now see a clearer picture of China, grim though it is, yet I feel I can now look at it in reality and not as if looking at it in a dream over a veil of haze. The idea of democracy has gotten hold of people. The unruling manners, attitudes and behaviors are expressions of long suppressed emotional strains. Education in all forms especially moral education is in great urgent need to guide the brusting flood into its rightful channel in order to be constructive in nature and attainment.

I also discovered China is not without mental power. Through the stormy periods during the meetings unexpected personality, quiet, unassuming, humble and sincere always seems to come out from the place to pacify the stormy waves in his quiet ways and to carry the meeting over the crisis. I noticed a number of such great souls who have never exerted themselves in any way and in anything before. If China still has a reserve of men like this there is still hope to escape a total ruin. The only trouble is that they always keep quiet and never exert themselves. Therefore on the surface people only know of the noisy and boisterous ones.

Something strange about Chinese characteristics is there to bewilder me. Once when different parties stood on unlike grounds and the meeting dispersed in chaos and comfussion. The meeting remain adjourned for a whole day the next day. I felt the end of China is here. But the meeting resumed on the third day. Matters went on smoothly and peacefully as if nothing happened. The ability to compromise is surprising. What has been done and how did they do it? Of course since I do not belong to any party I would not know the secret preceedings. But it is very amazing.

Furthermore the Chinese people is considered to be slow and never hurry. But the secretary of the assembly certainly has shown no sign of slowness. Whatever is discussed or suggested is always ready in print the next day. The minutes of the session in two volumes were ready on distribution on the second day after the close of the session. Written materials in connection with the meetings of the assembly are already out in volumes, only a number of the newspaper reports are rather distorted or ill-balanced.

In short, shouldering more political unrests and serious economic instability after years of war, naturally people are exhausted, discouraged and pent up with tremendous emotional upsets. This accounted for many seemingly unlawful activities- and such actions are rather too many. Undertakings of all shades and grades in China at present are comfronted with the same problem as the National Assembly. If one has not the proceedings at hand, to show his ability to solve the problem of war and economy, ready for immediate application and to show immediate results, he will be under suspecion and distrust. Without confidence and cooperation how can anyone do anything.

The majority of the illiterate people in China suffer the most and say the least. The war has laid waste about 60% of cultivated land in the occupied territories. Only about 20-30% were reclaimed after victory. But, at present, war disasters in the north, on the top of various national pestilence in the forms of flood and drought, have driven a continous out flowing column of emigrants leaving a much higher percentage of land to waste again. These poor children of the soil with long suffering in their struggles for living and life never make a sound while others scream at the top of their voices when even their skins are hardly touched.

Business people inspite of many difficulties seem to fare best, at present, while laborers, working people, are actually better off than formerly, comparatively speaking. The salaried class is having the worst of time. This naturally included the educational field and its effects are tremendous in all its manufestations.

Some professors and teachers are obliged by financial responsibilities to work in different jobs. That means they can not put their whole energy and attention to any particular work. The result is that they are not doing good work. They worry too much over the question of living. Among those who are devoting more attention to their teaching some are possessed by fear. They say the communists will won and Kwoh-min-tang will fail and they will die. Afraid of the communists, dis-satisfied with the Nationalists, they fuss and make most illogical moves. They are also the ones who are displeased with everybody including the Americans. Fear has driven them out of rhyme with everything and everybody. There are many of them. There are others who are more sane but they are terribly weak and quiet. With neither political nor finanical power, they can not move nor take action.

There is still a group who are educated but who have no definite jobs-and with mountains of unfulfilled desires. They too are dis-satisfied with everything, and become a great distructive current. I suppose they must recieve quiet a bit of subsidy in fermentating troubles. They are well organized and work in a rather effecient way. They are storming the students who want to be modern, want to do something and enjoy the feeling of exhilaration in self-expression, right or wrong, and to get some money in repay for whatever they do. They are up to series of activities since May in Antis and destructions. The trouble is they do not use their minds. They let money and emotion ride over them. If people with solid mind have the money and activities to meet another set of their fancies, the force might be led into a totally different channel.

Strange enough very little opinion is expressed in regard to the American aid to China by all groups but American aid to Japan is causing a great deal of comments in talks and in prints and is a great driving force for anti-American enterprisers-the last group [illegible] above. They are by far the minority but they are going

The discussions in the meetings were absolutely free, The way of voting the president and vice president was absolutely independent and by free will, Of course the candidates have done much to influence the voters, but in the last resort, each one is free to vote and the method is absolutely private, no one could find out whom the other voted for.

Rumours and criticisms by people who do not really take part and know not what the actual atmosphere of the meeting in the house is, often led astray by fanciful immaginations. Of course there are many difficulties, both the delegates and the parties have their faults and short comings. But it is better to see what is being done constructively under given circumstances than to criticize and tear apart whatever is being done.

Yet, in the avalanche of mixed emotions in regard to the National Assembly one thing was emerging clearer as I thought, democracy is in the process of taking shape. Sometimes I saw it in the dignified and daring out spoken speeches and sometimes in a chaotic mess of degrading noises and tragic events. Democracy and freedom are both excellent ideas when people are ready for it, otherwise they are means of choas and troubles. Anyhow everything must have a beginning. One only can hope to do one's own best and hope for the best. When there was conflicting ideas in the meeting house and "hunger strikers" struggled to get in at the front door, and students, shouting for public funds on the street, one felt the meeting can never reach anywhere. But it did and got normally adjurned.

Right after the close of the National Assembly, came May 4th the "Students" day. The storm of that is still on even though today is already May 13th. The students are to be pitied because they know not what they are doing. They only want the feeling of satisfication that they are doing something to release their suppressed emotional and financial strains.

On top of all this, my home town fall into the hands of the communists. My father and my sister-in-law and her five children arrived Nanking on April 24th. They escaped from Weihsien by the last plane to Tsingtau. One of my brothers and my sister could not get on the plane and walked to Tsingtau. They were held by the Eighth army for two weeks at Kaome when we had no word of them. We now got word that they have escaped to Tsingtau. While on the way to Tsingtau by foot they lived on wild vegetables. I suppose living under worse conditions than the refugees outside of my window. (The refugees outsides of my window is much reduced now because the police were forcing them to cross the river after, it was reported, pistols were found in some caves.) We are now expecting them to come to Nanking via Shanghai when they are a little rested. Trouble makers often disguise themselves as refugees.

Going into the deep cause of all troubles, the root is one of economic. After years of war people are all living on the edge of starvation, troubles soar. It is the root of evil from the lowly to the grand duches on high, only expressed by different fashions and commouflaged by different techniques. When the economic conditions are stable and people can live happily, over 50% of the difficulties will naturally disappear by themselves. The question is how. This solution do need some brain powers. Why don't people turn their destructive powers to the solution of this constructive ~~problems~~ one. This world certainly is a funny place. Isn't it?

Nature seems always to work naturally in a systematic way. My mind is still vivid with the memory of the snow covered hills, the white barren trees, before I noticed them, spring is fully here. The South hill, on which I am living is thickly covered by grasses and shaded by thickly leaf covered trees. Wisteria is blossoming. The air is sweet with fragrant flowers. Life and beauty is everywhere. Nature blossoms regardless of what man is doing. It is beautiful inspite of the neglect of man. Nature is a great comfort and a great teacher. Only man has no time for it.

With best wishes

Sincerely Yours

C Lan

Ginling College
Nanking, China
Nov. 24, 1948

Dear Dr. and Mrs. Casey:

While I am writing now, life is very much in the same sort of uncertain setting as the fall of 1937. No one knows exactly what is to happen the next day and what should be done. Should the College move or remain? Should we continue our classes as usual inspite of the fact that nearly 1/3 of our students have left. One only wishes one can have a magic eye to see into the future including all the changes we have to go through. Everyday brings something new and surprising. May be that is why life is interesting and that is also why life is gloomy.

When I wrote you in June we were in the midst of students agitations. They were exceedingly restless, rather unreasonable, however I like to label them as highly nervous. Fortunately the summer vacation did offer a let off, the tension was greatly relaxed by the decentralization ~~of~~ during summer vacation when they scattered to their individual homes.

Economically beginning from May, the old banished silver dollars(not paper bills) were risen from their places of long rest and began to pour into the markets in Nanking at the rate of $50,000.00 paper money per silver dollar. Then gradually increase to $500,000.00. The rate varied greatly from day to day and even vary by the hour and later by the minute. Many people simply stood on street corners selling and buying silver dollars as their occupation for living. One man may buy at the rate $500,000.00 per dollar and turn around and sold it immediately at the rate of $550,000.00 or more per dollar. The government began to interfere, police were put on the guard, that only drove the business into the black market and it was worse.

When a friend of mine came to Nanking from Changsha at the end of July, she said that the silver dollar became the current means of trade on the streets in Hankow, Wuchang and nearly everywhere in Hunan. No one seemed to trust the paper currency anymore and prices shoot up high. In fact silver dollars became the current currency everywhere except in Nanking and Shanghai where its circulation is forbidden under police force. People do not say they were dealing with silver

1.

刘恩兰致葛德石夫妇信（1948 年 5 月 24 日）

dollars, they talk about the equivalent value in amount of rice. By August the rate of silver dollars went up to $7,000,000.00 per dollar. Inflation was tremendously high. One needed a bundle of bills to buy an egg or a fish or anything. In fact there was nothing one could buy with a figure less than four zero that is less than $10,000. Figures went up so high counting became a real problem.

When the anouncement of the New Money System suddenly came on Aug. 20th, 1948 that Gin-yuan (Gold Dollar in paper) was to be used beginning Aug. 23 and commodity prices were to follow that of Aug. 19th. Each new dollar worths $300,000.00 of the original paper money bills. At the same time came the order that privately owned U.S. dollars, silver dollars and gold bars must be exchanged in the Central Banks for the New dollars, Gin-yuan, before the end of October. If not exchanged within the time limite, it will be confisticated ~~..........~~ and all C.N. paper bills must be exchanged to Gin-yuan by Nov.20.

It was with great hopes people accepted the new currency and the controlled price but somehow people entertain some kind of a doubt. They prefer to hold on to commodities rather than the new Gin-yuan bill. All rush to spend and eat.

As the days passed, store-keepers grew chary about selling goods. Gradually more stores became vacant of goods and some began to close up. The rice and oil stores were told to open and sell the rationed amount to buyers. Most people ~~who~~ had no storage in hand and they must buy everyday and long lines began to form. Commodities disappeared from the markets. Money became useless except in the black market. A ration system was immediately initiated. One can buy 1.3 catties of rice and 4 ounces of vegetable oil per day daily. One must go to stand in line before dawn in order to wait for one's turn. Often times about noon the store would declare that all rice or oil was sold out and those waiting in the later part of the line, have to leave empty handed inspite of the long hours of waiting. Suicides began to happen in the waiting lines and in shops. Finally the control on prices was up-lifted on November 1st. Commodities appear gradually but prices went sky high. Price of meat went up to $27 G.Y. (4 G.y.= 1 U.S. dollar at the time) per catty in Nanking and $51 G.Y. per catty in Shanghai.

Social disorder was brewing under this tremendous problem of food-shortage by hoarding. People began to rob the rice trucks coming into the city.

People carrying food on the streets were also constantly being robbed. The climax of disorder fell on November 8th. When a number of the food shops: meat, beans ric rice wheat and others were robbed by mobs of people and some of the stores were se set on fire after robbing. This economic revolution did bring out more goods on the market and with a drop in prices the next day. An anouncement of a proposed modification of the Gin-yuan was made, at the same time it was anounced civilians are permitted to have U.S. dollars, gold bars and silver with certain regulations, The tension was losened considerably.

However, before the first storm was over, another tempest was coming. Civil war was moving southward. People got excited over many descriptions of fears. People began to leave the city in crowds. Trains, boats and air planes were booked full and also/ahead of time/to a month even two months. People are again on waiting lists for travel and waiting in line for tickets. Life seems to be full of up-sets, difficulties and fears. Up to date families of the government officials and even some private institutions have already concluded their works or evacuated to Formosa or Hongkong. The long lines of waiting people are shifted from the front doors of stores to that of the ticket offices of stations. Indeed a strong nation, at least, needs three qualifications: leaders with wisdom, intelligent citizens and economic resources and security. All ~~with~~ Need a strong moral back bone, and a s ns sense of the presence of God and the love of one's fellow-men is absolutely e essential. Without these, there is no peace. The atmosphere at present is one of absolute darkness. However I still like to believe in the seemingly impossible. Inspite of all the miseries of life I still believe that God can work miracles, only if men would cooperate with Him, and I believe man's power of cooperation has not entirely expired yet. ~~Because~~ Inspite of these gloomy settings there seems to be still some intangible assests.

In the midst of inflation and economic pressure the geographical society of China along with nine other Science Socities did hold their annual meeting from October 9-11 in Nanking. There were a total of 600 members present out of which oe over one hundred are geographers. The papers presented and the works each has done in their own particular post has made great advancement from that of pre-war days. The annual meeting of the geological Society met from 25-28th of October. That again has given many signs of definite hard work and success in the field. It all indicates that man is still holding on to work with hope.

In the midst of economic pressure and chaos a project was launched to open four Companies such as Formosa sugar factory, Paper factory and Shanghai cotton weaving industries to civilians for shares, thus to gather stagnate money into circulation. At least ~~they~~ the attempt was made. Somewhere a screw is missing and the engine does not run.

On the way to Shwen Hwa village the fields were turned into soldiers camps since early ~~in the~~ summer. Every time I passed the place on my way to and back from Shwen Hwa I noticed some changes. The living conditions, ways of behavior of the soldiers and the management of the camps seem to be better than before yet the psychology is different too.

Yet all these and other characteristic incidents that lend perplexity to life, laborer strikes, rural poverty, business unrest, owe much to some undiscovered disease yet not correctly analyzed and properly treated. This disease naturally defeats the little good that is derived from rest and good nourishment. The disease is eating away the muscle of human confidence. Without the strength of confidence, and the love of mankind, life is nothing. Naturally other diseases creep in. The only hope lies in the salvage of human confidence. The solution depends on moral strength as well as intelligence and technique. I like to hold on to the faith that "all things work for good to those who love God". Inspite of the clouds I feel grateful that humanity is not all gone.

You know I am interested in the Rural district of Shwen Hwa and since I discovered water is what they need most, I wanted to help them with the repairing of the broken dams (reservoirs). We had, absolutely, no means of getting the funds. When the Rural reconstruction Commission came, we liked to get in touch with them but we have no ropes to pull. We studied our problem and worked just as hard as if we were going to have the means to carry it through. One student wrote her graduation thesis on the regional geography of Shwen Hwa. Two others did their summer field work there on irrigation system, land utilization and rural economy.

When I happened to meet Mr. John E. Baker of the Rural Rehabilitation Commission at a reception, I simply told him what was on my mind. He was interested in our findings and later wanted to visit the place himself. As he did not get my name and did not know who I am, he was not able to find me. After some delay he did find me through Dr. Wu and we did go to Shwen Hwa, inspite of the threats of war and the excitements of evacuation, he is so deeply interested in the project that he is sending an engineer. And there is a great chance the work is to be done this winter if circumstances permit. This is all beyond our expectation though we did hope for it. Aren't we funny?

I have decided to remain in Nanking regardless of what is to happen because I believe in "Do what one can and leave the rest to God". No one can see clearly what the morrow is going to bring forth. Anyhow, life can be interesting. It depends how one is taking it.

Even though nearly one third of the girls have left, work is going on just the same. I feel time is more pressing due to additional meetings and other extras. But it is better to be absorbed in some kind of work all the time than to be confussed by all kinds of gossips and fears.

Let us all pray for the birth of Christ into all human hearts during this Christmas season, so that there will truly be "pleace on earth and Good will among men".

Merry Christmas and a Truly Happy New Year to you and family

Sincerely Yours
En-lan
Liu En-lan

（3）师生通信

涂长望

涂长望（1906–1962），湖北武汉人，英国利物浦大学地理系肄业，中国近代气象学的奠基人之一。1926–1929 年间涂长望就读于沪江大学地质地理系，师从葛德石，深受其影响。

此后，涂长望是无论负笈英国，还是任职中国，与葛德石师生情深，二人通讯从未间断，一直持续至四十年代末。1949 年之后，涂长望被任命为中央气象局局长。当葛德石在中国地理学界被人人喊打的时候，作为门生的涂长望保持了沉默。师生二人的通信现存数十封。

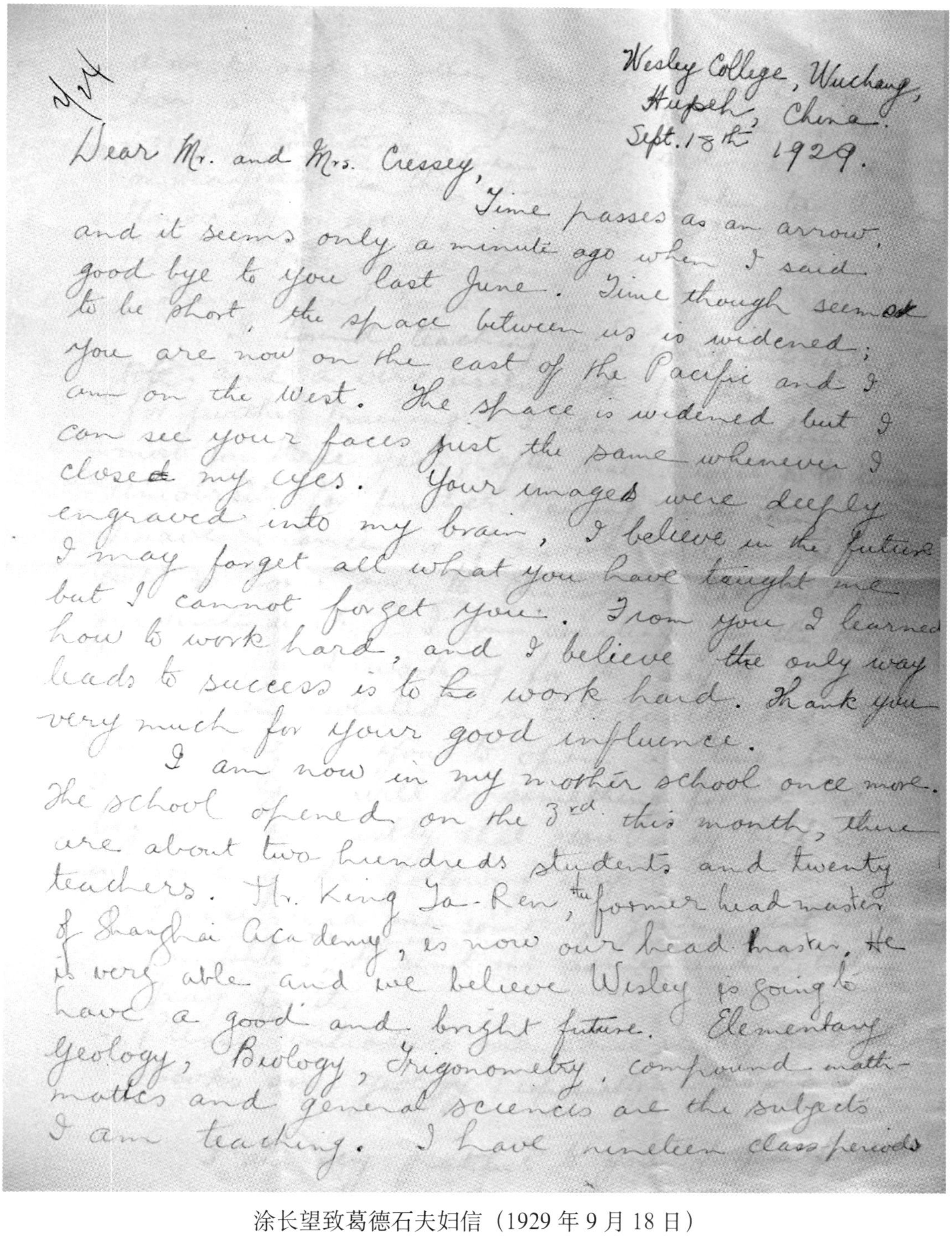

2/24

Wesley College, Wuchang,
Hupeh, China.
Sept. 18th 1929.

Dear Mr. and Mrs. Cressey,

Time passes as an arrow, and it seems only a minute ago when I said good bye to you last June. Time though seems to be short, the space between us is widened; you are now on the east of the Pacific and I am on the West. The space is widened but I can see your faces just the same whenever I close my eyes. Your images were deeply engraved into my brain, I believe in the future I may forget all what you have taught me but I cannot forget you. From you I learned how to work hard, and I believe the only way leads to success is to work hard. Thank you very much for your good influence.

I am now in my mother school once more. The school opened on the 3rd this month, there are about two hundreds students and twenty teachers. Mr. King Ta-Ren, the former headmaster of Shanghai Academy, is now our head master, He is very able and we believe Wesley is going to have a good and bright future. Elementary Geology, Biology, Trigonometry, compound mathematics and general sciences are the subjects I am teaching. I have nineteen class periods

涂长望致葛德石夫妇信（1929 年 9 月 18 日）

time to help me. I hope you will guide me an
lead me as usual.

Mr. Hou Yi Hwa is now in Nanking, he int
to join politics, perhaps he got a job already.
Mr. Teng Shao Tang is teaching in some middle
school in Kuangtung. My brother-in-law Mr.
Tsai-Lin-Sheng is taking his post-graduate
work in Chemistry in Chicago University now.
I wrote to him last time and told him to see
you sometime, and he is a stranger ~~to th~~.
perhaps he needs your help in some respects.

I believe you have a very nice ti
with your parents and friends now. How a
your two children? Are they getting alon
very nicely?

Best regards to you and your
family.

Yours affectionately,
Yi Chang Wang.

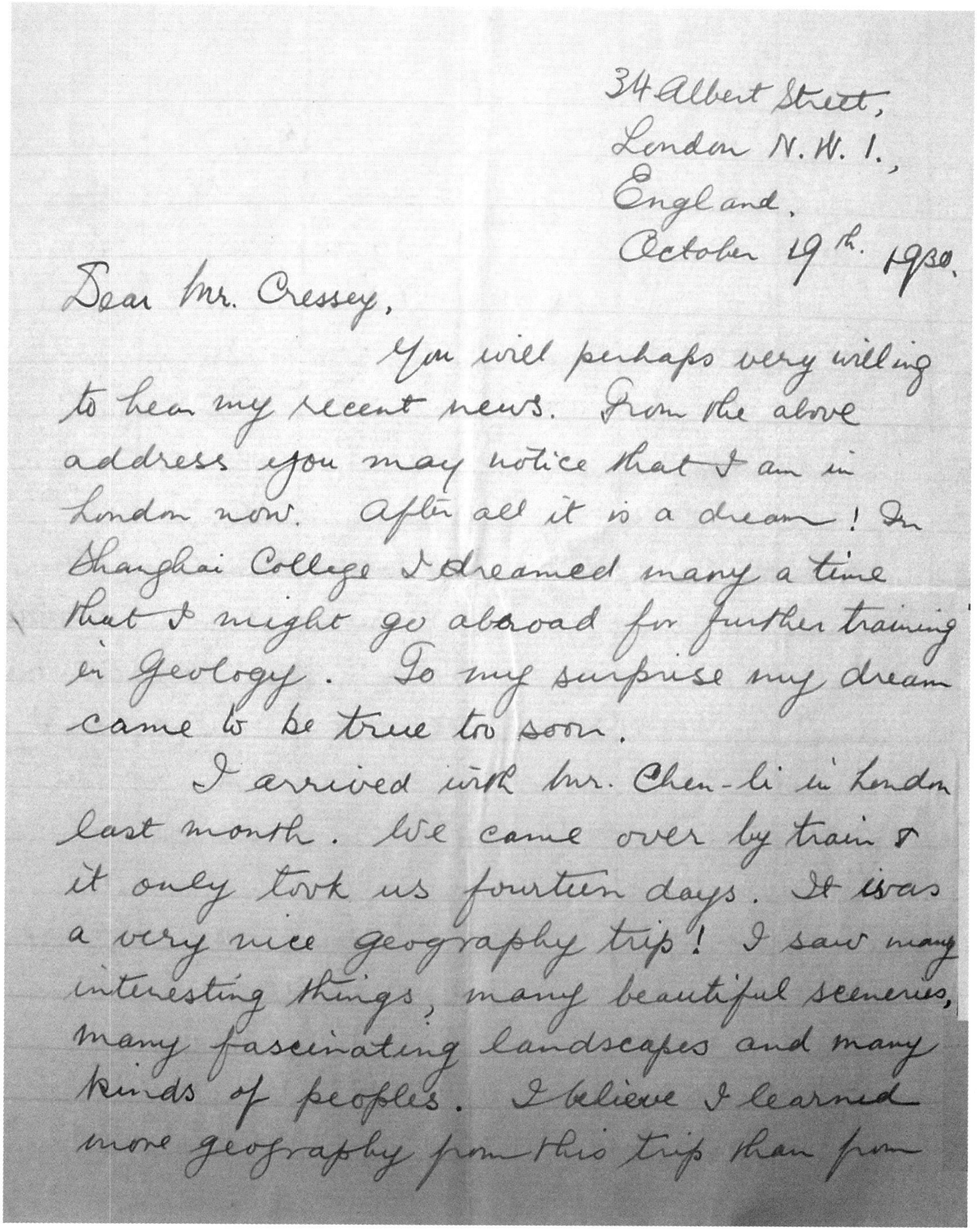

34 Albert Street,
London N.W. 1.,
England.
October 19th. 1930.

Dear Mr. Cressey,

You will perhaps very willing to hear my recent news. From the above address you may notice that I am in London now. After all it is a dream! In Shanghai College I dreamed many a time that I might go abroad for further training in Geology. To my surprise my dream came to be true too soon.

I arrived with Mr. Chen-li in London last month. We came over by train & it only took us fourteen days. It was a very nice geography trip! I saw many interesting things, many beautiful sceneries, many fascinating landscapes and many kinds of peoples. I believe I learned more geography from this trip than from

涂长望致葛德石信（1930 年 10 月 19 日）

2.

the text-books. It took me ~~to~~ a long time to get into the University of London and it took even a longer time for me to find a nice and comfortable 'digs'.

I am now studying my principle subject geography in London School of Economics and Political Science, and my subsidiary subject geology in Kings' College. I am working in the second year. If I have luck perhaps I could manage to take my final examin. in B.A. (Honour) in two years. And then I shall spend another three year for in research work. The courses I am taking this year are the following,

Geography.	Geology.
1. Europe (Reginal Geog.)	(1). Petrology
2. Map work	(2). Paleontalogy
3. North America (.. ..)	(3). Stratigraphy.
4. Physical Basis of Geography.	(4). Practical work.

3.

I like the practical work better than the lectures. It seems to me that the professors, assistant professors and lecturers are only good writers. I can hardly appreciate their lectures — at least at present.

London is a very interesting place, it is a world rather than a town. Many people asked me about my impression of London and I found this question very hard to answear. I have not seen enough London yet and it is impossible for me to pass a sound description at present. There are some very famous writers who can write a book about any place in the world after spent a week-end there. I am no such writer and I hope I will never be. London is still very strange to me and I am searching it with open eyes.

Would you please kindly tell me something about the geography courses that are offered in American Universities? I wish I could come over to America for a few years. At present I don't know what is the best for me to do. Your advice and instruction are heartily welcomed.

Where are you now? How are you and Mrs. Cressey? I am very anxious to hear from you.

With best regards to you all,

Yours respectfully,

C. W. Li

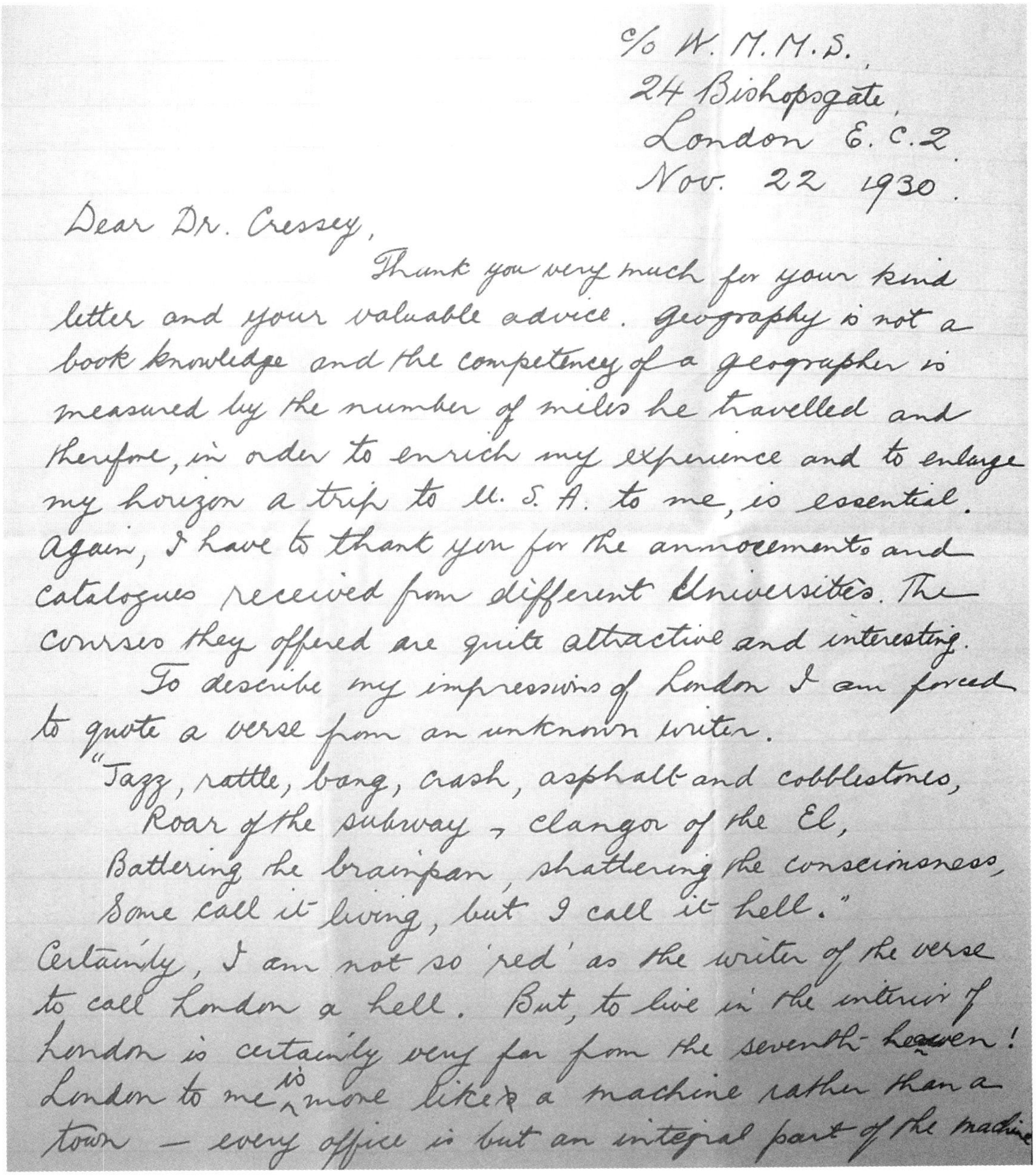

c/o W. M. M. S.,
24 Bishopsgate,
London E. C. 2
Nov. 22 1930.

Dear Dr. Cressey,

Thank you very much for your kind letter and your valuable advice. Geography is not a book knowledge and the competency of a geographer is measured by the number of miles he travelled and therefore, in order to enrich my experience and to enlarge my horizon a trip to U. S. A. to me, is essential. Again, I have to thank you for the annocements and catalogues received from different Universities. The courses they offered are quite attractive and interesting.

To describe my impressions of London I am forced to quote a verse from an unknown writer.

"Jazz, rattle, bang, crash, asphalt and cobblestones,
Roar of the subway, clangor of the El,
Battering the brainpan, shattering the consciousness,
Some call it living, but I call it hell."

Certainly, I am not so 'red' as the writer of the verse to call London a hell. But, to live in the interior of London is certainly very far from the seventh heaven! London to me is more like a machine rather than a town — every office is but an integral part of the machine

涂长望致葛德石信（1930 年 11 月 22 日）

and every human being is but a fraction of that power which keeps the wheel going. Every morning and evening I enjoy myself by watching the rushing-in crowd and the pouring out mass. Sometimes I said in silence to myself 'This is life'. I quite agree with Huntington that climate does exert influence on the development of a race's character but to my mind inherited racial temperament plays a greater role to determine the kind of civilization we are going to have. Even the yellow race has the same kind of stimulating climate as you have in New-York I don't believe the same kind of civilization will result. Taste differs. Racial temperatoment counts. Though I was born in a big port, trained in a big town, had ample chance to come into contact with foreigners and equipped with western ideas, nevertheless, I am prejudiced ~~to~~ against western civilization to some extent. I don't like this kind of living. I ~~rat~~ prefer to live in a deserted village rather than a crowded town. Too crowded, ~~and~~ too mechanical and too artificial!

Sometimes London looks like a big zoo to me and of course I am a member of the zoo. Masses of animals move in and out, daily weekly, yearly and lifely! Black animals, yellow animals, white animals and red animals pass each other and look at each other but ~~each~~ every one of them wears a contenance of satisfaction, because they call themselves 'MEN'. This is not philosphy but it is my impression of London.

The English people at once win my admiration. They are very kind and exceedingly polite. Politness shall I say is the key to success and there is no ~~doubt why~~ wonder that English people are successful everywhere in the world. To my mind politness as a weapon is more effective than battleship, fortunately they have both. Most of the English people are gentlemenlike and I believe the art ~~of~~ to be gentlemanlike is another good character that a Chinese should learn. Much to my disappointment I learned from Bertrand Russell last week that gentlemanlike is the enemy of the English people. As a whole I should say the English people are very moral but there are exceptions For example, in the geography library of L.E.C. about one hundred and fifty books were missing last year. This certainly strikes me, but a moment's thinking leads me ~~to~~ to realize the great principle that possessive instinct is universal. This is my impression of the English people.

I don't quite know whether I have any impression of my work in geography or not. You might say that I have not started my work yet. I am just attending a few lectures on Europe, North America and Physical Basis, and that is all. The lectures are far from interesting. I often heard from my fellowstudents saying that they are fed up with so and so's lecture. Nature always balances his children; a good writer does not necessary mean a good teacher and vice versa. Of ~~to~~ course there are exceptions. Professors R. Jones and L. D. Stamp are our two best professors and ~~both~~ of them have written many books. This term I take more geology courses than geography. Stratigraphy, Petrology, Paleotology and Practical geology are the courses I have to take for the subsidiary. At present, as lecture goes, geology is more interesting to me. It takes time for me to adjust to my environment and to get acquanited with the libraries and laboratories. A new student can hardly get hold of the books he wants, old students always dominate. I am an old student ~~the~~ next year and it won't be long for me to get really started in my work. It is quite true that the English geographers have a big lead in descriptive geography but it is equally true that they have very few College text-books on geography. Geography of Europe by Coster is less than three hundred pages, ~~and~~ very simple and elementary and yet it is a recommended text-book for college student! A great many of the text-books we use here are written by American geographers. English scholars are quite behind in text-book writing business.

Yesterday I went with my friend to the British Geological Museum and I was stupified ~~with~~ by what I saw. I sighed many a deep sigh in the museum. I sigh because I realized how little I know about geology. My knowledge about geology is nothing in comparison with what I saw yesterday. I determined to spend my winter vacation in the museum.

I am afraid that I have taken too much of your time and I shall leave the rest to the next letter.

Remember me kindly to Mrs Cressey.

Yours respectfully,

Tse Chang Wang.

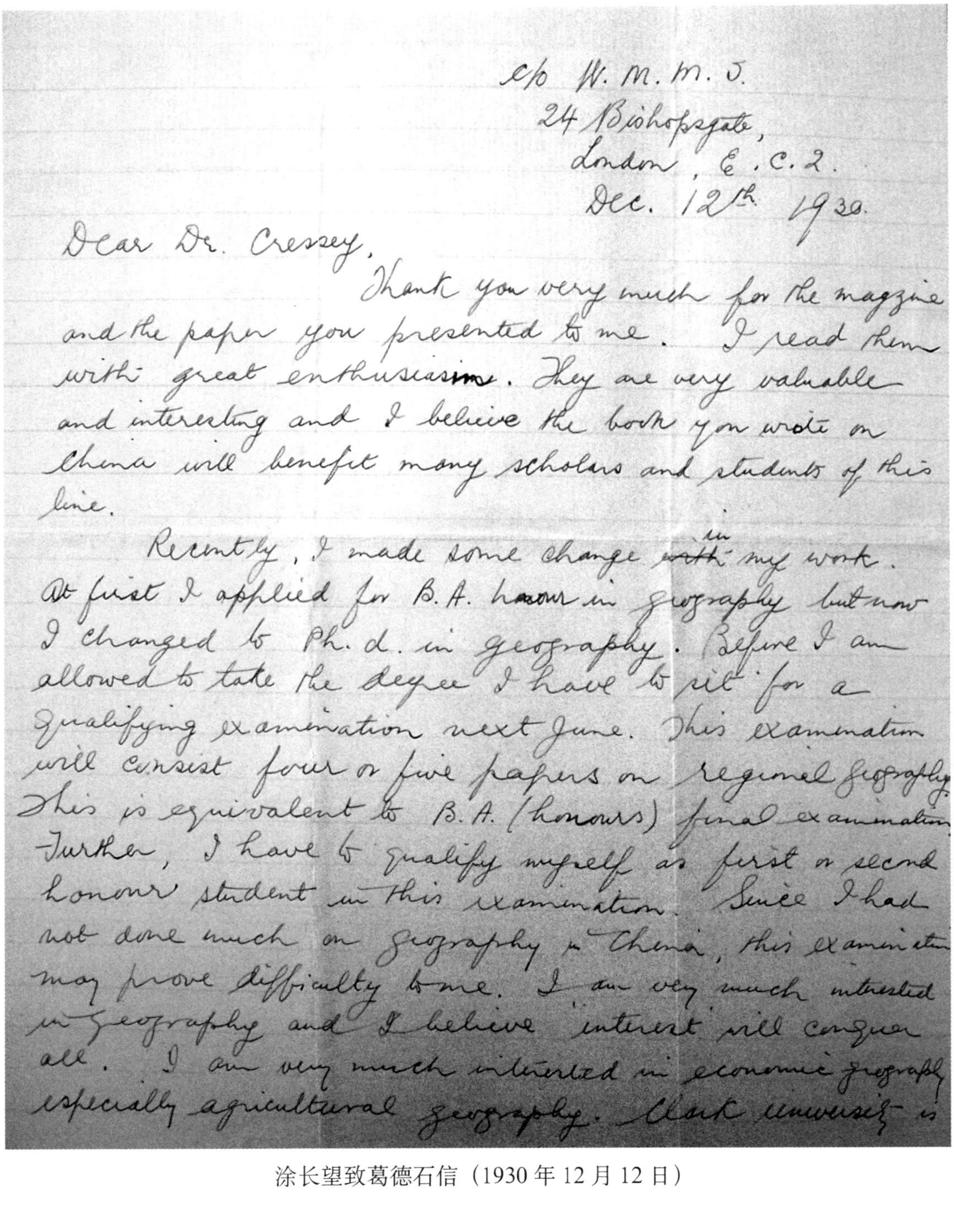

c/o W. M. M. S.
24 Bishopsgate,
London, E. C. 2.
Dec. 12th 1930.

Dear Dr. Cressey,

Thank you very much for the magazine and the paper you presented to me. I read them with great enthusiasm. They are very valuable and interesting and I believe the book you wrote on China will benefit many scholars and students of this line.

Recently, I made some change ~~with~~ in my work. At first I applied for B.A. honour in geography but now I changed to Ph. d. in geography. Before I am allowed to take the degree I have to sit for a qualifying examination next June. This examination will consist four or five papers on regional geography. This is equivalent to B.A. (honours) final examination. Further, I have to qualify myself as first or second honour student in this examination. Since I had not done much on geography in China, this examination may prove difficulty to me. I am very much interested in geography and I believe interest will conquer all. I am very much interested in economic geography especially agricultural geography. Clark University is

涂长望致葛德石信（1930 年 12 月 12 日）

quite strong along these lines and I hope I can spend two years in Clark University with you. Meterology is my favorite subject too and I am just studying several books on this line. As a matter of fact I have two many favorite subjects and I don't know which one shall I specilize in. Meterology combines with agricultural geography may be very useful to China.

Our school closes down for Christmas today, fortunately the library does not close. I have not done much last term and I am trying to catch it up during this vacation.

Best regards to you and Mrs Cressey.

Yours respectfully,

C. W. Tu.

On board President Hoover
Yokohama
October, 12, 1934

My dear Mr. Tu:

I am sorry not to be able to welcome you back to China, but on the day when you are leaving Venice I am sailing to America. I have heard of your new position in Nanking, and wish to congratulate you on such a splendid opportunity. You are indeed fortunate to be able to start in so well.

I have had a very pleasant and busy summer myself, most of it in China, with some time also in the Philippines, Korea and Japan. In addition to my studies of land utilization, I have been making a geographic survey of Chekiang and Kiangnan for the National Agricultural Research Bureau of Nanking. Unfortunately I must hasten back to the States for my classes are already under way.

One of the things in which I have been interested in China is the very favorable reception which my book seems to be receiving. Of course you have also seen Roxby's fine reviews, etc., but I was particularly anxious that it be acceptable to Chinese scholars. Already 600 copies have been sold in China, 300 more in Japan, and several thousand in the United States.

I am particularly sorry that I shall not be seeing you in Shanghai, for I wanted to talk over with you the matter of translating the book into Chinese. I have searched the country, and find noone whom I should prefer to yourself. The qualifications, as I see them, are ability in both English and Chinese, geographic competancy, and dependability. The only other person who is a possibility is Mr. Pan En-ling, formerly at the College but now with the Shanghai Commercial and Savings Bank in Shanghai. I have talked matters over frankly with Mr. Pan and he is willing to undertake the job, but we both agree that you are better qualified, and I am therefore now asking you to be my translator. If you happen to have time in Shanghai I should be glad to have you see Mr. Pan; in any case will you be good enough to write him so that he will know your decision. This will save time for letters to America and back.

葛德石致涂长望信（1934 年 10 月 12 日）

Mr. Tu Chang-wang - 2 - Oct. 12, 1934

I need not tell you that I have put ten years into the writing of the book and that I am exceedingly anxious that the translation be extra well done. The preparation of the manuscript has been a very expensive proposition, the total costs running to U.S. $4000.00. Part of this has been paid by various foundations, but I shall never get back my costs. That is quite alright, for this is my contribution to China. I mention it only that you may understand my financial position.

The Commercial Press has agreed to publish the translation, which will probably sell for around Mex $4. They will pay me fifteen per cent royalty, of which I shall be glad to pay you as translator one-third or five per cent until the total of the payments to you amount to Mex. $1000.00 In addition I shall be willing to pay you Mex $100. at the time of publication to cover your various incidental expenses. Your task will include translation, preparation for the printer, proof reading, and general superwision of publication in Shanghai.

I have written to Mr. Y. W. Wang, Chief Editor of the Press, and I would suggest that you get in touch with him if you are willing to go ahead. He asks that you submit a sample translation of a dozen pages so that they may check your style. My agreement with you is of course conditioned upon their approval of your Chinese style of writing. There is no particular time limit, but I should like to have the book appear as early as possible next spring. In any case I would not want your work to extend more than five or six months.

I talked briefly with Dr. Chu in Nanking about your doing this work and he has no objections, although of course it would come outside your time at the Observatory. No doubt you are also busy with thesis and will have many things to pick up on coming home. I very much hope that you will this job, partly as a favor to me, incidentally to make some money, but chiefly as a major geographic contribution to China.

If you agree, you may proceed at once and I shall write in full detail. In any case notify Mr. Pan. I am anxious that the translation be a complete and full translation, sentence by sentence. Where you dissagree, you may feel free to insert a translators futnote.

Hopefully yours,

George B. Cressey

P. S. I am sending one copy to the boat and another to Wusueh.

TITUTE OF METEOROLOGY
ACADEMIA SINICA
PEICHIKO, NANKING, CHINA

涂長望
氣象研究所
南京：北極閣

April 8th,1937.

My dear Professor Cressey,

Thank you ever so much for your nice and long letter. I am very glad to hear all the good news but sorry to learn that your department suffered slightly from water in the midst of flames, and hoping that the damage so incurred would not hinder the smooth running of your courses. It seems that you are very busy with geological conferences and geographical sessions and I presume that you are one of the outstanding leaders. By sheer coincidence your letter arrived in the very time when we are busy with meteorological sessions and geographical annual conferences. They took place in Nanking and lasted for three solid days.

I am so glad to hear your projected plan of visiting Soviet Russia in this coming summer and do hope that you could come to our country for awhile. I was on a sightseeing trip in Russia in May,1934 for about one month. Our tour extended as far south as the Black Sea and had visited most parts of southern and central Russia. From what I had seen and experienced in different parts of that country I was convinced that Soviet Russia is on the right road towards an enlightened civilisation,if not entirely a new one. The new social and cultural pattern in the making is entirely different from what I have experienced in western Europe though the tools of production are essentially the same. Soviet Russia deserves the special attention of geographical experts for it presents a new socio-economic problem, a new challenge to civilisation. And this is the reason why I am particularly interested in your Soviet trip. May I wish you a very successful trip!

I must thank you for the valuable publications you sent me from time to time and needless to say that I am always interested in your writings and found them very helpful. In reciprocating your kind favour I have arranged with the Meteorological Institue and the Meteorological Society of China to send to you

涂长望致葛德石信（1937 年 4 月 8 日）

INSTITUTE OF METEOROLOGY
ACADEMIA SINICA
PEICHIKO, NANKING, CHINA

涂長望
氣象研究所
南京：北極閣

all the current memoirs and the Meteorological Magazine. These publications just indicate to you what we are doing here but they do not necessarily represent words of wisdom.

You will notice from the writing paper that I am no longer teaching at Tsinghwa University. I was called back from Peiping last fall when Coching Chu was about going to head the Chekiang University, Hangchow. He has been the chancellor of the Chekiang University for one year already and if he does not choose to resign he could stick to the job permanently. At the same time he is acting head of the Institute, but sorry to say, owing to the great demand of time made on him in the University he could hardly spare any time for the Institute. We all feel the great loss. Most of his former work is passed on to me and so I am having a very busy time indeed; supervising all the publications, editing the Meteorological Magazine, acting as the English secretary and beside I have to research on the problem of seasonal forecasting of weather and flood stage. In view of this circumstance I find it impossible to do any work on geographical problems though my interest in these problems seldom waned. It seems to me that degrees of any sort have not direct bearing on my research problem and so I am not very interested in this question at present.

Geographers in China are few and many of the names listed below are known to you, but I do hope that you will find the list of names useful.

With very kind regards,

Respectfully yours,

Changwang Tu.

Chang-wang Tu.

中央研究院氣象研究所
INSTITUTE OF METEOROLOGY
ACADEMIA SINICA
PEICHIKO, NANKING, CHINA.

Chungking, Szechwan,
March 26th, 1938.

Dear Prof. Cressey,

I am so glad to hear from you in this time of the crisis and more so to learn what the American people are doing to help us in spite of their difficult times at home. It is needless for me to mention here that our people are very grateful to the American people for what they have done to us and in return our 450 millions have determined to fight to the bitter end, regardless of consequences, showing to our friends in the other side of the Pacific that we have courage and are worthy of your support and assistance. We knew from the very start that we have to fight a powerful and ruthless foe all by ourselves, nevertheless, we took the challenge, for the alternative to fight is surrender. Hundreds and thousand of our peasants, workers, stundents and professional men march to the battle field side by side with soldiers singing and joking even they know that they are using only rifles and swords to fight against field guns, tanks and aeroplanes. But what a nobler cause than fighting for our existence? And who can tolerate Japanese rule?

You ask me in your letter as what the Americans can do to help China. The answer is that we don't want the Americans to fight for us, nor ~~do you~~ against us. The Americans are very intelligent people and I am not in the position to advise you as to the best method of assisting us. But in passing may I just let you know that Stimson's open letter to the New York Times has created a profound impression in the minds of our teeming millions. The choice is between peace and righteousness! We are on the side of righteousness and we are confident that righteousness will eventually win. But who can deny us the final victory if we are determined to fight to the last man?!

涂长望致葛德石信（1938年3月26日）

中央研究院氣象研究所
INSTITUTE OF METEOROLOGY
ACADEMIA SINICA
PEICHIKO, NANKING, CHINA.

Now let me write something about our Academia Sinica and our institute. In order to find a safer place to continue our work we moved to Hankow in the begining of last September and some institutes moved down to Changsha. Since the fall of Nanking then Hankow and Changsha became the target of Japanese bombers and we were forced to move once more. This time our institute alone moved up to Chungking and the other institutes moved to Kweiling, Kwangsi. In spite of the present difficult time we are carrying on our work as usual and at present we are engaged in writing a book entitled "Climate of China" in both English and Chinese. If circumstances permit we would like it finished by the end of this year.

Your little map is very fascinating and I am so glad to learn that you have travelled far and wide in Soviet Russia and central Asia. And I am sure some work of importance will soon come out of your pen, but may I ask in advance to have the privilege to read your words of wisdom.

In closing please remember me kindly to Mrs. Cressey.

With kindest regards,

Yours respectfully,

Changwang Tu

National University of Chekiang,
Tsen-yi, Kweichow, China,
November 22nd 1940.

My dear Professor,

Please forgive me for not writing to you for such a long time and, no doubt, you will understand the present war condition is so bad that nobody has any courage or time to sit down to write a long letter. The Japanese bombers have literally bombed us to pieces, at least morally. These brutes came regularly day and night for the past five months, ~~and~~ we had practically no air defence and our air raid cellar is not too safe. Sometimes, we could not sleep at all and even could not get anything to eat for one or two days. And who could work under such difficult circumstances! It is really a great pity and a great loss to China for there are so many hundreds of intellectuals just wasting their time in a game of hide and seek with the Japanese bombers. Personally, I could do nothing under such frightful circumstances, so Dr. Coching Chu, now chancellor of the Chekiang University, has recently transferred me to this university and helping him to organize a geographical department. This University has experienced a gipsy's life in the past three years, it first moved to southern Kiangsi, then to northern Kwangsi (Ishan) and lastly to Tsenyi, northern

涂长望致葛德石信（1940 年 11 月 22 日）

Kweichow. Tsenyi 遵義 is not too far away from Chungking and air alarm is of daily occurrence. Our life here is far from happy. Early in the morning we have just time to manage a hurried breakfast and then scatters to the country ready for the air alarm. The bombers usually appear about 10 o'clock, circlingaround and looking for trouble, then fly northwards to Chungking, after bombing Chungking they return to their base and fly over here again about 2 o'clock. Then, we all hurry back and have a few classes.

I have the ambition to write a book on "The Climate of China" in Chinese and English but unfortunately such difficult conditions render my writing of such a book almost impossible. I only wish I could come over to work and finish such a book with you, so that my time would not be totally wasted. Your experience and valuable advice are indispensible in such an undertaking. But this is only a wish! The Boxer indemnity funds have suspended payments during these war years otherwise, I would apply for a scholarship. I don't know anything about the Rockfeller fellowship, please kindly make inquiries for me.

Dear Professor, what research work are you working on now? I believe, you are very busy as usual and must have written many papers since I wrote you last. Please send a few copies to enlighten me. We are living in a dark age, completely cut off from the world of science. The subscribed magazines and Journals have not arrived for one year! This is no doubt due to Communication difficulties.

I am glad that your government is gradually taking positive steps against aggression, the re-election of President Rosevelt will mean a lot to the Dictators. I do hope the world choas will be soon over, after all homo sapiens is homo sapiens!

I do hope this letter will reach you sometime before Christmas so that it can bring to you and your able wife and lovely children our Christmas greetings.

Yours respectfully,

Changwang Tu.

P.S. In a separate cover I am sending you a paper of mine, written one year & half ago but just comes out of the print, and part of which had already appeared in "Physik der freien Atmosphäre" 1939, pp. 233-240. C.W.Tu

随信附涂长望全家福

NATIONAL UNIVERSITY OF CHEKIANG
Tsen-yi, Kweichow, China

February 23rd, 1941

Prof. G. B. Cressey
Department of Geology and Geography
Syracuse University
Syracuse, New York

My dear Professor,

Thank you so much for your lovely letter and we are very happy to learn that your family is growing in size and is rapidly approaching the size of a large chinese family. My family joins me in shouting " three cheers to Mrs. Cressey and her big family!" We have a saying "將門多虎子" and tiger cubs are badly needed in this time of world choas. My humble family is growing too but at a very slow space and a girl has come to our family since we came to the university.

As an expert on Far eastern problems many of us were convinced that you must have played a lion's part in forming a more realistic public opinion and shaping the present American foreign policy towards the east. From your letter we learn that our friends are doing their utmost in helping us and for our part we must carry the war to the desired end. It is not an easy matter for a poor agricultural China to fight against a highly industrialised Japan, the odds are tremendous! What is more, the enemy has occupied the best part of our soil and mineral resources, and this makes the war more difficult, even impossible. The miracle is that we can still carry on the war even sometime without any outside help ! This is not to say that we are self-sufficient, far from it. We need money, gasoline, bullets, aeroplane, trucks, tanks, medicine, food and everything that is necessary for a mordern war very badly. Owing to the shortage of gasoline passengers have to wait many a week before they could move a few hundred miles and our troops got to walk the whole way from the northern front in Shansi to the southern front in Yunnan. Our communication system is practie

涂长望致葛德石信（1941 年 2 月 23 日）

cally frozen and troops immobile at the present moment. The food problem is also serious, last year the harvest is non-too good and the prices of cereals have already trebled last October's prices. If this year's harvest were bad there would be widespread famine. There is also the danger of inflation, the amount of notes issued is unknown but the rate of increase of prices is alarming. We are very grateful of your help but we hope that the financial as well as material aid should be more substantial and come at the right moment, otherwise it will be too late. Our people has many weak points but after all he is a good neighbour and judging by the means and manner he is fighting the Japanese he may prove a worthy partner.

In closing I must thank you for making arrangements to enable me to come over for continued research. The best thing I can do for my country to is do my utmost in a most efficient manner. To continue my research work, I think, is what I could do in the most efficient way. I am so glad to hear that your new book "Asia's Lands and Peoples" is soon to appear and I also sinecerely hope that you could come over to China in her time of great distress and need, afterall you are her best firend and interpreter.

With kind regards to all of your family.

Respectfully yours,

THE NATURAL SCIENCE SOCIETY OF CHINA
c/o. National Central University,
Sa-ping-ba, Chungking.

April 20th,1944.

Professor G.B.Cressey,
c/o. The American Ambassy,
Chungking.

Dear Professor Cressey,

We have the great pleasure to inform you that during our recent Committee Meeting you have been elected as the adviser of our Committee for Micro-film Extension Service of our Society. And Prof. J.Needham is the other adviser elected,representing Great Britian. Owing to the difficulties in obtaining electricity and projectors in many parts of China our Society is going to mimeograph some of the important articles and abstracts from the microfilms for distribution and for permanent keeping. The project is divided into four sections,namely: Physical Sciences (Mathmatics,Physics,Chemistry,Geology and Geography), Biological Sciences(this include medical science),Enin-gineering Sciences, and Psychological Sciences. The first two sections are ready and will be mimeographed presently. We are very anxious to have your valuable suggestions and advices on this matter and please favour us with your words of wisdom.

With our warmest Greetings,

Yours faithfully,

The Natural Science Society of China.

per. Chang-wang T'u (secretary)

Chang wang Tu

涂长望致葛德石信（1944 年 4 月 20 日）

THE NATURAL SCIENCE SOCIETY OF CHINA
c/o. National Central University
Sa-ping-pa, Chungking.

May 23,1944.

My dear Professor,

My wife and children want me to write and thank you for the chocolate bars,the orange drops and the gums. The children had a thrilling time with the gums because this was their first ~~time~~ experience with the American civilisation! And I want to thank you particularly for the fountain pen and the nice afternoon that I had spent with you last Saturday.

I have the pleasure to report that I have already written to the Institute of Meteorology asking for the monthly rainfall and temperature records of Lahsa of the last ten years. I have also made contact with the headquarters of the Generalissimo about the planes to Sinkiang,but nobody can guarantee nowadays because everything depends upon the temperament of one man. And I have also found out that Mr. K.C.Huang is in town at the present moment.

During the last few days I have made inquiries about the translation of your books and I have also given some serious thought on this matter. The failure of my translation of your first book still weighs heavily on my conscience and I will try my best to find some qualified person to have it translated for you. The reason why I could not do it myself is because my Chinese is nothing comparable with your beautiful English. The following particulars about translation are supplied to me by my neigbour who is a well-known translator.

a. Since China has not joined the international copyright association nobody has ever paid any attention to the copyright. (This is ,of course,improper.)

b. In selling translated work the rate varies from 100 to 200 dollars per 1000 characters.

c. The cost of printing is one dollar per one character for 3000 copies.(This includes paper,binding etc.)

涂长望致葛德石信（1944 年 5 月 23 日）

THE NATURAL SCIENCE SOCIETY OF CHINA
c/o. National Central University
Sa-ping-pa, Chungking.

d. The biggest circulation of translated work during the war time is 10000 copies.

e. The author of the book will get 15% of the sale minus the amount paid to the translator.

These particulars may be useful to you but I don't know whether the Commercial Press can give you better terms or not.

Enclosed is the copy of names which you have sent it to me. I have made a few alterations in conjunctions with colleagues of our department.

Dean Hu told me this morning that you have mentioned to him that you have brought a letter from the Geographical Society of your country for the Geograhical Society of China. He would like to know whether you still have the letter with you because he want tow write a letter to thank them.

The Natural Science Society want me to find out from you whether there is any possibility for the Cultural Division of the State Department of Washington to contribute a type-writer(desk), a mimeograph machine and some stencils towards the smooth running of our Mimeograph Service. At the present moment we are using those belong to the Central university which is very inconvenient during crowded hours.

I have also recieved your letter of invitation and I am only too pleased to come and meet Prof. Buck and Hall.

Looking forwards of seeing you soon,

Your pupil,

Changwang T'u

Changwang T'u.

THE NATURAL SCIENCE SOCIETY OF CHINA
c/o. National Central University
Sa-ping-pa, Chungking.

May 29th.1944.

My dear Professor,

Thanks very much for your nice party and we believe through your effort and ~~t~~ enthusiasm you may be able to instill into the hearts of our geographers the sense of responsibility,the spirit of co-operation and the atmosphere of concerted action towards a common idealogy,the lack of which would not only delay the geographical reserch work in China but also introduce choas and confusion in the related circles.

Through my repeated inquiry the dairy farm at the long last has produced a cupful of semi-fluid butter and asked me to ~~brought~~ bring it in for you. I do'nt know whether it will keep in this hot weather or not. If it wont keep, we are going to consume it and will bring you a tin of butter for compensation next week.

Enclosed herewith is a short paper written by me recently please correct the English for me. I don't know whether any American magazine would publish it. I am a christian by birth and an internationalist by faith. Theviews stated in my paper may not be acceptable to many,and particulqrly will not be acceptable to many of our narrow minded scholars.

I have studied "The Objectives of Geography" with great interest. It is the best two paged paper I ever read on this topic. The foggy vagueness and the intangible confusion of geography are swept aside by such exact phrases such as "to clothe the map with meaning","to give significance to the varied personality" and by such cathhing words as " Integration","Place" and "Relationship". To my mind the old geogrpahy is static,in the sense that it empheasizes too much on geographical control,and the future of geography lies in its dynamic forces. The value of experimental science such as physics and chemistry lies in their forecasting value. Other things beign equal,it is nearly always possible for

涂长望致葛德石信（1944 年 5 月 29 日）

THE NATURAL SCIENCE SOCIETY OF CHINA
c/o. National Central University
Sa-ping-pa, Chungking.

the physcist or chemist to pronounce cause and effect, at least to the satisfaction of common man. I am not a determinst either in the realm of natural philosophy, but I firmly believe that if the new geography is going to play a valuable part in natural as well as social sciences in the future it must possess some of the virtues of experimental sciences, i.e. to be able forecast effect from some similiar causes. In order to be able to do so, the students of geography must adopt some new technique, or radically change their "birdeye view" technique to approach this problem. I often heard geography is quoted as human ecology, but few has ever pointed out, the method adopted in studing plant or animal ecology are quite different from those methods used by most of geographers. Travelling is essential in geographical research, but travel is not enough in modern geogrpahy. Modern geography demands many years' careful observation, scientific analysis and if possible, experimentation. Since statistical method is one of the most important weapon used by social scientists and since, geography is said to be the link between natural and social sciences, a geographer therefore must master the experimental technique as well as the statistical method. Geography, as a science and as an art is a very difficult subject to master and that is the reason why we have some many gramophone records and a very few geographers in China. And that is also the reason why I take refuge im meteorology temporarily. I shall take up geography again only until I know more about social and natural sciences.

I am sorry to wast too much of your time.

With kindest regards,

Your pupil,

Changwang Tu

THE NATURAL SCIENCE SOCIETY OF CHINA
c/o. National Central University
Sa-ping-pa, Chungking.

June 1st,1944.

My dear Professor,

Herewith enclosed is the climatical record of Lahsa you desired. Mr. P.K.Chang of the Institute of Meteorology write to say that the records before the year 1935 were already published ~~by~~ in the Meteorological Magazine of the Chinese Meteorological ~~ma~~ Society and in the Quaterly Journal of the Royal Meteorological Society. Owing to the difficulty in communication the records later than 1937 are incomplete and he promised to send them on to you as soon as ~~th~~ he has them.

Have you got your Russian visa yet? If you are going home by way of India then when are you leaving ? I must see you once before you leave.

Several months ago I remember I have written you a letter asking you to help us to get a few books and journals of meteorolgy for us. I wonder whether you have received it or not ? In case you didn't,I am writing down them once more.

Meteorological Journals.

Meteorological publications of the department of Meteorology of M.I.T. later than 1937.

Monthly Weather Review and Supplements later than 1940.

Bulletin of the American Meteorological Society later than 1940.

Meteorological Books:

B.Haurwitz: Dynamic Meteorology

Pettersenn: Weather Analysis and Forecasting.

Landsberg / Conrade : Physical Climatology.

Thanking you in advance,

your pupil,

Changwang Tu

涂长望致葛德石信（1944 年 6 月 1 日）

Department of Meteorology,
National Central University,
Sa-ping-ba, Chungking,China,
May 10th,1945

Prof. G.B.Cressey,
Chairman of the Department of Geology and Geography,
Syracuse University,
Syracuse,New York,U.S.A.

My dear Prof. Cressey,

I am so glad to receive your letter today, and very happy to learn that you have collected enough material from Central and South Siberia on you way home that enabled you to print a separate book on Russia. " The Basis of Soviet Strength " must be a very attractive book and I do hope our department will get a copy soon. It seems to me the real strength of Soviet Russia does not rest only on her large resources or vast land or large population. These are fundaments of a great nation,but,to me,their system of government ---democracy built upon solid economic basis for all---is the road to greatness and prosperity. Geographical factors,at least physical factors,have remained practically unchanged from the last war to the present war,but what a contrast between the czarist Russia and the present Soviet Russia ! It is needless to say that human element is more important than physical environment but few realizes that cultur ural environment is even more important than human element. For example, the human elment, so as as the race is concerned,remains unchanged, but under the Czars the Russians were hopelessly week while under the present regime they are dangerously strong. Political system,the most important cultural environment of all,has worked wonders in the past and is transforming the world now. No doublt, cultural environment is the product of man so many people argue that

涂长望致葛德石信（1945 年 5 月 10 日）

latter is after all more important than the former, but we must not forget that the difference in quality and ability between individuals of a race is much greater than the difference between the average qualities of different races. This is to say a few genius of a race will determine the fortune or future of a whole race while the majority of the people will work on a model that was pre-designed by some great thinkers and politicians. That is to say, a good cultural institution will benefit all while an absolete cultural institution will plant the seed of hardship and suffering. China is still suffering from all sorts of ancient and obsolete institutions and I must say we have paid too heavy a price for them. Westerners often praise the good works of Confucius and Mencius but they have not realized the great harm these two gentlemen had done to our race. Change is the catch word for new China. We got to break away completely from those harmful old institutions, otherwise we are doomed to failure and serfdom, because the essence of our ancient culture was to teach people how to remain silence in face of force and violence and how to be obedient and amiable before your new masters, or old Gods. But alas ! those traitors, fools and cunning politicians are trying their best to dig these two gentlemen out from their graves. The struggle is going on and it is needless for me to forecast which side will win the war. But one thing I am certain and that is the side who has the full support of the mass and the intellegensia will win the day.

Things have changed a good deal since you left China but it is not wise for me to write them here, afterall you have heard enough from your own reporters . But I must tell you one thing and that is we have a new meteorological department. The baby was born naked and remains so now and I hope some generous American friends

3

will contribute some books and journals to make her ~~her~~ a little bit more attractive.

Hou Yu-hwa is now in Chungking. He has some terrible experience in Kwangsi last winter when Japs were chasing our poorly clothed and underfed army .He has lost everything except his wit and optimism and wishes to be remembered to you.

My family ploughs on as usual. The field is rocky, the road muddy and the weather gloomy but in the far distant we can see the rising sun. I am so fortunate to be born a Chinese because there are so ~~much~~ many things we can do in the near future.

We were grieve striken to learn the tragic news of the untimely death of our world leader Rosevelt. The world has never seen such a geneerous leader before. To say that world peace is shaken to its foundation by the fall of such a great star(in Chinese sense) is not too much of an exaggeration. His wisdom, his experience and above all his devotion to common man and his generosity to all would have certainly ~~lead~~ lifted the world to a better and brighter horizon.

How are Mrs. Cressey and her lovely children and I do hope they will come back to China again .

With kindest regards to you all.

Yours respectfully,

Changwang

Changwang T'U

NAKING,CHINA
April 20,1948

Dear Prof. Cressey,

Thank you very much for your letter and since you demand a frank reply from me I,therefore, decided to make the following comments which I believe are not acceptable to many Americans,especially to the capitalists.

First of all Chinese liberals have no faith in the kind of capitalism that is practiced in America and the kind of democracy that is nourished by selfish monopoly and private interests of the big families. They are equally opposed to rigid state control and tatalitarianism. Chinese liberals stand for Min Sen Chui I(The Principle of People's Livelihood) and the Four Freedoms preached by the late President Roosevelt. They beleive that freedom from want is the material basis of the other three freedoms. A semi-starved person does not worry about the freedom of speech,the freedom from fear or the freedom of religion. All he cares is some hot steamed rice. Thousands and thousands of our hungry farmers rushed to the Army,not because they love fighting and danger, but because the Army can keep them alive by offer them some meager meals. A hungry peasant cannot make any use of the freedom of expression because an illiterate person has neither the power to express himself by writing nor the power to articulate intelligently. An ignorant peasant is free to believe anything that is handed down to him by his parents ,old customs and traditions. They believe the business of a rational government is to provide every citizen with a filled ricebowl first and some basic education so that he or she can have the physical energy and mental alertness to make use of the other freedoms bestowed to him or her by a democratic government. Freedom does not mean the victory of one individual at the expenses of others. Free enterprise and free competition as practiced in America,they believe , do possess many admirable qualities,but in the last analysis they are nothing but Jungle rule. The aggressive ones, the ones with financial resources and family or political backings can always crush and destroy their less fortunate competetors. Has not Rochefeller ruined many of his competitors by financial pressure and other illegal means ? One swallow does not make a spring so one victim does not make a capitalist. The success of one capitalist means the ruination of many small traders. Perhaps this is reason that Jesus said that it is easier for a camel to get through a needle's eye than a richman to go to Heaven. Individual genius has climbed to the top of American society,but not every man or woman is a genius and the business of the government is to protect the interest of the majority and not permitting it to be exploited by some clever and selfish individuals. If they are asked to choose betwen initiative and social justice ,they do not hesitate to choose social justice. If Communism cannot destroy initiative as demonstatrated by its great vitality in the last war, then no other system of government can. Viewed from this angle, there is then no need for Americans to worry about the spreading of totalitarianism in other parts of the world, nor need the Russians worry the spreading of western democracy in China.

So much for the introduction now let the Chinese intellectuals answer your questions.

涂长望致葛德石信（1948 年 4 月 20 日）

Should we keep our hands off entirely,or extend only economic aid,or provide partial or all-out military support ?
ANSWER: If American Government believes in democracy and has faith in national determination and non-intervention of some other countries's domestic affairs then it is only too natural for America to keep her hands off entirely. There is no need to pretend that American aid to China is intended to save the Chinese people from the Red Terror. Chinese people knows how to make their own choice and they know perfectly well who is their enemy and who is their friend. The Chinese people,especially the liberals,are very much worried about the American policy toward China,not because it will prolong the civil strife but because it will drive them to the opposite camp. American people ought to know that Chinese Universities,especially American Christian universities, have become the hot-beds of anti-Americanism or anti-American policy. This is an important fact which cannot be ignored by any American stateman. Marshall knew the political conditions in China better than anybody else and his testimany in the Congress worths close study. He is certain of one thing,and every Chinese liberals agrees with him,that any amount of financial and military aid,short of direct intervention,cannot save the tottering regime from collapse.

If American people and the Government have something private on thier minds then it is not our business to answer this question. Because Wedmeyer, MacArthur,Chennault, Buillit and Judd knew the military importance of China to America much better than all of us. But we doubt very much that they can realize their cherish hopes.

As the Chinese people value American friendship very highly and economical China will look upon America as base for supplying us with capital,machines and technical experts in the future,we are very certain that a new government formed by the Chinese people would not and cannot be hostile to the American people,provided the American people act wisely now.

Marshall was convinced that the present regime is incapable of drastic reforms. He was perfectly right because the present election and the revision of the Constitution to suit the purpose of one person proved it beyond any doubt. You were in China four years ago and you had some experience of Chinese politics,but the present conditions are ten times worse. Our atmosphere is stifled and every Chinese,farmers, workers,students,bankers,religious leaders and Y.M.C.A workers, is expecting a change. Science can cure everthing but whether it can cure a regime that is rotten to the core need to be seen.

For your reference I have taken the liberty to enclose herewith some clippings from the Shanghai Evening Post, an American newspaper in Shanghai.

Sorry to bother you with this long letter but as an obedient student of yours I have to keep you informed about the feeling of the Chinese people,especailly the Chinese intellectuals and liberals.

With love to you all,

Yours affectionately,

C.W.

Department of Meteorology,
National Central University,
Ssu Pai Lou, Nanking

July 20, 1948

Dear Mr. and Mrs. Cressey,

Thank you ever so much for sending us another valuabl parcel. It is really very kind of you to take so much trouble in packing and post the parcel. We have a saying:
But certainly your parcel is much more valuable than a feature from a distant land. The children were thrilled to find so many tools, candies and balls in the package and wanted me to thank you all for such nice and beautiful presents. Every member of the family was benefited by the parcel.

Situations in China have taken a worse turn lately, or perhaps a good turn for the Chinese people eventually. Nationalist troops have suffered defeat after defeat. The strategic towns Hsiangyang (northern Hupeh) Yencheng (strong military outpost of Hsuchow) and Yenchow (military nerve center of Shantung) were occupied by the Communist last week. Other strategic towns such like Taiyuan, Paoting, Kaifen, Hsuchow and Tsinan will fall into bandits hands very shortly. It seems that the Communists have started a general offensive on all fronts. Only a miracle will save the present regime from collapse.

Inflation is accelerated by military defeats. A pre-war silver dollar is quoted at CNC 4,000,000 to 1. That is to say the paper money has inflated more than 4 million times. Greenbacks are quoted at 8,000,000 to 1. I am now getting 60,000,000 paper dollars per month which is equivalent to US$7.50 per month! What price civil war!

Perhaps you would like to know something about the Anti-American movement in China lately. The Chinese people are not against the American people but they are, however, bitterly oppose the American policy in the Far East, particularly in Japan and China. The fostering of Japan by U.S. Government is feared by Chinese people of all walks. Naturally, the American people will blame the Chinese people for being unable to unite and become a strong country in the Far East. But the Chinese people also blame the American people for prolonging the civil war in China by helping a reactionary and corrupt regime. Herein lies the true cause of the present Anti-American movement in China. The movement is so-wide-spread and spontaneous that even Ambassador Stuart admitted that it was not engineered by some plotters. So far as we can see "hands off" policy is the best policy for the American Government. After all the Chinese people are not hostile to the American people. But if the American Government insists on backing the wrong horse she will suffer ~~in the future~~.

Cultural works in China are dying a slow death. Professors, teachers and students are starving, physically, culturally and spiritually. People in America will perhaps wonder why a third party cannot rise into power in China. If the other two parties have their armies how can on earth, an unarmed third party survive the cross fire ? This is the tragedy of Chinese intellegensia. Our love to you all.

涂长望致葛德石信（1948 年 7 月 20 日）

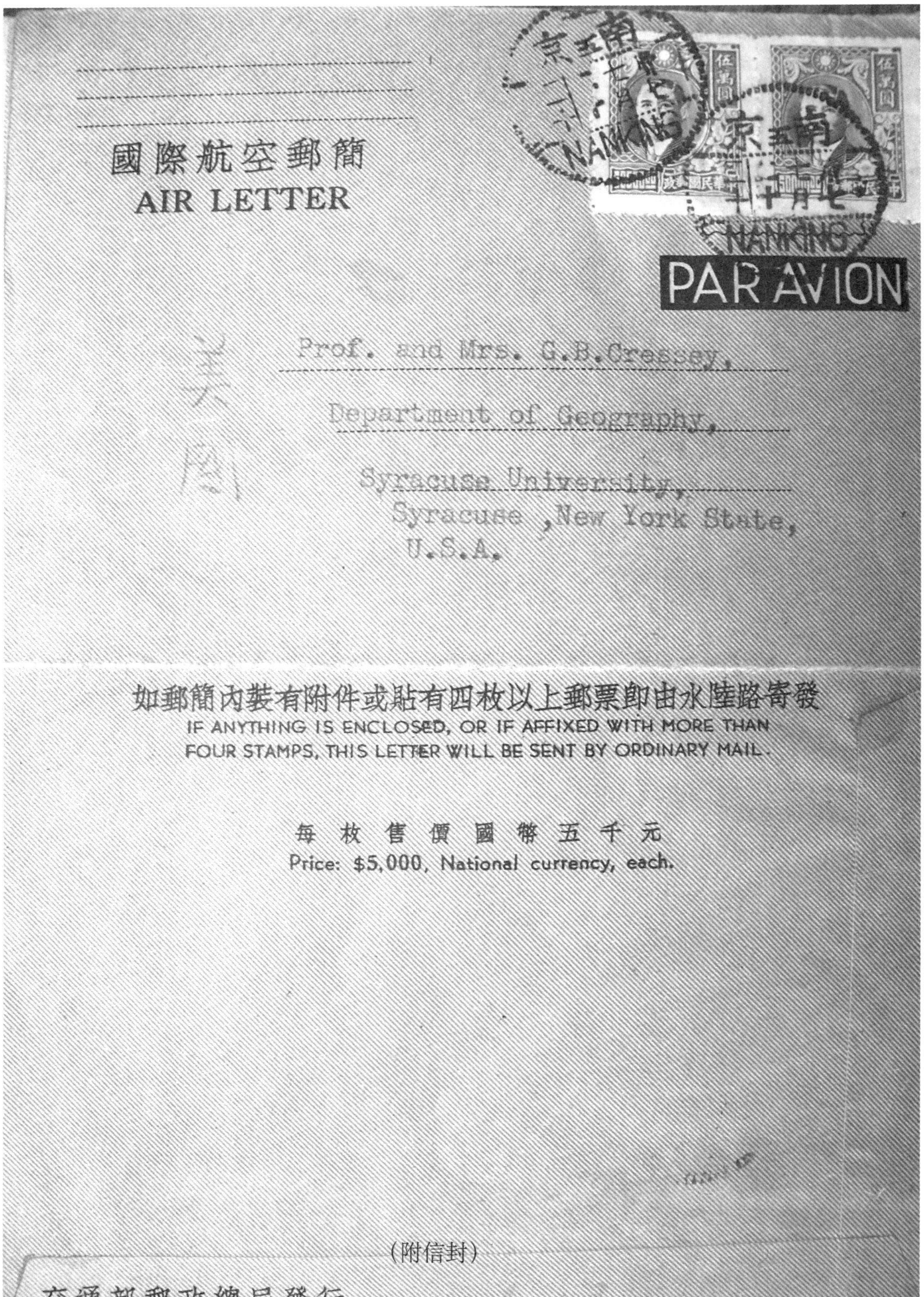
國際航空郵簡
AIR LETTER
PAR AVION
美國
Prof. and Mrs. G.B.Cressey,
Department of Geography,
Syracuse University,
Syracuse ,New York State,
U.S.A.
如郵簡內裝有附件或貼有四枚以上郵票即由水陸路寄發
IF ANYTHING IS ENCLOSED, OR IF AFFIXED WITH MORE THAN
FOUR STAMPS, THIS LETTER WILL BE SENT BY ORDINARY MAIL.
每枚售價國幣五千元
Price: $5,000, National currency, each.
(附信封)
交通部郵政總局發行

附信封

第二卷

葛德石书信档案

第二章
葛德石与中国地质学界的通信

葛德石不仅以研究中国地理闻名，而且与中国地质学有极深的渊源。20 世纪 20 年代的中国，地理学者寥寥无几，而地质学已相对成熟。而葛德石的地质学训练也使得他的交流对象首先是中国的地质学者。1924 年葛德石成为中国地质学会为数不多的外籍会员之一。中国地质学会 1922 年创立于北京，依托中国地质调查所，是民国时期中国最具有国际水准的学会之一。葛德石以地质学会为媒介，来往的学者主要不仅有中国地质学者如翁文灏、李四光等，而且还有在华的外国地质学者，如葛利普和巴尔博等。

翁文灏

翁文灏（1889—1971），字咏霓，浙江鄞县人，比利时鲁汶大学地质学博士，中国地质调查所所长，是民国最具国际声誉的中国科学家之一。翁文灏自 1934 年后步入政途，官拜经济部长、行政院院长，是民国学者从政的代表人物。翁文灏为葛德石在中国最早接触的学者之一。1924 年葛德石成为中国地质学会会员，开始与翁氏的交往。在葛德石的《中国的地理基础》的中国地质部分主要源自翁文灏等主持中国地质调查所的研究成果。抗战期间，葛德石再次访华，得到翁文灏的多方帮助。两人的通信现存六封，跨度十余年。

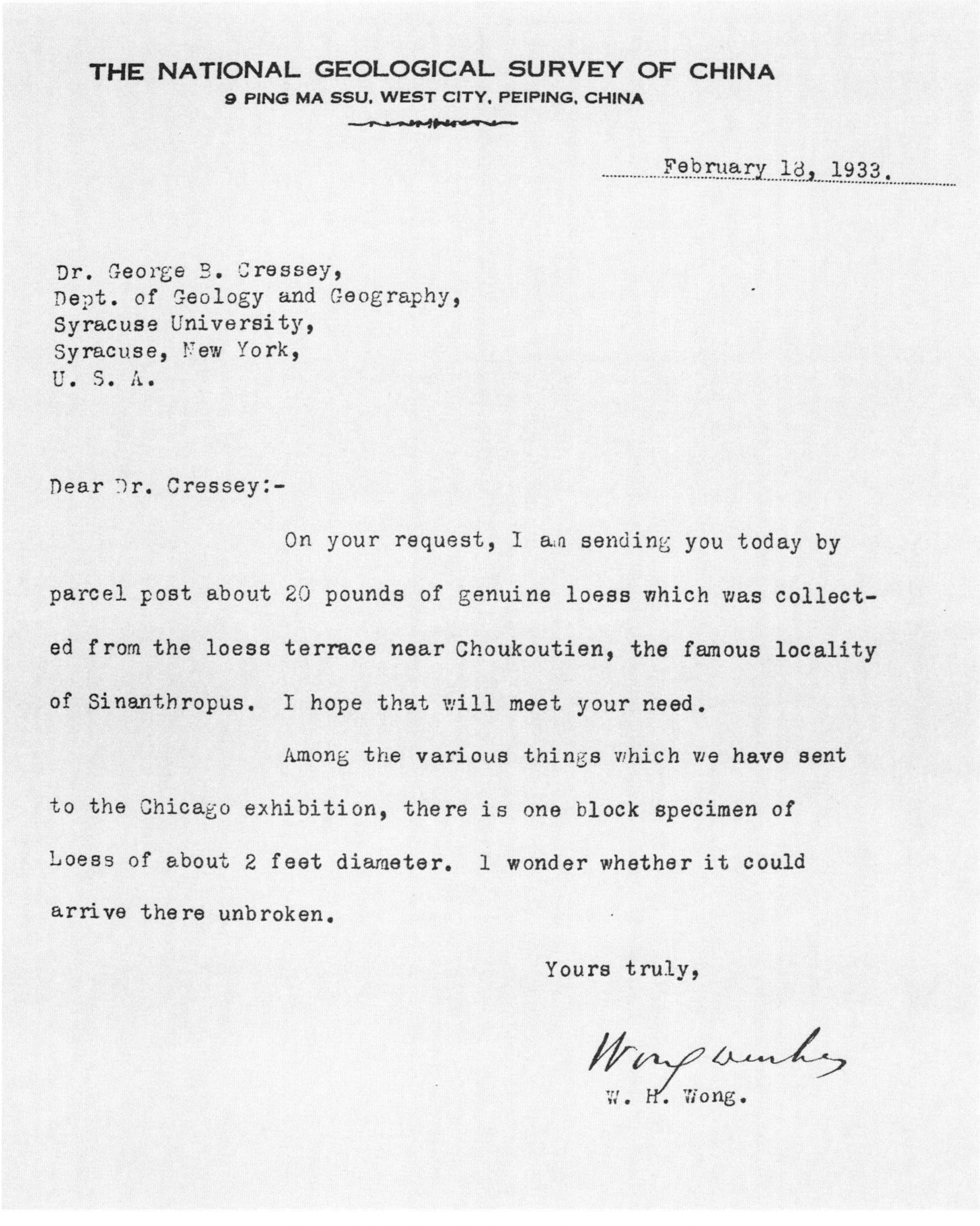

THE NATIONAL GEOLOGICAL SURVEY OF CHINA
9 PING MA SSU, WEST CITY, PEIPING, CHINA

February 18, 1933.

Dr. George B. Cressey,
Dept. of Geology and Geography,
Syracuse University,
Syracuse, New York,
U. S. A.

Dear Dr. Cressey:-

On your request, I am sending you today by parcel post about 20 pounds of genuine loess which was collected from the loess terrace near Choukoutien, the famous locality of Sinanthropus. I hope that will meet your need.

Among the various things which we have sent to the Chicago exhibition, there is one block specimen of Loess of about 2 feet diameter. I wonder whether it could arrive there unbroken.

Yours truly,

Wong Wenhao

W. H. Wong.

翁文灏致葛德石信（1933年2月18日）

THE NATIONAL GEOLOGICAL SURVEY OF CHINA

PEIPING ADDRESS
PING MA SSU, WEST CITY

NANKING ADDRESS
SHUI CHING TAI, CHUKIANG ROAD

NANKING, October 27, 1936.

Dr. George B. Cressey,
Dept. of Geology & Geography,
Syracuse University,
Syracuse, New York,
U. S. A.

Dear Sir,

I am sending you a copy of the third edition of the "New Maps of the Chinese Provinces" published in August 1936. The first edition of these maps was published in 1933 by the well known Chinese news paper Shunpao in commemoration of the Sixtieth Anniversary of its foundation. Many important additions and corrections have been introduced in the third edition. The essential content is as follows:

Relief map of China in plastic colours 1:27,000,000.

Political map of China 1:18,000,000

Physical map of China 1:18,000,000

Map showing mineral resources 1:18,000,000

Charts of Climate provinces

Isogonic chart 1:23,000,000

Soil map 1:23,000,000

Map showing important cities and distribution of farms 1:23,000,000

Map showing linguistic distribution 1:23,000,000

21 maps of provinces, topography shown in layered colours 1:3,000,000

2 maps of Kukunor and Heilungkiang, topography shown in layered colours 1:5,000,000.

2 maps of Tibet, Sikang and Sinkiang, topography in layered colours 1:7,500,000.

翁文灏致葛德石信（1936 年 10 月 27 日）

In addition to the many astronomical determinations (more than one thousand) of latitude and longitude fully utilized in the previous editions, sixty new determinations made by the members of the Chinese Geological Survey have been introduced in the present issue. The maps of the provinces Shansi, Kansu, Ninghsia, Chinghai (KukuNor) and Szechuan have been improved as more detailed materials on scales of 1:50,000 and 1:100,000 have been available at the time of revision. More than one corrections have been made in the region KukuNor, Amnemachin and Gashun Nor and Sokho Nor according to the latest observations. The general topographical feature of China is well represented by the colour layers.

The maps contain about 10,000 geographical names instead of 6,000 in the previous editions. In addition to the Chinese index, there is an English index so that the maps although printed entirely in Chinese can be of easy use to foreigners who know how to find the geographical names. The railways, roads, telegraph stations and other important features are well recorded and quite up-to-date.

These maps are chiefly reduced from the "New Atlas of China" issued by the Shunpao in 1934 although many points have been revised. The handy size ($7\frac{3}{4}$ X $10\frac{1}{2}$ inches) and very reasonable price ($3.00 Chinese currency per copy) will make these maps welcome by many people who like to have a convenient guide to the geographic knowledge of China.

I present you this copy in the hope that it may be useful to you and also that you may have opportunity to make it better known to the larger public.

Yours sincerely,

Wong Wenhao

Wong Wenhao

per T. C. Lu [?]

NATIONAL RESOURCES COMMISSION

MINISTRY OF ECONOMIC AFFAIRS

Chungking, June 3, 1944.

Dr. George B. Cressey,
American Embassy,
Chiu Ching Middle School,
Chungking.

Dear Dr. Cressey,

I wish to forward my hearty thanks of the valuable publications presented to the National Geological Survey of China through your attention and care.

The fine volume of the Soviet World Atlas Vol. II presented by the United States Department of State is specially highly valued because it just meets the requirement felt by the Chinese Geological Survey which already possessed Vol. I of the named Atlas.

The two volumes respectively on Oil Fields and Source Beds of Petroleum from the American Association of Petroleum Geologists are also welcomed as they well supply the new data and ideas on the mineral oil in which the Chinese geologists become more deeply interested in recent years.

The geologists of the Survey will all appreciate your thoughtfulness in bringing these volumes and the really helpful and friendly attitude of the American Government and scientific organisations toward China.

Thank you therefore for these gifts and the delightful dinner last evening.

Enclosed please find my letter of introduction to General Sheng Shih-tsai, Governor of Sinkiang Province.

Yours sincerely,

Wong Wen-hao

Wong Wen-hao.

翁文灏致葛德石信（1944 年 6 月 3 日）

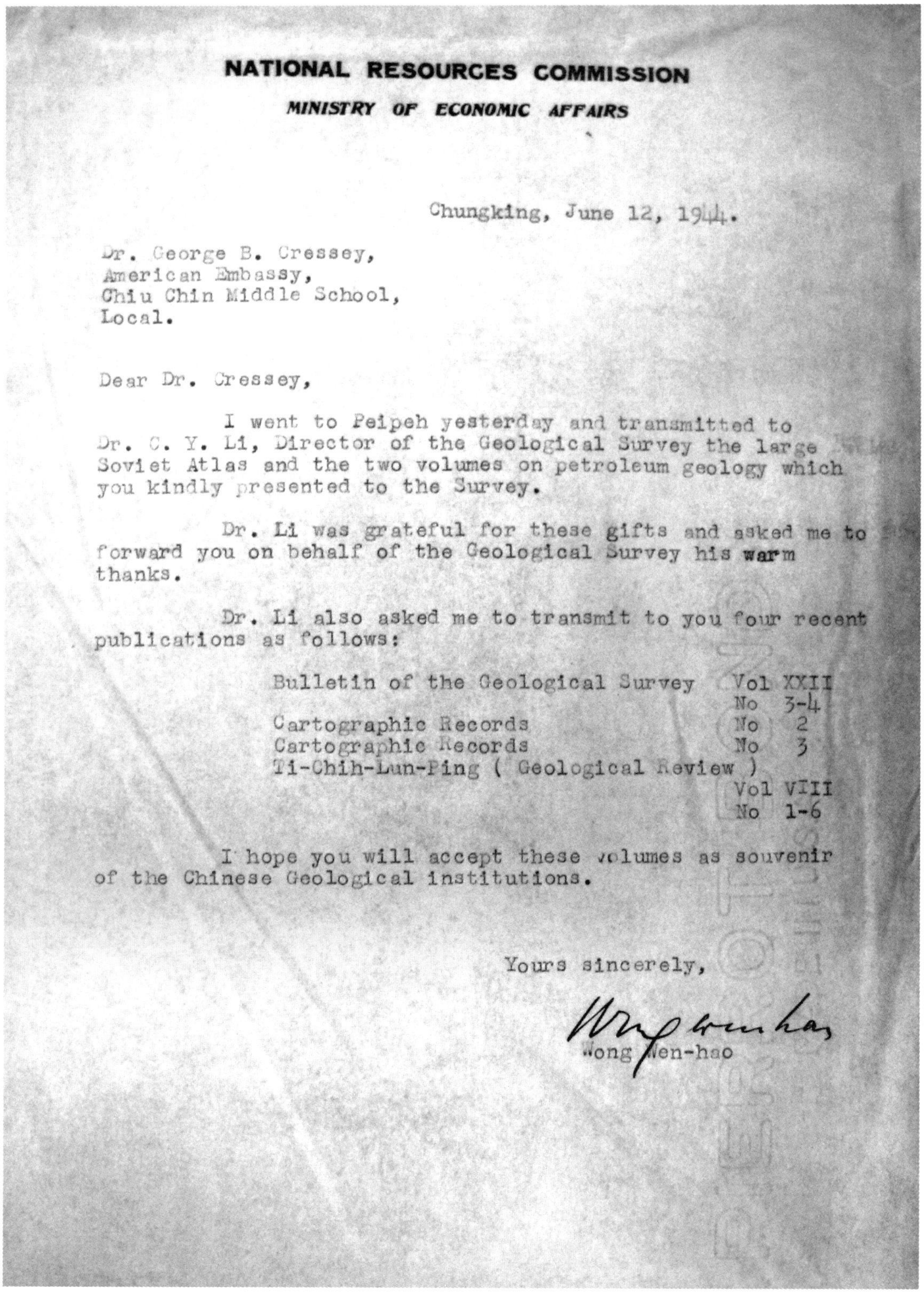

NATIONAL RESOURCES COMMISSION

MINISTRY OF ECONOMIC AFFAIRS

Chungking, June 12, 1944.

Dr. George B. Cressey,
American Embassy,
Chiu Chin Middle School,
Local.

Dear Dr. Cressey,

I went to Peipeh yesterday and transmitted to Dr. C. Y. Li, Director of the Geological Survey the large Soviet Atlas and the two volumes on petroleum geology which you kindly presented to the Survey.

Dr. Li was grateful for these gifts and asked me to forward you on behalf of the Geological Survey his warm thanks.

Dr. Li also asked me to transmit to you four recent publications as follows:

Bulletin of the Geological Survey	Vol XXII No 3-4
Cartographic Records	No 2
Cartographic Records	No 3
Ti-Chih-Lun-Ping (Geological Review)	Vol VIII No 1-6

I hope you will accept these volumes as souvenir of the Chinese Geological institutions.

Yours sincerely,

Wong Wen-hao

Wong Wen-hao

翁文灏致葛德石信（1944 年 6 月 12 日）

NATIONAL RESOURCES COMMISSION

RE.

CHUNGSHAN ROAD, NORTH
NANKING, CHINA

April 7th, 1948.

Prof. George B. Cressy
Department of Geography
Syracuse University
Syracuse 10, New York
U. S. A.

Dear Professor Cressy:

I have to thank you for your letter of March 20, and I appreciate your continuing sympathetic interest in Chinese problems.

In order however to reply to the questions you mentioned in your letter, I must first explain that we have now to deal with the critical world problem.

The world situation has been described in some alarming way by the manifesto of the Cominform in early october last year. According to that document representing the opinion of the communist parties in many European countries presided by Zhedonov and Malinov from Moscow the world is divided into two camps. On the one side there are "imperialistic" countries led by the United States, and on the other side there are "democratic" countries including of course the USSR. The duty of the USSR and other "democratic" country is to work against the imperialist actions of the United States. And in order to do so they will appeal to the deep feeling of sovereinty of all the nations of the world.

Although the terms such as "democratic" and "imperialistic" were used, purposely of course, in the reversed way, such is actually the soviet movement going ahead continuously. The communist party in China, according to their official declarations, is now not working for the communism but for what they call the "new democracy".

China has been advised after VJ day by the Special Envoy of America to negotiate with the Communists in order to include them in the Government. One year was completely spent on such negotiation during which the Communistic forces widely expanded and occupied what they called "liberated areas" meaning areas liberated from the Chinese Government and laws. The recent talk of President Truman explained that it has been the intention of the America to invite Chinese Communists to join the Government. Such is indeed a fine policy. But before that some contrary action did take place resulting in practical consequences.

There is of course our treaty of friendship with Soviet Russia with regard to Manchuria largely based on the Yalta agreement. The Russian side does not observe the treaty at all so that North Korea and

翁文灏致葛德石信（1948年4月7日）

NATIONAL RESOURCES COMMISSION

RE.............................

CHUNGSHAN ROAD, NORTH
NANKING. CHINA

Prof. George B. Cressy - 2 - April 7th, 1948.

the largest part of Manchuria now already constitute strong base of communists from which the Soviet influence grows and extends.

The true democratic side of the world headed by the United States has to face and halt the overwhelming Soviet-Communistic combined force which is conquering and expending incessantly and formidably. Failing to stop such invading force there can be no true liberty in the world. Several countries such as Yugoslavia, Czechoslovakia, Finland have already fallen. Manchuria and Korea are now all falling. The task of the United States is surely not to blame the bad intention or inability of such countries but rather to realize the menacing attitude of the Soviet-Communist combine and quietly decide on the practical measure to take.

I do not deny the weak position of the Central Government of China. But I feel surprised to observe the opinion of many American friends who seem to forget the deeply disturbed world situation and prefer to spend time in blaming China. Such attitude would rather confirm the accusation of the other side and give no help to the real improvement.

Let us remember the period before the Japanese attack on Pearl Harbour when merchants of your country continued to sell to Japan scraps and oil despite the good understanding which your Government already has had. The present hard situation from the Soviet side is already too evident to require any thing to be called foresight.

I hope, as a geographer familiar with the practical feature now prevailing, you will agree with me in the understanding of the true international condition. And then the questions you asked me in your letter will require no other explanation.

Yours sincerely,

Wong Wen-hao

Wong Wen-hao

WWH:mtl

行 政 院
THE EXECUTIVE YUAN
NATIONAL GOVERNMENT. CHINA.

June 24, 1948.

Prof. George B. Cressey,
Department of Geography,
Syracuse University,
Syracuse 10, New York,
U. S. A.

Dear Prof. Cressey,

Your letter of June 14th was read with great delight and thankfulness. It is indeed very heartening to hear from an old friend of distant lands like you an expression of approval and encouragement for my new appointment. As you are already aware, the new appointment of mine carries with it heavy responsibilities and immense difficulties and while there is yet no panacea worked out for the solution of all China's problems, I shall, however, exert my utmost to see that some real good be done to our country as far as circumstances could allow me.

You have always been a genuine and sincere friend of China and the interest you take in our national affairs represents your real concern for our country. To you, therefore, and to all other similar friends of your country, I should like to express my highest esteem and also my sincerest wish for a common effort towards the promotion of Sino-American understanding as well as cooperation.

With best regards,

Yours sincerely,

Wong Wen-hao

WWh/HSC

翁文灏致葛德石信（1948 年 6 月 24 日）

李四光

李四光（1889—1971），字仲揆，湖北黄冈人，著名地质学家，北京大学地质系教授兼系主任。1927 年，李四光从英国伯明翰大学获得地质学博士回国。随后，在中央研究院设在上海的地质研究所担任所长。在上海沪江大学的葛德石与其有地利之便，两人时有过往，今存李四光致葛德石信三封。

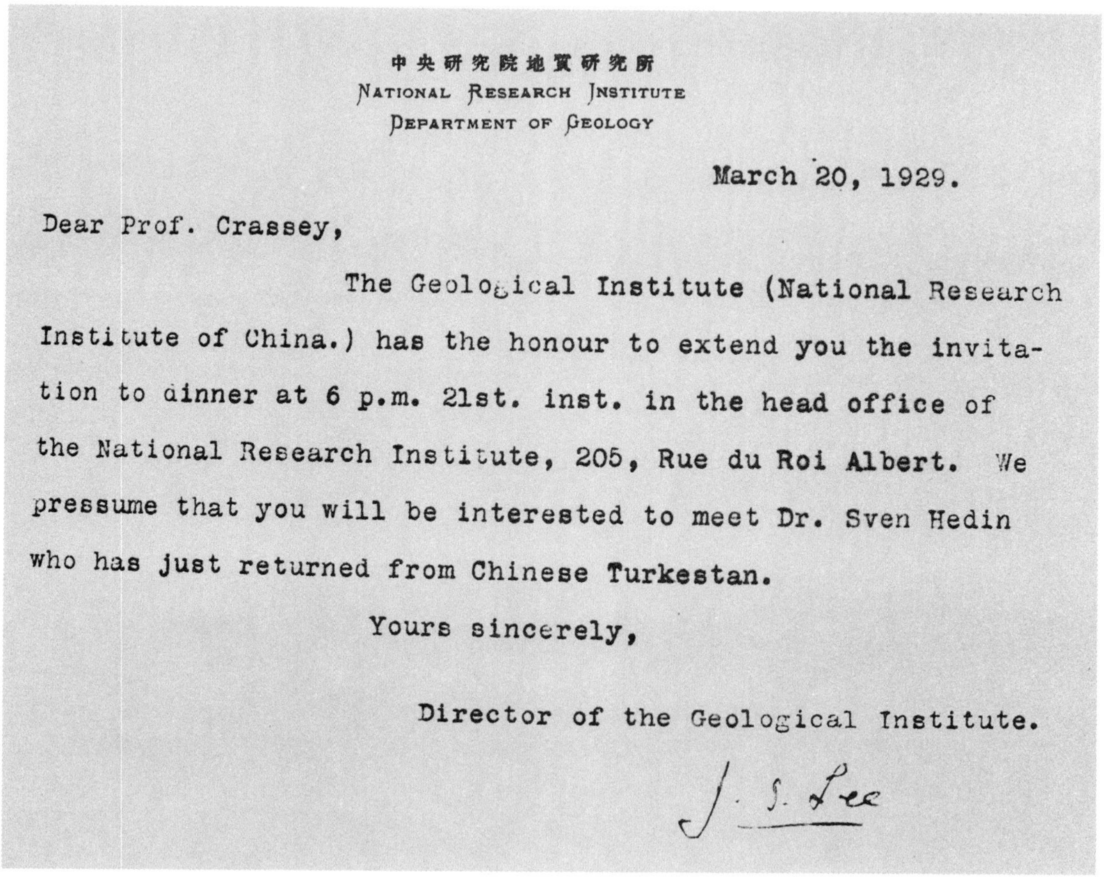

中央研究院地質研究所
NATIONAL RESEARCH INSTITUTE
DEPARTMENT OF GEOLOGY

March 20, 1929.

Dear Prof. Crassey,

The Geological Institute (National Research Institute of China.) has the honour to extend you the invitation to dinner at 6 p.m. 21st. inst. in the head office of the National Research Institute, 205, Rue du Roi Albert. We pressume that you will be interested to meet Dr. Sven Hedin who has just returned from Chinese Turkestan.

Yours sincerely,

Director of the Geological Institute.

J. S. Lee

李四光致葛德石信（1929 年 3 月 20 日）

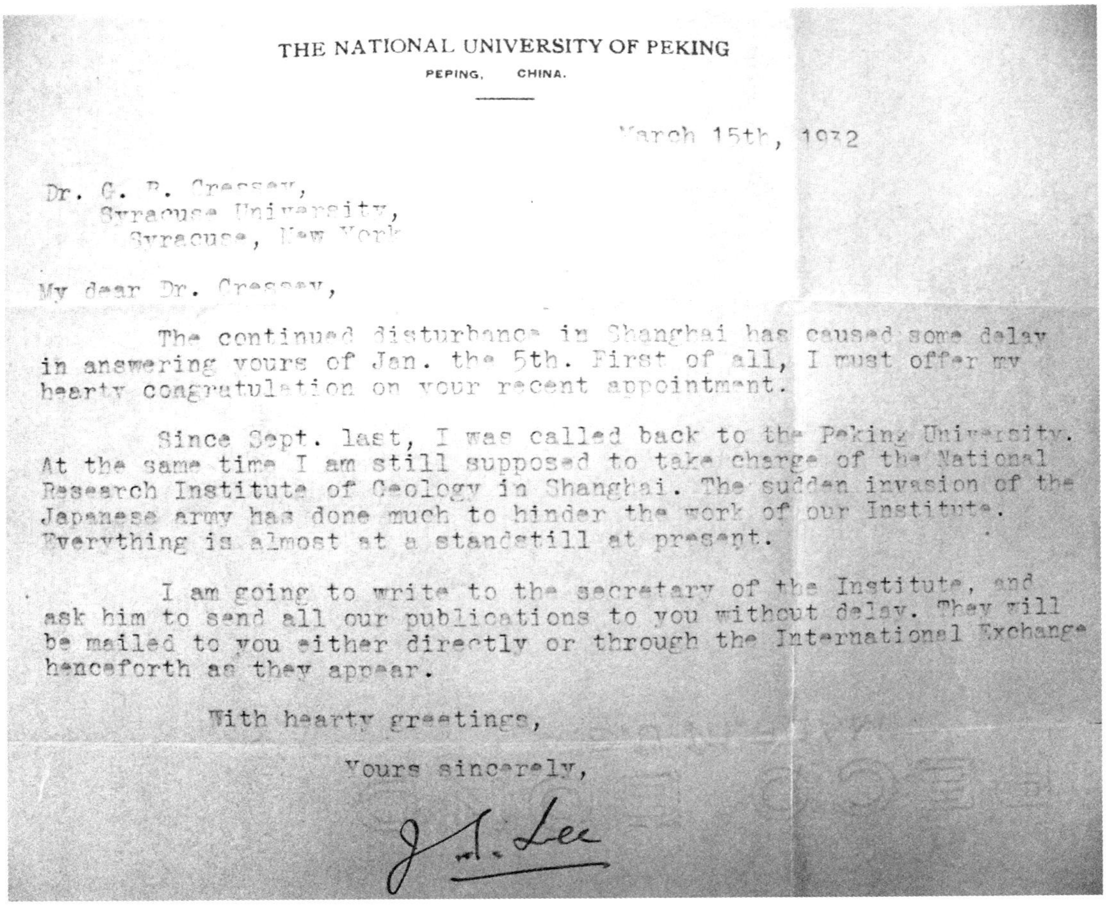

THE NATIONAL UNIVERSITY OF PEKING
PEPING, CHINA.

March 15th, 1932

Dr. G. B. Cressey,
Syracuse University,
Syracuse, New York

My dear Dr. Cressey,

The continued disturbance in Shanghai has caused some delay in answering yours of Jan. the 5th. First of all, I must offer my hearty congratulation on your recent appointment.

Since Sept. last, I was called back to the Peking University. At the same time I am still supposed to take charge of the National Research Institute of Geology in Shanghai. The sudden invasion of the Japanese army has done much to hinder the work of our Institute. Everything is almost at a standstill at present.

I am going to write to the secretary of the Institute, and ask him to send all our publications to you without delay. They will be mailed to you either directly or through the International Exchange henceforth as they appear.

With hearty greetings,

Yours sincerely,

J. S. Lee

李四光致葛德石信（1932 年 3 月 15 日）

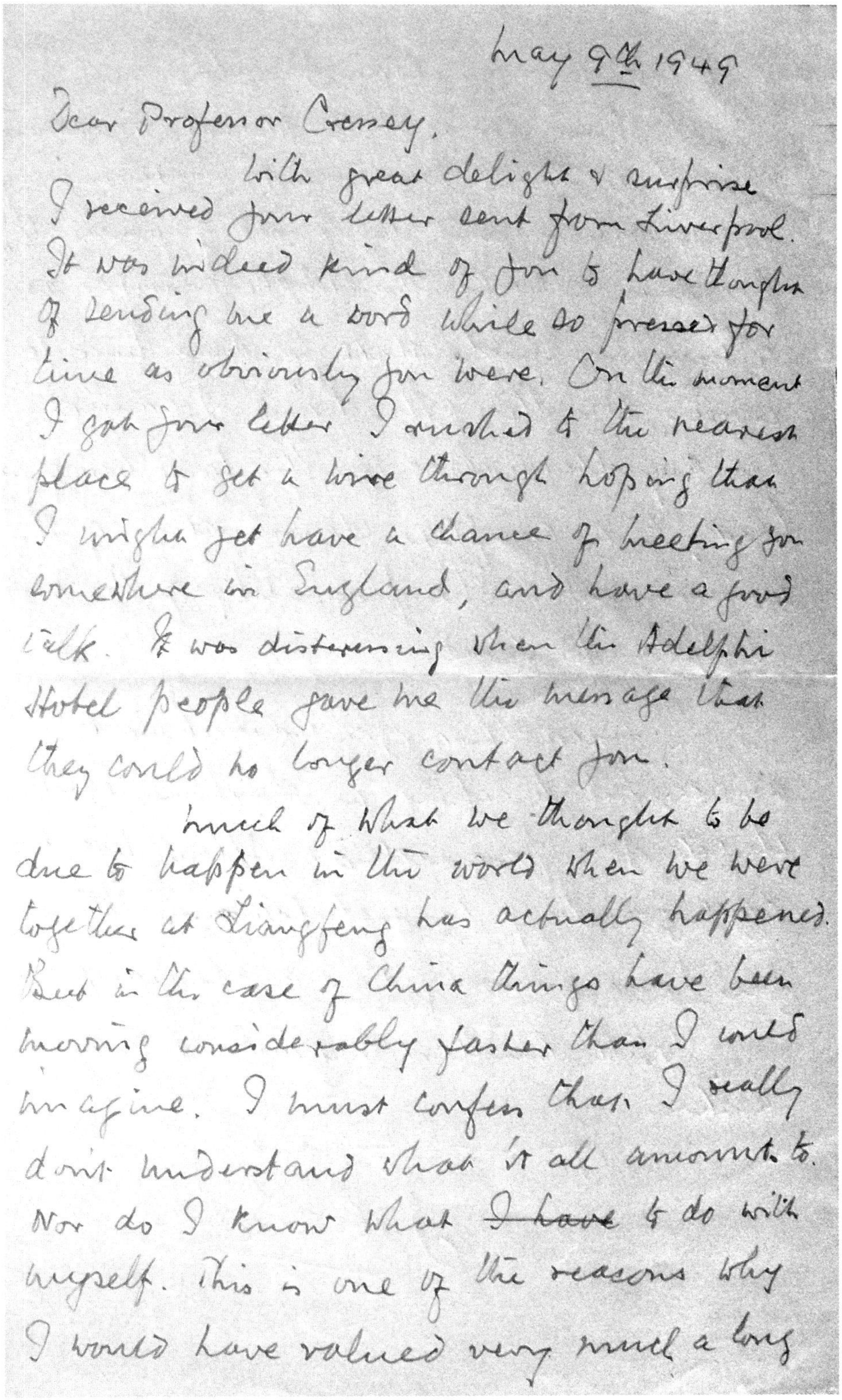
May 9th 1949

Dear Professor Cressey,

With great delight & surprise I received your letter sent from Liverpool. It was indeed kind of you to have thought of sending me a word while so pressed for time as obviously you were. On the moment I got your letter I rushed to the nearest place to get a wire through hoping that I might yet have a chance of meeting you somewhere in England, and have a good talk. It was distressing when the Adelphi Hotel people gave me the message that they could no longer contact you.

Much of what we thought to be due to happen in the world when we were together at Liangfeng has actually happened. But in the case of China things have been moving considerably faster than I could imagine. I must confess that I really don't understand what it all amounts to. Nor do I know what ~~I have~~ to do with myself. This is one of the reasons why I would have valued very much a long

李四光致葛德石信（1949 年 5 月 9 日）

talk with a friend like yourself.

I have some geographical arguments against a stable government, whatever may be its nature and its source of power, that professes to rule the whole country as a uniform, single state for some time to come. On the other hand I cannot see any alternative, for the time being at least, to a complete domination of the communists. The plurality of the word may be the clue.

I trust that you have had a successful meeting in Lisbon over which you presided. Allow me to offer you my congratulations. Hoping your home journey was a pleasant one.

With kindest regards & best wishes.

Yours sincerely,

J. S. Lee

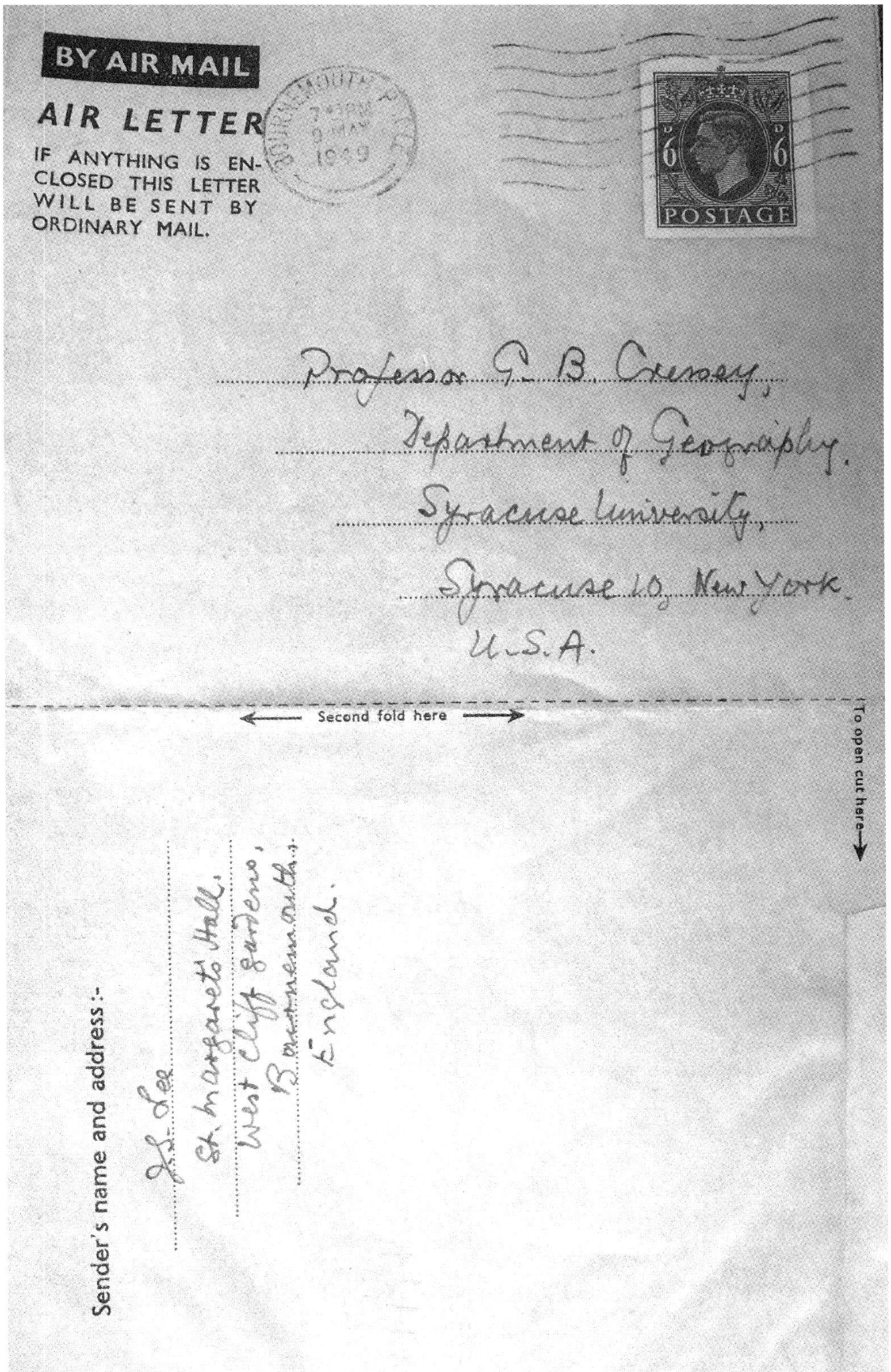
BY AIR MAIL

AIR LETTER

IF ANYTHING IS ENCLOSED THIS LETTER WILL BE SENT BY ORDINARY MAIL.

BOURNEMOUTH POOLE
7 45 PM
9 MAY
1949

POSTAGE 6D 6D

Professor G. B. Cressey,
Department of Geography.
Syracuse University,
Syracuse 10, New York
U.S.A.

Second fold here

To open cut here

Sender's name and address:-
J. S. Lee
St. Margaret's Hall,
West Cliff Gardens,
Bournemouth,
England.

附信封

裴文中

裴文中（1904—1982），河北丰南人，法国巴黎大学博士，古生物学家，是北京猿人第一个头盖骨的发现者。现存与葛德石通信两封。

PEIPING UNION MEDICAL COLLEGE
PEIPING, CHINA

DEPARTMENT OF ANATOMY

Dr. George B.Cressey,
Department of Geology,
Syracuse University,
Syracuse,New York,USA.

Peiping,27th.Sept.-38.

Dear Dr. Cressey,

Sorry I could not write to you at an earlier occasion because my wife and children have been ill successively all the time since two month ago. At present they are all recovered and except my wife, are out of the Hospital. I come to my office constantly just two days ago.

I have recieved your letter of 21st. July mailed to Peiping but never that to Changsha which you speak about.

I am very glad to know that you are delighted to have one copy of Thorp's work. I have still a great number of the publications of the Survey ready to send them away. If you, your department or your friend need some thing published by the Survey don't hesitate to let me know. I am willingly sending them away and like to have them properly placed.

We have no precise information from the south. I may tell you what I have heard from the people who escaped from Nanking. All the maps, rare books, and type specimens of the Survey have been transfered to somewhere and are all safe.Some of the ordinary reference books, a great part of the Survey's publications, and the specimens under study are transported from NK at the critical moment so only a part of the shipments arrived safely. All the apparatus sent away but damaged. A great part of the books in Library and specimens for exhibition in the Museum only partly packed either transported to outside of NK or left in the buldg:all get lost, we guess.Now the Survey is moved again from Changsha to Chungking. But we have somebody in Hongkong for looking for the painting and publications. Only one no. of Geological Soc. bulletin has so far been sent away(Vol.17,nos.3-4). Have you recieved it ?

In Peiping we are doing our research work ordinaryily and quietly. We are planning to publish a 2nd. edition of Fossil Man in China, a no. of Geol. Soc.'s bulletin, and a big volume on a late Palaeolithic cave at Choukoutien.etc. Our excavation work can't be resumed in the near future on account of the local trouble at the place.But we ahve still much to do in the Lab.

Weidenreich has had great success in Copenhagen during the international congress of Anthropology and his trip to Europe. He is arriving here after two weeks. Father Teilhard went to France

裴文中致葛德石信（1938年9月27日）

three weeks ago where he will have a series of lectures. He has been elected as professor of high study of the French association of the scientif institutions. He will go to USA in March or April next and then come back again to Peiping.

Wong is now in Chungking and Huang is acting his service in our connection. CCYoung is in Yunnan and has established one office like what we have had in Peiping.I am planning to go to Yunnan in two months for having an exploration of the caves there.

Old Grabau is in Peiping and will be here all the time. He is working veyy hard for his theory. His fourth volume on the pulsation theory already published. He expects to have 15 volumes more.Very recently he catches cold and entered the Hospital. I know he is quite all right in PUMC and hope to be out in a short time.

Sincerely yours,

W. Pei

THE NATIONAL GEOLOGICAL SURVEY OF CHINA
PEIPING BRANCH
9 Ping Ma Ssu. West city. Peiping. China.

Peiping, Dec. 14th 1948

My dear Cressey,

When I was in the field in north west China your letter of July 23rd with the enclosed clip forwarded to me. I came back from Lanchow only sometime about a month ago and during the last few weaks I did nothing but to complet my report of my last trip of this year in North West. I am sending a copy of a summarized report of my two last trips, which was prepared actually for the World Radio University of Washington, and you will see what I have done during the last two years,

Certainly you know the situation in China was very bad, so my expeditions were carried out with much difficulties, especially the finance business. I was only supported by some private persons who have the interest in the study of origin of Chinese culture. In a near future Peking is going to have a great change. And the communication between us may be cut for a short time. I hope after a few month the diplomatic relation between USA and China will be resumed.

Perhaps it is very hard to you to understand the real situation in China. The sucess of the change certainly is not caused by the military force but by the union of the people. In future we have the hope to do some large scaled scientific work, especially in geology, anthropology and archaeology. After a certain time I hope I can arrange an invitation sent to you to come to China for the third time.

Sometimes ago the people of the present Nanking governement proposed to me to go to the States for continue the work of late Weidenreich. But I saw the situation and refused. However in future I may have another chance to go to USA and hope you may help me in some way. In future we may short of foriegn exchange to support me in the States.

I may write a book on the "origin of Chinese Civilization" or lecture on the same subject. I wonder in USA if there was some publisher or university could grant me some fund or fellowship. Of course my main work in the States will be the study of Upper Cave Man of Choukoutien and of the Djalai Nor Man(similar to the Upper Cave Man and the actual specimens are in my hand); and some newly discovered actual specimens of Sinanthropus(the others all lossed during the War).

I will stay in Peiping and the Geological Survey in Nanking and Peiping can't move away because we have no money and no transport. Acdemia Sinica is moving to Formosa.

My best regards to Mrs. Cressey and other friends.

Very sincerely yours,

W.C.Pei.

裴文中致葛德石信（1948 年 12 月 14 日）

黄汲清

黄汲清（1904–1995），字德淦，四川仁寿人，瑞士纳沙泰尔大学博士，地质学家，中央地质调查所所长，对中国石油天气勘探贡献甚巨。今存与葛德石通信一封。

Geological Survey,
9, Pingmassu,
West City, Peiping.
August 18, 1946.

Prof. George B. Cressey,
Department of Geography and Geology,
Syracuse University,
Syracuse, N. Y., U.S.A.

My dear Professor Cressey:

We haven't heard from you since your visit to Pehpei in 1943. We don't know either, if you succeeded in traveling through Sinkiang to Soviet Central Asia. I am sure, however, you have seen much more of China in your last trip, and I dare say you know China better than any other foreign student of Chinese geography.

Geology forms one of the foundations of geography. As you might well know, the geology of China as we understand it today is very different from that of 15 or even 10years ago. I have, in recent years, given much thought to the wider problems in Chinese geology and have written a book entitled "On Major Tectonic Forms of China" one copy of which has been forwarded to you through the U.S. Embassy. Since April 1945, I have been busy in compiling a geological map of China and hope by next spring the work will be completed.

Having been blockaded from the outside world for nine years, we Chinese geologists are out of touch with recent advances and discoveries in our Science and that is why I am looking for an opportunity to go to the United States. Since the Geological Survey of China is financially unable to support me, I am asking my American friends what they think I could do. I have written to both Bailey Willis and Eliot Blackwelder but haven't got any reply from them. I should be exceedingly glad to know what you could advice me. Suppose I am to give lectures in Chinese geology in some American university. Do you think that is feasible?

The Survey is moving back from Pehpei to Nanking, while a branch office is now established in Peiping. I am here to continue my work in the compilation of the geological map of China--especially for the Manchurian part.

With kindest regards,

Yours very sincerely,

T. K. Huang

黄汲清致葛德石信（1946 年 8 月 18 日）

斯行健

斯行健（1901–1965），字天石，浙江诸暨人，德国柏林大学博士，古植物学家，中央研究院地质研究所研究员。现存与葛德石通信一封。

THE CHINA FOUNDATION
FOR THE PROMOTION OF EDUCATION AND CULTURE
DIRECTOR'S OFFICE
SPECIAL NO. 3, MAIN STREET, LITSEPA
CHUNGKING, CHINA

December 10, 1943.

Dear Prof. Cressey:

My wife and I shall be most pleased if you can come to tea with us on Monday the 20th, at four o'clock in the afternoon. We are especially anxious to have you meet a small group of friends who have been disappointed not to have had a chance to meet and talk with you at the reception held in your honor by the Academia Sinica last week.

Please do not let our invitation be a pressure on your time, but we thought you may be interested to meet some of our people informally and freely. If Monday does not suit, please choose another day around the 20th, and favor us a reply at your earliest convenience, so that we may invite the other friends.

Inclosed pleased find a slip of paper with our address and direction in Chinese for coming to our place.

With best regards

Sincerely yours,

H. C. Zen

P.S.
In case you prefer another date to the 20th, will you not consult with Dr. Kates who has also been invited?

斯行健致葛德石信（1943 年 12 月 10 日）

葛利普

葛利普（A.W. Grabau，1870—1946），美国纽约州布法罗人，美国哈佛大学地质学博士，哥伦比亚大学地质学教授，在古生物学及地层学研究上享誉世界。一战期间，葛利普由于同情德国而遭到哥伦比亚大学解聘。1920 年应丁文江之聘而前来中国，担任农商部地质调查所古生物室主任，兼任北京大学地质系教授。葛利普一生在华 26 年，著作等身，诲人不倦，中国地质学会自 1925 年即设有葛氏奖章以示尊崇。葛德石与葛利普的交往始于葛德石 1923 年在北京学习汉语期间，直至葛利普在中国逝世。虽然两人书信仅存一封，但是葛利普是葛德石在中国的重要联系人。

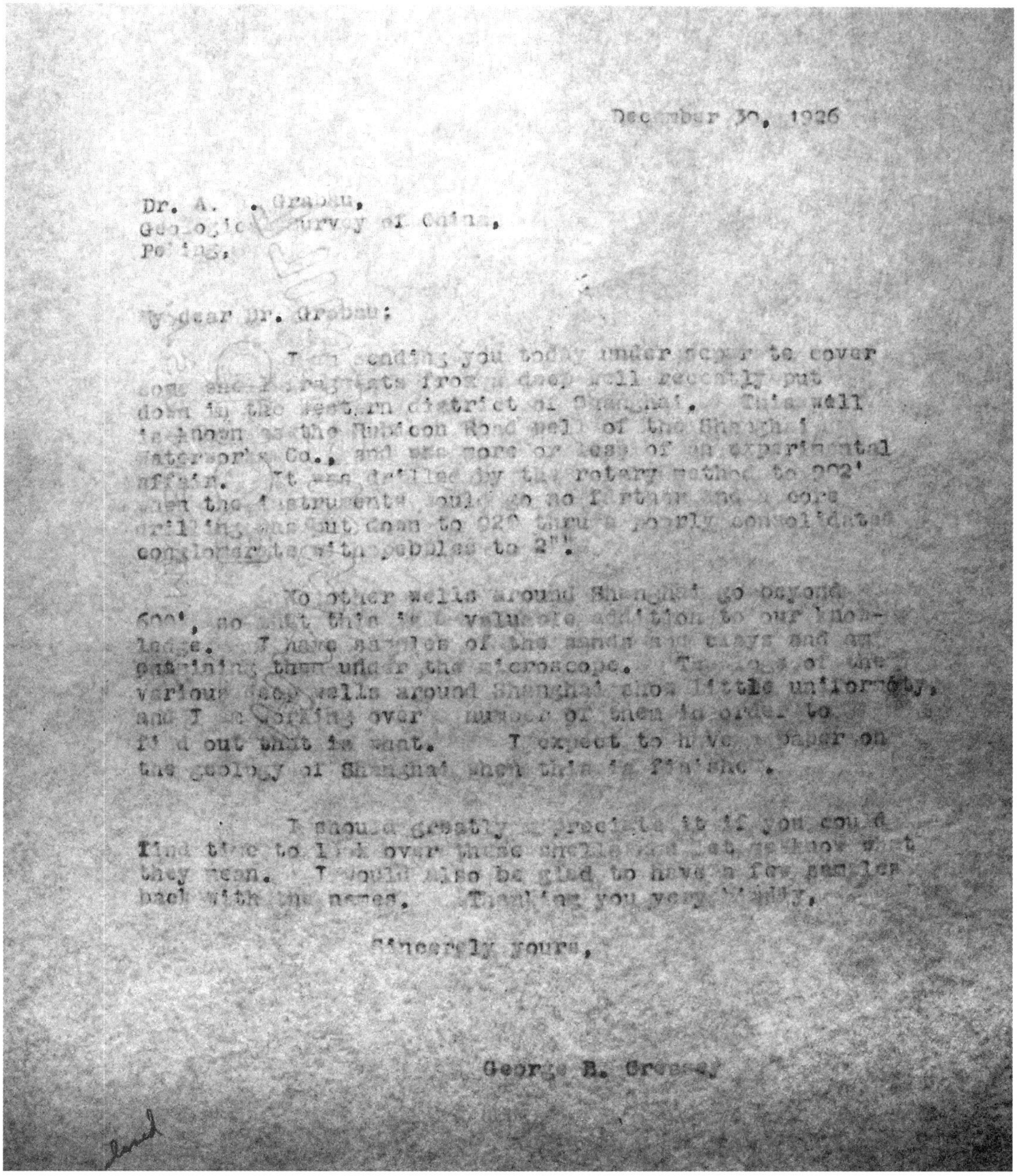

December 30, 1926

Dr. A. [illegible] Grabau,
Geological Survey of China,
Peking,

My dear Dr. Grabau:

I am sending you today under [illegible] to cover some [illegible] fragments from a deep well recently put down in the western district of Shanghai. This well is known as the [illegible] Road well of the Shanghai Waterworks Co., and was more or less of an experimental affair. It was drilled by the rotary method to [illegible]' when the instruments could go no farther and [illegible] core drilling was put down to 020 thru a poorly consolidated conglomerate with pebbles to 2".

No other wells around Shanghai go beyond 600', so that this is a valuable addition to our knowledge. I have samples of the sands and clays and am examining them under the microscope. The [illegible] of the various deep wells around Shanghai show little uniformity, and I am working over [illegible] number of them in order to find out what is what. I expect to have a paper on the geology of Shanghai when this is finished.

I should greatly appreciate it if you could find time to look over these shells and let me know what they mean. I would also be glad to have a few samples back with the names. Thanking you very kindly,

Sincerely yours,

George B. Cressey

葛德石致葛利普信（1926 年 12 月 30 日）

巴尔博

巴尔博（George B. Barbour，1890—1977），苏格兰爱丁堡人，1920 年巴尔博担任燕京大学地学系教授。至 1932 年，巴尔博才阔别中国，后来转而执教辛辛那提大学地质系。巴尔博对华北和长江流域的地质均有较深研究，与葛德石的研究区域有一定重合，因此两人往来密切。现存巴尔博致葛德石通信四封，均为两人返回美国之后所写。

Dear Cressey,

I see with interest the summary of your paper to the G S A - I was interested still more recently to have your name submitted to me for approval as one of the elect! Welcome where you belong!

As I am at the moment at work on a paper on the geomorphology of the Nanking Area at the request of the Academia Sinica,(who recently made me an honarary member in order to extort a week's work and a report out of me) - in true Sinian fashion) I want to take up at once with you several points which were doubtless fully treated in your paper but do not appear in the abstract except implicitly.

My problem is this;(and I shall state it categorically together with implied questions regarding your own position and conclusions, so as to elicit a clear reply:)- (Darn this type-writer for not having the keys where they ought to be! - here ends the parenthesis):-

You refer to loess at Nanking and in the North-west of China and I am aware of your familiarity with it in both regions; I have looked at it as far as Lanchow, in Shensi,Honan and up the Fenho to Tatung, in Shantung and at Nanking. So that we each know what the other has in mind. My work in Shansi as confirmed by independent observations of Teilhard elsewhere seems to be able always to separate an upper true aeolian yellow-khahi loess with a vertical cleavage which becomes practically columnar in its best developments; this is essentially of Middle or Upper Pleistocene age, always breaks vertically except where you pass into the sandy or gravel facies in the base of depressions formerly occupied by water even in loess days (though perhaps intermittently), and only attains thicknesses of over say 20 feet where it settled on an incised topography in the subjacent formation.

Under it is the Sanmenian series with its several facies including a type that closely resembles the Malan (yellow-khaki) loess above-mentioned, but which is distinct in a number of respects, so much so that I feel obliged to postulate at least a history different in certain important climatic respects if not a composite origin; its color is distinctly redder, its clay component greater, its tendency to columnar cleavage less marked, its concretions larger, more rounded and of different tint; though sharp stratification is absent(except in the definitely fluvio-lacustrine facies into which it grades) it is banded in layers from two to eight or even more feet in thickness whose trend of slope conforms to the successive depositional surfaces during its time of formation; the aggradation associated with its deposition produced a much more mature topography than was present before or since except perhaps at the close of the Malan epoch when the incoming aeolian loess practically restured the same topography.

I need not go into the reasons for the confusion between the two deposits, It was only at the time of my trip into Kansu that I came to realize the fact that the confusion existed; I though previously that Andersson's"redeposited loess" and his "loess" of the Malan stage (as defined in terms of the Malan Terrace in the Western Hills) were a clear-cut issue. I now find that his "loess" is mainly of Sarmenian age, at least that the large bulk of it is of this material and that the problem is in confusion from which only one or two of us can

巴尔博致葛德石信（1932 年 1 月 29 日）

rescue it. As a temporary expedient to avoid cutting the Gordian know too soon I have so far referred to the Sanmenian variety as loessic-loam (at Nanking it is so clayey that the flour-like xxx texture of pure loess is often almost entirely absent) and I am convinced that we have to do with a deposit which after its coming to rest was further considerably changed by soil-forming processes under xxxxxx climatic conditions more nearly tropical than those of today. Also that it was largely contributed to by the weathered producsts of the locality brought down by rain-wash and solifluction. Some such processses seem essential to explain (1) the concretions (2) the layered structure (3) the composition (4) the relation of the topographic surfaces to the reduced bedrock summits of the epoch, all of which show a subdued xxxxx well matured type of lanform.

I feel that the uniformity of character of the stuff demands probably the introduction of material in bulk from the outside, and this of course must somehow be fitted in with the erosional and ablational history of the deserts to the North and North-west. I noted you give the Ordos as a source rather than the Gobi. Personally at present I disagree in view of the equal development of the same facies at Lanchow itself. The Ordos is not big enough a gathering ground, moreover. In addition, I have thought of the sands of the Ordos as the heavier material which the wind could not carry far and swept along to the edge of the plains - unless of course you propose to set up an Ur-Ordos whose limits ran north west over to the other bank of the Yellow River.

Anyhow, now send me anything you have written to let me quote you where possible. And give me your reactions to this screed. I'll send you a copy of a recent paper on Taiku and shall be interested to hear what you have to say in reply. Also you may be able to prevent my making mistakes by premature statement. I have a copy of your excellent Shanghai paper (China Journal) in my boxes, but not accessible; if you have plenty, send me another copy as a loan as I cannot get the China Journal here. Also, let me know how to get a thing of yours cited as one of the grounds of your qualification for fellowship - on the Ordos Desert.

I am now working at the California Institute of Technology as we had to leave China for the boys' health and education and until I settle on another job, or learn of one, I felt the time was well spent in getting ideas onto paper that should have been in print many moons ago.

Give our warm greetings to your wife. If I come east I shall look you up; I'll bring you some slides I can show your boys on the Peking Man discoveries if they would be of interest. I know your neighbor Harold Alling and his wife pretty well and have close friends in Syracouse - if they have not moved -

Au revoir

Yours ever

George B Barbour

1865 Woodland Road
Pasadena
29 Jan 1932

UNIVERSITY OF CINCINNATI

January 11, 1933

DEPARTMENT OF GEOLOGY AND GEOGRAPHY
OLD TECH BUILDING

Dear Cressey:

Answering yours; - re the Hwang-ho:

You are correct; there are no terraces on the Ordos loop immediately flanking the River; they lie back against the hard-rock ridges, and are clearly visible just behind Paotou and all along the Ta Ching Shan; for the Alashan, etc., I cannot speak, but Teilhard's Palaeolithic sections in the Ninghsia neighborhood suggest alternation of cut and fill. Now my point is that similar terracing is found markedly at Lanchow and Tungkwan where there are constrictions and where the local stream base is not much different from what it was in early Pleistocene, that where trenching has been deep (as along the gorges) and the valley has stayed narrow, all terraces of superficial material have been scoured and only, therefore, left in favorable localities; however, it should and does exist in those localities as shown by Teilhard and Young's sections at half a dozen points (see their Memoir) showing that a stream of magnitude comparable with that of today flowed where the Yellow River does in early Pleistocene and probably late Pliocene. In places where the late Pliocene topography was not one of basin-range type, relief remaining unmodified for a longer time, the river developed the most perfect characteristics of full maturity, i. e. the Ordos; the processes in that basin were such as to preclude high terrace formation of the kind mentioned and wide meandering was the course of the day. Going downstream, however, the warp-axis had to be crossed and if upwarp was rapid enough, ponding at the Paote bend and above was a possibility, only to be drained as cutting down proceeded; where the maximum relative uplift occurred the gorge-cutting would be most marked, the terraces least likely to be preserved by rock-defence and most certain of being scoured except in the favorable localities (connected with tributary mouths) as above mentioned. Here also should be the greatest difference in elevation between the old channel-bottoms of the successive aggradation epochs, as is in fact the case.

Hence a coherent history is traceable back to the beginning of the Pleistocene and possibly somewhat further back; the presence of Pontian fossiliferous gravels and sands at considerable elevation above the present stream level in the gorges indicate a Miocene river along approximately the same axis but it may have been a Pliocene tributary of the Wei-ho which captured the Ordos drainage at a time when the headwaters of the present Hwangho entered the Weiho south of Lanchow, if they ever did. I am, therefore, not pressing the point back beyond the end of the Tertiary, because the earlier history predates the latest important rifting and the structural geology of that part of Kansu is not yet worked out; the travellers' tales of explorations following the southern route from Sianfu to Lanchow instead of the direct ridge route via Pinchow, etc., are very vague on the character of the divide crossed

巴尔博致葛德石信（1933 年 1 月 11 日）

2

between the two basins; I a little assume that had there been no structural block interposed south of Lanchow the opener valley across the divide would have been the Great Road in preference to the Pinchow-Pingliang route.

Carrying the point of possible capture further, we have as I see it at present, only three possibilities - and now I become speculative; and in so doing am putting at your disposal ideas that still wait for publication. Did the Ordos drain east originally out along the north of Suiyuan or Shansi? The Tatung graben might seem to be a possible channel, linked with the Yangho, Huaiho system. But on field examination I see no reason to postulate any cause beyond ordinary rift-valley filling of the basin-range type; there is no indication of a single great drainage channel traceable for any distance that suggests an Ur-Hwangho. Maybe it lies in Mongolia and runs round into the Lao-ho, certainly the Peking grid right to Jehol shows no obvious channel.

Hence I feel the history back to the late Tertiary is increasingly clear. Beyond that I have made no analysis, beyond half-thought out ideas which need field corroboration.

I note you say "In view of the complex history...I wonder whether it is safe to attempt correlations between the Lanchow and Tunkwan areas..." Yes, because the entire stretch of road from Honan to central Kansu shows a unity of history (Sanmen-Chingshui, Malan and recent) discernible over the entire country and fitting in precisely with the river history; I struck north from Kuyuan towards the river, along a tributary which from its trend must have gone into the west corner of the Ordos region rather than into any Lanchow-Weiho drainage system, and found the same terraces and structural features there as well. I am surprised at your failing to pick it up in west Shansi. It is of course not so striking, but present nevertheless, though obviously aggradation is less ~~obvious~~ in a region undergoing uplift.

Have you still a copy of the multigraphed geography you issued at Shanghai which I could glance at for three days to see whether there is anything of which I am in ignorance?

Yours ever,

George B. Barbour

George B. Barbour

THE BRITISH BROADCASTING CORPORATION

Broadcasting House, London, W.1

TELEPHONE: WELBECK 4468 TELEGRAMS: BROADCASTS, LONDON

13th May, 1935.

Dear Cressey,

I have promised to help the B.B.C. to secure material for some of its geographical talks next winter. They have already in the past made use of a number of your illustrations and I am writing at the moment to find out whether you will grant permission, which I have no doubt you will, for the use of several of your excellent illustrations.

In particular they would like to make use of four of your own maps showing distribution of crops, the ones you repeated in Economic Geography, Vol. X; four only of these would be used, reduced to meet their needs and of course with full credit given.

Do you happen to have the original of the picture taken by Ato Photographic Association on your page 188? If not, can you tell me whether the address is correctly given as

Sanyei Building,
21, Sanchome Atagocho,
Shibaku,
Tokyo.

Am I right in assuming that I can obtain from you permission to use other photographs as required, or must I refer to McGraw-Hill? Have the originals been preserved, or are they obtainable by application to the publishers? For a reason you will see immediately, I am saving time by sending a carbon of this letter direct to your publishers, since I see they hold the copyright. I do not imagine they will be averse to the use of your material in this fashion, since it inevitably means wider publicity for an excellent book.

I have promised to take the Summer Course at Stanford, beginning on June 20th, but will pass through west-bound rather hurriedly, so I shan't be in Boston and therefore unlikely to come via Syracuse, unless I go by night to Toronto, where I have

巴尔博致葛德石信（1935 年 5 月 13 日）

- 2 -

13th May, 1935.

to spend twenty four hours. If you care to send a postcard of immediate reply, I would get it before my departure, and thus learn of your plans for the summer. It is possible our tracks will cross somewhere.

Greetings to your wife.

Yours sincerely,

Barbour

(George B. Barbour)

Professor George B. Cressey,
Department of Geology,
Syracuse University,
Syracuse,
N.Y.

UNIVERSITY OF CINCINNATI
McMICKEN COLLEGE OF LIBERAL ARTS
CINCINNATI 21, OHIO

OFFICE OF THE DEAN

February 14, 1946

Dr. George B. Cressey
School of Humanities
Stanford University
Stanford University, Calif.

Dear Cressey,

I am glad that the few adverse comments in my review of your book were taken in good part. Before I consented to review the book, I warned Rollin Chamberlin that a superficial glance at it revealed points open to criticism which I would feel bound to include with any comments of praise well merited by the book as a whole. He still insisted that in the long run an honest appraisal would serve you better than the encomiums of a publisher's blurb. Since I know the pressure under which you had to work, which would be recognized by all who appreciate what you have done, I did what I could to make a fair statement.

Ting wrote me directly in the usual Chinese friendly fashion, and indirectly through one of his proteges. In neither case was the idea of a research fellowship indicated. When I knew him in China he was still very second rate, callow, and plagiarist-minded, but he seemed to have elements of individuality which, to judge from your letter, have developed well under responsibility. I assume from your letter than you are interested in having him at Syracuse and shall be glad to see him when he comes. Thanks for his message. I take it that since I have written to him directly within the last two months no further immediate action is called for.

Yours ever,

George B. Barbour

George B. Barbour

巴尔博致葛德石信（1946 年 2 月 14 日）

梭颇

詹姆斯·梭颇（James Thorp，1896—1984），美国宾州人，1921—1933 年任美国农业部土壤局调查员。1933—1936 年被聘为中国地质调查所土壤研究室主任技师，著有《中国之土壤》一书，集中反映了 20 世纪 30 年代中国土壤的研究成果。葛德石本人对中国土地利用有相当研究，与梭颇的研究有异曲同工之妙，两人有一定的交往，现存梭颇致葛德石信函一封。

UNITED STATES DEPARTMENT OF AGRICULTURE
AGRICULTURAL RESEARCH ADMINISTRATION
BUREAU OF PLANT INDUSTRY
Soils, and Agricultural Engineering
WASHINGTON

DIVISION OF
SOIL SURVEY

Lincoln, Nebraska
July 6, 1943

Dr. George B. Cressey
Department of Geology and Geography
Syracuse University
Syracuse, New York

Dear Dr. Cressey:

Your manuscript arrived the latter part of last week and I have spent the last couple of days going over it. I have gone over it just once and have made quite a number of penciled notations on the margins and between the lines. I think most of these notations are self-explanatory. Some of them are in the form of questions where I felt some doubt in my mind as to the accuracy or adequacy of your statements, and a few involve corrections of obvious typographical errors. I made no consistent attempt to change the method of expression, since I realize that every man has his style and there would be no object in my trying to impose my style on you.

I shall give you a few of my impressions that I obtained from this rather hasty perusal of your manuscript.

I have the distinct feeling that the first six pages are somewhat disjointed and I do not get the feeling of coherence from this part of the text. On page C-1-4, I felt as though you overemphasized the importance of virgin forests, except perhaps in the more remote parts of Manchuria and possibly of the southern Tibetan borderland. In China Proper, or as you prefer to call it, "Cultural China", I do not recall seeing any important areas of truly virgin forest. Throughout the book I get the impression that you are writing as though Japan had been defeated and as though Japan no longer has any chance of winning the war. Of course we hope that Japan will be defeated, but if the book is published before the end of the war, it is quite conceivable that Japan may retain many of her territorial gains in the Orient even though she may not defeat the United States. This would leave you "out on a limb". This statement is made not because I hope Japan will win because that is the farthest possible from the truth, but because of the feeling of not wanting to count too many chickens before they are hatched.

Regarding soils, I have made quite a number of changes in the text. Some of these are made to bring the material a little more in line with nomenclature developed since the book of the geography of the soils was written, and some of them to correct actual mistakes. For example, in a number of places you use the term "alkaline" soils where you actually should have used the word "alkali". Alkaline soils are any soils in which the pH is above 7, regardless of whether or not they contain calcium carbonate or easilty soluble salts. Alkali soils, in the popular

梭颇致葛德石信（1943 年 7 月 6 日）

usage, are all soils affected by excessive accumulation of soluble salts. In a strictly scientific sense, we do not like this term, but it has been used so widely in the literature that we tolerate it. Ordinarily, in a scientific sense, we prefer to use the term saline or salty soils instead of soils commonly called "white alkali". Soils with an excess of "sodium clay" or of sodium carbonate are more accurately called alkali soils.

I noted in the section on vegetation that you used "semiarid" and "arid" as adjectives to modify plants. We know what you mean, but it hardly seems to be good usage inasmuch as those are climatic terms. It is on the same plane as speaking of semiarid and arid soils.

In several places I note that you use the term "plant foods" to mean the nutrients obtained by plants from the soils. In recent work of plant physiologists it is customary to speak of these as plant nutrients and to save the term plant foods to cover the food that is elaborated in the tissue of the plants through the action of the sun and moisture on chlorophyll. I used the term plant foods in my book in the same sense in which you have used it because the distinction which I just made has not been emphasized very long and I was not up on this point at the time I wrote the book.

You mention that Shachiang soils are unique in China. My conversations with Milne of Africa indicate that Shachiang soils are the same as some of the Vlei soils of Africa. I think it likely, from descriptions I have had verbally from Pendleton, that the Shachiang soils may be duplicated on the Hindo-Ganges Plain. On my trip to south Texas last winter, I saw some soils near Corpus Christi which are very much like some of the Shachiang soils of China. They are developed over the thick caliche deposits of which you have doubtless heard. Some of the Shachiang soils of China are developed from a similar material and at the present time are in a well-drained position brought about by recent dissection of uplifted plains. Much of the Shachiang-like soil which I saw in Texas has been similarly drained by recent dissection, but I think it would not be difficult to find areas where conditions are similar to, if not the same as, those in China. This is a problem which I hope to work out in the future, and I just want to let you know that Shachiang soils are probably not confined to China.

In one place you speak of "Brown Forest soils". We have used the term Brown Forest soils in the United States as an equivalent of "Braunerde" as described by Ramann. The soil of which you speak is not of this type. In other words, it is a brown soil of the forests but is not a Brown Forest soil. It is distinctions such as this that forced us to capitalize the names of all of our Great Soil Groups in the United States.

In a number of places in the text you have repeated the impression you have of the swarms of people which occupy China. I think this repetition is justified, but it would add to the rhythm of the text if you could state it in a little different way each time and so add variety to the expression. I realize that

3--George B. Cressey--July 6, 1943

this is a criticism of style and you do not need to give it any special consideration.

I suppose I am partly responsible for your converting the term "Red Basin" to "Purple Basin" because of my characterization of the soils of that region. The colors of many of the soils to my eye have a definitely purplish tinge, and I find that many others have the same feeling. I do find, however, that color experts state that the soils we commonly spoke of as purplish in color are the only soils which approach a true red and that the soils we commonly call red nearly always contain a very large amount of yellow in the color mixture and belong more to the strong browns and reddish-browns. I like the term Purple Basin for more reasons than one, but there might be some question as to the advisability of introducing this term, since the term Red Basin already has such wide usage among geologists and geographers in China. I do not wish to urge the point either way but did wish to call your attention to the above facts.

In the discussion of the modernization of China's cities, involving the broadening of streets, you laid considerable stress on the narrowness of streets in the older cities. When I was in Nanchang, I was told that the national government justified the widening of the streets for automobile traffic to the population by stating that the streets were formerly much wider than at present, and that they became narrow through the gradual "squatting" of merchants in front of the buildings of the wide streets. The gradual encroachment of merchants on the streets eventually resulted in the narrow alleyways which are so common in the old cities. I was told this by, I believe, Dr. Brown of the Methodist mission at Nanchang, and you may take it for whatever it is worth.

In my travel in the loess region with Dr. Buck, Professor Shen, Professor Shao te-Shing, and Mr. Brian Lowe, I had the same impression that you have that there is no room for immigration of people from other parts of China on any large scale. I felt that the best solution was rather to adjust the population that was already there in a manner so that cultivation would be restricted on the more hilly parts and the population would be concentrated where the land is more nearly level and where irrigation could be initiated. I felt that there was an abundance of people in northwest China to cultivate efficiently all of the land that might be brought under irrigation without bringing in people from outside. Actually, if erosion and floods are to be brought under any kind of control, it seems to me that it will be almost imperative for quite a large number of people to be evacuated. This is almost certainly not practicable, since there is no place for these people to go and I do not expect to see soil erosion brought under control in northwest China to a much greater extent than is already the case. This is a pessimistic viewpoint for which I have been criticized by a number of people, but the people who have criticized have not given satisfactory evidence that any program can be initiated that will improve the situation very greatly.

This brings up the question of the Malthusian principle. While you have stressed the teeming population of China and the vast total number of people in that

4--George B. Cressey--July 6, 1943

country, I do not think you have stressed sufficiently the importance of education in the limitation of births as a means to improve the economic lot of the Chinese. I realize that this is a very unpopular proposal with many Chinese and with people of Catholic faith, but I do not see how it is possible for the Chinese people to be well fed for any important length of time without new crises being developed in the food situation. It has been well demonstrated that as soon as any large group of Chinese are well fed, the rate of infant mortality decreases and the population spurts ahead very rapidly. I hope it will be possible for the idea of reasonable birth control to be sold to the Chinese as well as to other Oriental and European people. Perhaps this is because I am somewhat of a humanitarian and do not like to see people die the hard ways that are brought about by over-population.

I shall try to get together the photographs which you requested and perhaps a few others. This morning I discovered that my ticket to Denver is for tonight instead of tomorrow night, and in case I cannot get all the material together myself, I think it will be possible for Mrs. Thorp to have prints made of the pictures. Unfortunately, many of the films were not very well exposed and I do not know whether or not we can get sufficiently satisfactory work done in any of the photgraphic shops in Lincoln. Hartung's in Peiping reproduced nearly all of my photographs, and they took special pains to make allowances for imperfections in the films when they were printing my pictures. I do not know whether or not we can get such painstaking care in this city. I have a few extra enlargements left over from my work in China and I may be able to find some satisfactory prints among those. I hope you will receive them within a few days and I shall send the manuscript by express collect today or tomorrow.

With best regards,

Sincerely yours,

James Thorp

James Thorp
Regional Inspector
Great Plains

第三章
葛德石与中国其他学者的通信

在中国地理学和地质学之外，葛德石与中国其他学界领袖也有往来。其中包括胡适、朱家骅、王云五、刘大钧及陈裕光等。他们代表了中国学术界、教育界及出版界的精英。葛德石与胡适的往来则源于胡氏出任美国大使，葛氏曾邀请他到雪城大学演讲。胡适后来还为葛德石的著作题写章节汉语名称。在政界，葛德石与朱家骅的往来是在 1943 年至 1944 年葛德石访问中国之时，主要是例行公务，私交不深。在出版界，葛德石与王云五书信来往则是关于《中国的地理基础》一书的出版以及之后中文译稿的出版事宜。在经济学界，葛德石与刘大钧来往甚密，获取中国经济统计信息。在教育界，葛德石与金陵大学校长陈裕光的来往，主要涉及聘请和访学等。

胡适

胡适（1891—1962），字适之，安徽绩溪人，美国哥伦比亚大学博士，曾任北京大学校长，中国驻美国大使，中央研究院院长。1939 年葛德石邀请时任中国驻美大使的胡适前来雪城大学演讲，之后在家中设宴款待。现存胡适致葛德石信函一封。

CHINESE EMBASSY
WASHINGTON, D. C.

November 20, 1939

Professor George B. Cressey
Department of Geology and Goegraphy
Syracuse University
Syracuse, New York

My dear Cressey:

I appreciate your very kind letter of November 16th. I hope you and Mrs. Cressey will accept my most sincere thanks for the many kindnesses I received during my last visit to Syracuse. I thoroughly enjoyed those two days and,in particular,the party in your house and the several conversations with your good self. Kindly express my thanks to Dr. Piper and the members of Syracuse-in-China.

Sincerely yours,

Hu Shih

Hu Shih

胡适致葛德石信（1939 年 11 月 20 日）

朱家骅

朱家骅（1893–1963），浙江湖州人，德国柏林大学地质学博士，历任中山大学和中央大学校长，浙江省府主席，中央研究院总干事、院长，教育部部长，国民党组织部长等要职，一身纵横学术、教育、政府和政党之间。作为国民政府要员，朱家骅一直倡导重视地理学，主持中英庚款选派地理留学生，创建中国地理研究所。1943–1944 年，葛德石作为美国国务院教授访问重庆，朱家骅作为中央研究院院长出面招待，并聘请葛德石为中国地理研究所兼任研究员。现存朱家骅致葛德石信函三封。

國立中央研究院
ACADEMIA SINICA
HEAD OFFICE:
CHUNGKING, CHINA

30th November 1943.

Dr. G. B. Cressey,
American Embassy,
CHUNGKING.

Dear Dr. Cressey,

I wish to acknowledge with thanks your letter of the 27th November addressed to the Academia Sinica and in which you enclosed formal letters of greetings from the National Academy of Sciences and the American Council of Learned Societies. The Academia Sinica will reply direct to these learned bodies to thank them for their friendly greetings.

The cultural ties between China and America have always been close. We welcome your appointment as Visiting Professor to China by the U.S. Department of State and we are confident that during your stay here with us, you will do much in fostering and cementing the friendship that exists between our two peoples.

Sincerely yours,

Chu Chia-hua.

Chu Chia-hua

朱家骅致葛德石信（1943 年 11 月 30 日）

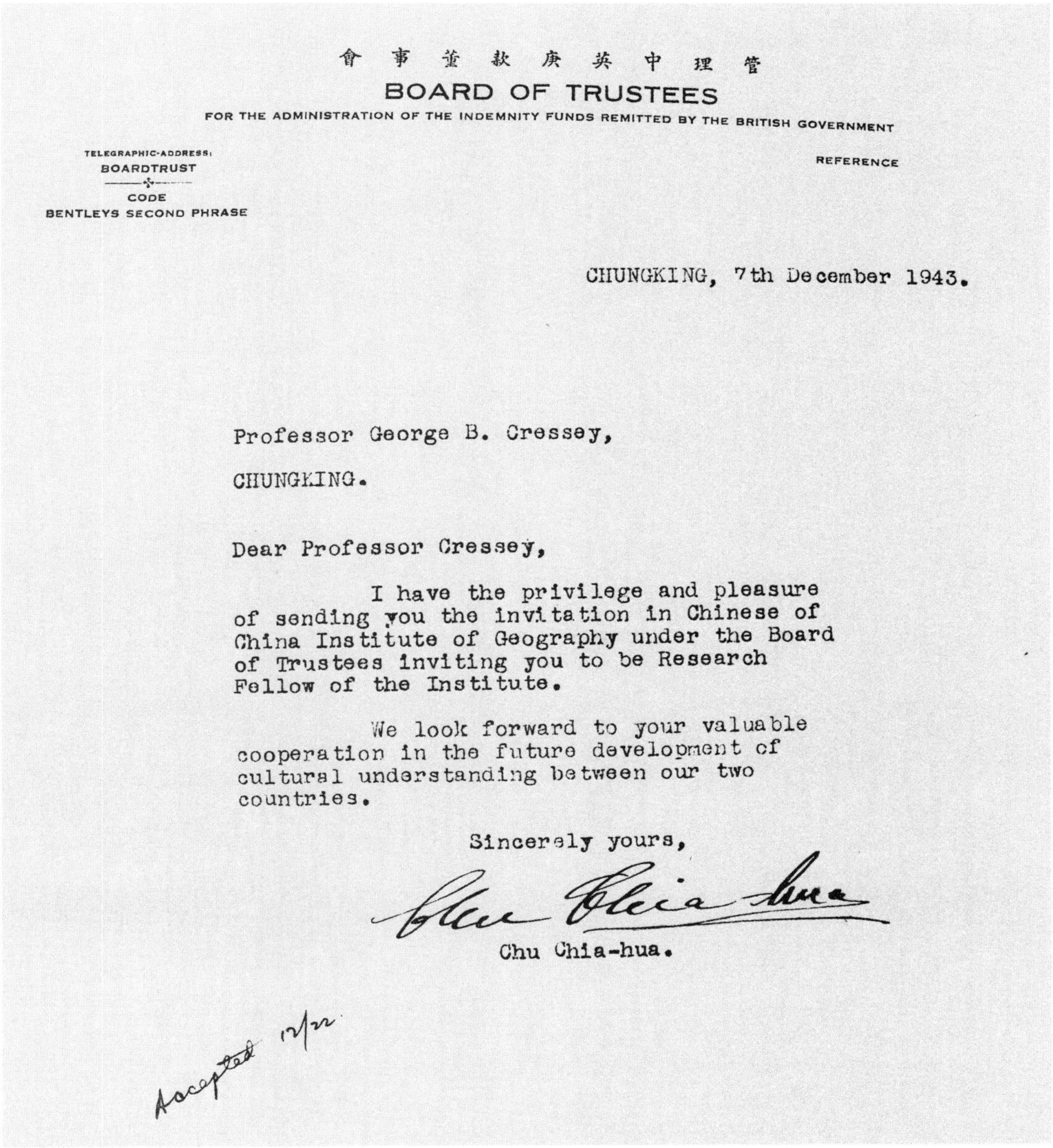

管理中英庚款董事會

BOARD OF TRUSTEES

FOR THE ADMINISTRATION OF THE INDEMNITY FUNDS REMITTED BY THE BRITISH GOVERNMENT

TELEGRAPHIC-ADDRESS:
BOARDTRUST
CODE
BENTLEYS SECOND PHRASE

REFERENCE

CHUNGKING, 7th December 1943.

Professor George B. Cressey,

CHUNGKING.

Dear Professor Cressey,

I have the privilege and pleasure of sending you the invitation in Chinese of China Institute of Geography under the Board of Trustees inviting you to be Research Fellow of the Institute.

We look forward to your valuable cooperation in the future development of cultural understanding between our two countries.

Sincerely yours,

Chu Chia-hua

Chu Chia-hua.

Accepted 12/22

朱家骅致葛德石信（1943 年 12 月 7 日）

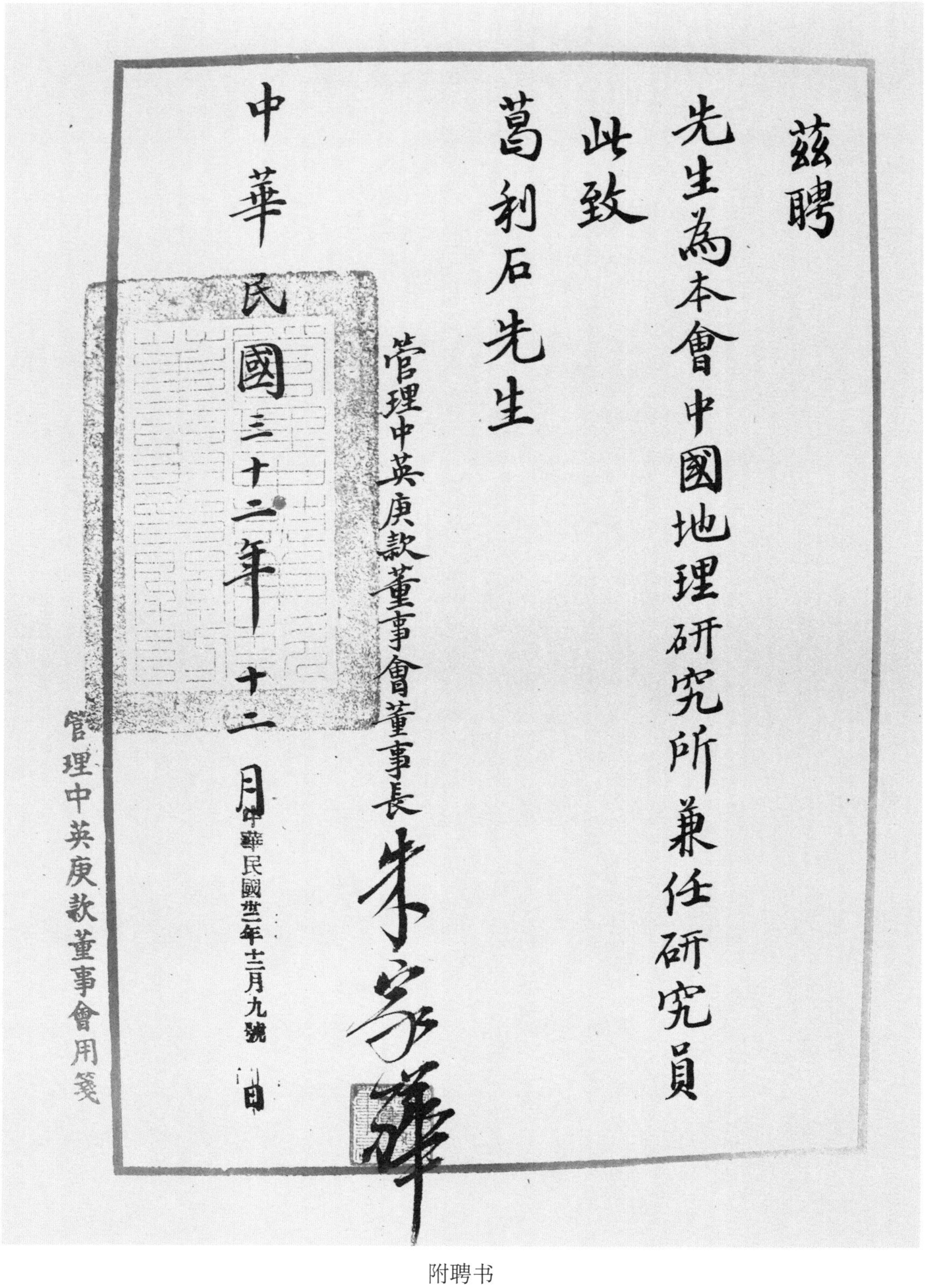

茲聘

先生為本會中國地理研究所兼任研究員

此致

葛利石先生

管理中英庚款董事會董事長

朱家驊

中華民國三十二年十二月　日

中華民國卅二年十二月九號

管理中英庚款董事會用箋

附聘书

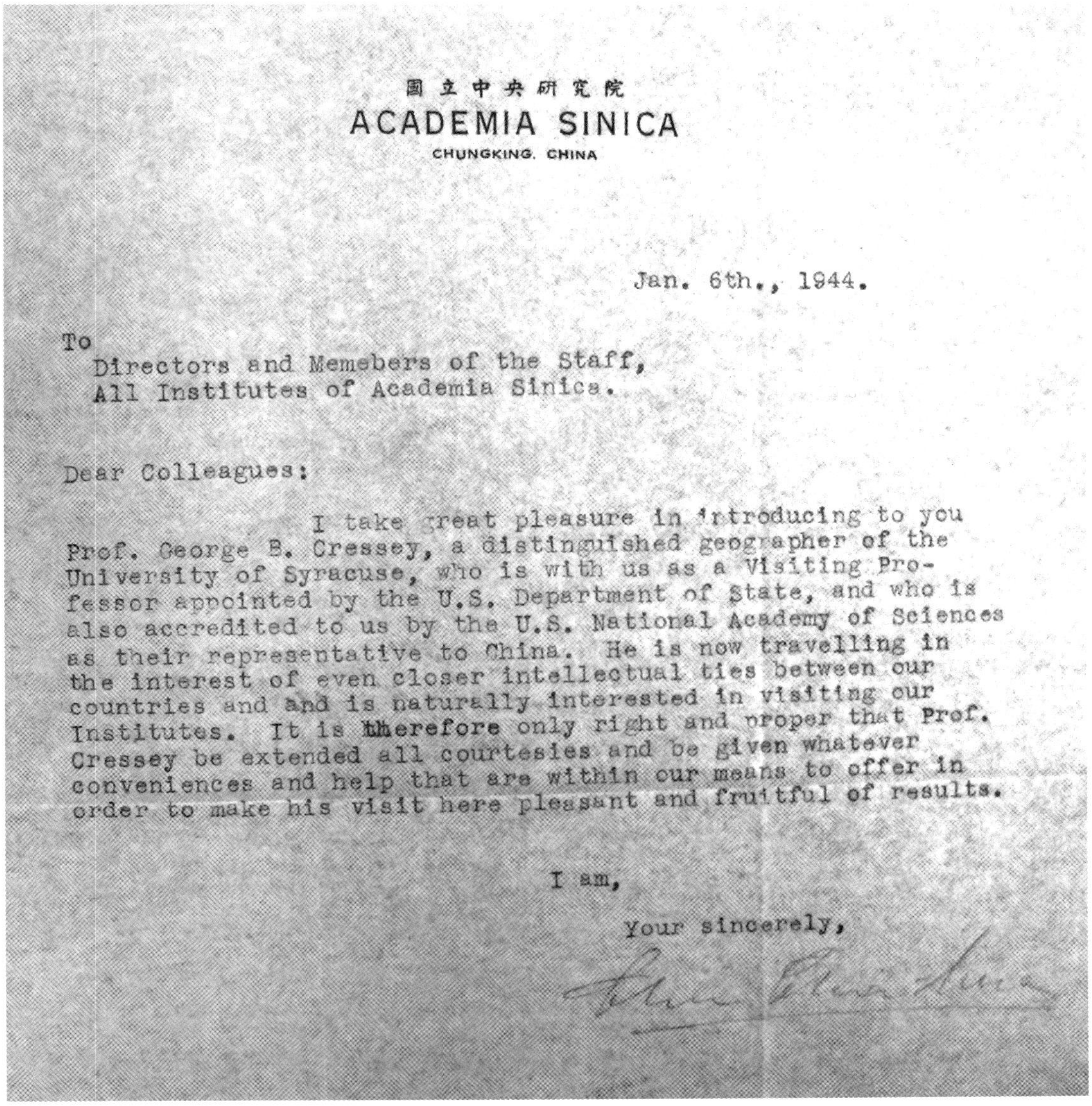

國立中央研究院
ACADEMIA SINICA
CHUNGKING, CHINA

Jan. 6th., 1944.

To
Directors and Memebers of the Staff,
All Institutes of Academia Sinica.

Dear Colleagues:

I take great pleasure in introducing to you Prof. George B. Cressey, a distinguished geographer of the University of Syracuse, who is with us as a Visiting Professor appointed by the U.S. Department of State, and who is also accredited to us by the U.S. National Academy of Sciences as their representative to China. He is now travelling in the interest of even closer intellectual ties between our countries and and is naturally interested in visiting our Institutes. It is therefore only right and proper that Prof. Cressey be extended all courtesies and be given whatever conveniences and help that are within our means to offer in order to make his visit here pleasant and fruitful of results.

I am,

Your sincerely,

朱家骅为葛德石开具介绍信（1944 年 1 月 6 日）

附朱家骅赠葛德石照片（1944 年 6 月）

王云五

王云五（1887—1979），字云五，广东香山人，出版家，1921 年任商务印书馆编译所所长，1930 年至 1946 年任商务印书馆总经理，对中国出版与文化贡献甚巨。1929 年葛德石曾计划将《中国的地理基础》交由上海的商务印书馆出版。1932 年书稿因战火被毁。抗战期间，葛德石再次计划将此书中文译稿交由商务印书馆出版，因此有了与王云五长达十余年的业务来往。现存两人之间的通信九封。

April 29, 1929

Mr. Y. W. Wang,
Editor-in-chief,
The Commercial Press,
Paoshan Road,
Shanghai,

My dear Mr. Wang:

In response to your request, I am sending you my understanding of our agreement concerning my book entitled "The Geography of China". These items have been covered in our conversations and in my letters of March 26th, March 2nd, and December 4th, and in your letter of April 4th, that of Mr. Hu dated March 11th, and in a letter from Dr. Fong of December 11th.

1. I agree to your printed contract entitled "Conditions re Lease of Copyright", with the following additions:

a. I am to receive 30 copies of the book free of charge.

b. The royalty is to be 15% of the list price.

c. In consideration of my heavy expense in preparing the book, you agree to pay me the sum of $500.00 upon the completion of the manuscript.

d. All rights of translation, in part or in whole, are reserved by me, but the Commercial Press shall have first chance to publish any Chinese edition.

e. In the case of my death, the royalty shall be paid to Marion Chatfield Cressey, my wife.

f. The copyright shall cover all text, illustrations, diagrams or maps supplied by me, which may not be reproduced without permission. In case either party desires to make occasional use of some of the ilustrative material, permission will freely be given, provided that in each case due credit is given to the book.

g. The base map, hsien map and any other material prepared by the Commercial Press under my supervision shall be held under joint copyright. For three years after the date of publication of the book, the use of such maps shall be restricted to this book, except that the Commercial Press shall have full liberty to sell copies of the maps separately, without royalty, provided that the maps carry a credit line such as "reproduced from Cressey: The Geography of China". After the period of three years, either party shall have unrestricted use of the maps.

葛德石致王云五信（1929 年 4 月 29 日）

Mr. Y. W. Wang - 2 - April 29, 1929

2. I am glad to take this opportunity to again assure you that my purpose in writing this book and in having it published in China is to render some service to China. I have written as a professional interpretative geographer, not with the object of minutely describing places and conditions or of making a critical study of problems and possibilities, but rather with the object of showing man's adjustment to the physical environment in definite geographic regions. It will be a book for the mature reader, both in China and abroad.

With this object in mind I shall welcome any suggestions concerning clarity of expression or geographic principles. The book is in no sense political propoganda and contains nothing to which fair-minded objection can be raised. The book is the product of five years of teaching a course on China to Chinese students, and practically all of its statements have been tried out orally. In case there are sentences to which you take exception, I agree to modify or omit them in so far as it does not interfere with the presentation of geographic principles.

3. We are agreed that the book is to be reproduced in the best manner possible, as to the quality of paper, half tones, color work on maps and binding.

I understand that you agree to undertake the preparation of the book immediately upon the preparation of the manuscript. I have already supplied Mr. Hu with most of the diagrams and photographs and with the copy for one chapter. I shall expect to have two-thirds of the copy in your hands by June first.

I am very anxious to see the galley proof before it is set in page form. I shall return to Shanghai on June 20th, and hope that you will have a considerable amount of proof ready at that time. I trust that you will be able to give the work right-of-way so that as much as possible may be done before my departure for America on July 13th.

Sincerely yours,

George B. Cressey

商務印書館股份有限公司

THE COMMERCIAL PRESS, LTD.

ESTABLISHED 1896

TELEGRAPHIC ADD: "COMPRESS" SHANGHAI
A. B. C. 5TH EDITION, WESTERN UNION
BENTLEY'S
TELEPHONE 92310

HEAD OFFICE

HEAD OFFICE SALES OFFICE
211 HONAN ROAD
SHANGHAI, CHINA

REFERENCE NO. BA

November 5, 1934.

Dr. George B. Cressey, Chairman
Department of Geology & Geography
Syracuse University
Syracuse, New York
U. S. A.

My dear Dr. Cressey:

I am glad to learn from your letter of October 12, 1934 that you have secured a more congenial person to take up the work of translating into Chinese your book on China's geographic foundations.

We shall keep you informed of our opinion as to the acceptability of the manuscript when it reaches our hands. When the complete translation is accepted, we shall conclude an agreement for its publication on royalty basis. The royalty is to be 15%, of which we shall pay a part to your translator, as mutually agreed upon between your goodself and the translator.

Sincerely yours,

THE COMMERCIAL PRESS, LTD.

Y. W. Wong

Managing Director

YWW:T

王云五致葛德石信（1934 年 11 月 5 日）

商務印書館股份有限公司
THE COMMERCIAL PRESS, LTD.
ESTABLISHED 1896

"COMPRESS" SHANGHAI
ION, WESTERN UNION
ITLEY'S
ONE 92310

HEAD OFFICE SALES OFFICE
211 HONAN ROAD
SHANGHAI, CHINA

HEAD OFFICE

December 26, 1935.

Dr. George B. Cressey
Syracuse University
Syracuse, New York
U. S. A.

My dear Dr. Cressey:

I have your letter of Dec. 4, concerning the Chinese translation of your China's Geographic Foundations.

We shall not have much difficulty in securing for you a reliable person to take up the translation work, provided that you will be responsible for advancing a sum of some eight hundred dollars Chinese currency ($5 per thousand Chinese characters) as remuneration for this undertaking. We shall then publish your Chinese version on royalty basis as you offer. The full claim of royalty, of course, will be yours, and likewise the copyright in this country. The royalty we can possibly give on this edition is fifteen per cent. A contract will be drawn up, if you will agree on these points.

Yours very truly,

THE COMMERCIAL PRESS, LTD.
Y. W. Wong
Managing Director

YWW:T

王云五致葛德石信（1935 年 12 月 26 日）

(H1-1000:9-29)

商務印書館總管理處駐港辦事處

THE COMMERCIAL PRESS, LIMITED

HONGKONG OFFICE

TELEGRAPHIC ADD.: "COMPRINT" HONGKONG
BENTLEY'S
TELEPHONE 24766

NORTH POINT, HONGKONG.

Ref. No. 30/70

August 8, 1941.

Mr. George B. Cressey,
Syracuse University,
Syracuse, New York,
U. S. A.

Dear Mr. Cressey,

We beg to acknowledge the receipt of your letter dated May 28, 1941 concerning the publication of a Chinese edition of "China's Geographic Foundations" for which we thank you.

In reply, we wish to inform you that, after exchange of correspondences with Mr. Y. T. Shen, we are satisfied that the portion which he has already translated is sufficient for the Chinese reading public. We are, therefore, pleased to accept Mr. Shen's manuscript on a royalty basis by giving you a 15% royalty on all copies sold. Meantime, you are requested to pay Mr. Shen for his translated services as agreed upon by you.

Enclosed please find two copies of our royalty contract one of which kindly sign and return to us at your earliest convenience.

Sincerely yours,

THE COMMERCIAL PRESS, LTD.

Y. Wong

Managing Director

YWW:Y
Encl.

王云五致葛德石信（1941 年 8 月 8 日）

September 12, 1941

My dear Mr. Wong:

I am glad to have your letter of August 8 enclosing the contract for China's Geographic Foundations. It is indeed a pleasure to again have a contract with the Press, and I trust that we will have no recurrence of 1932. I am enclosing my Chinese card so that you will have the correct characters for my name in Chinese. I have signed the contract today and am sending it with one copy of this letter by boat, while the other goes by air mail so that you may proceed at once with the publication. In view of the long delays since the writing of my original manuscript and the years which have elapsed since Mr. Shen completed his translation, I earnestly hope that you will be able to start printing at once.

My agreement with Mr. Y. T. Shen, the translator, was that I would pay him $1,000 in Chinese currency upon publication, but since there has been so much delay, I shall be glad to forward the money to him as soon as I hear from you that you have started printing. I am writing him today in care of the Commission of Civil Service Examination, Goh-lo Hill, Chungking, but I am not sure whether this is his present address.

In the letter which goes by ordinary mail, I enclose several pages of corrections which cover mistakes that appeared in the first and second printings. I am also sending a new preface for the Chinese edition. If you plan to include any of the bibliography, I can send you a few important additions which have appeared in recent years, but you may have decided that the bibliography is less important for the Chinese edition.

I am also sending by parcel post the original photographs for all of the pictures except 12, 59, 86, 92, 123, 137, and 186. For these you will have to copy the half-tones in the original volume. I will not send the

葛德石致王云五信（1941 年 9 月 12 日）

Mr. Y. W. Wong 2 September 12, 1941

drawings unless you want them. You can probably make satisfactory cuts from the printed copy. In the case of the climatic charts, figures 206, 227, and 374, the cut in the English edition is incorrect and I enclose new copies from the French edition.

Sincerely yours,

George B. Cressey

Mr. Y. W. Wong
The Commercial Press
North Point, Hongkong

gbc:ejs

Care American Embassy,
Chungking,
May22, 1944

My dear Mr. Wang,

I am sending youthis note in anticipation of our call at three o'clock this afternoon. Youmay recall that from 1923 to 1929 I taught at the University of Shanghai. I am now in China as Visiting Professor under the Division of Science, Education and Art of the United States Department of State, and concurrently representing the National Academy of Sciences.

Late in 1941 I signed a contract with you for the publication of a Chinese version of China's Geographic Foundations, and accordingly sent the illustrations to you in Hongkong. I understand from the Post Office that they arrived November 20. Can you give me any further word as to the matter of publication?

I have recently completed a new volume entitled "Asia's Lands and Peoples", the folios for which I have just received by air mail. I also enclose a letter from McGraw-Hill, the publishers. Since this book contains a large amount of data dealing with post-war strategy and reconstruction not only in China but in the Soviet Union and other parts of Asia, I would be especially pleased to arrange for a Chinese translation.

In order that you may be able to give me your judgement, I am sending you a copy herewith. Can you undertake to translate and publish a volume of this size within the next year or so? Can you include the maps, even though the half tones may be out of the question. If I have it translated by geographic friends rather than by your own service, what compensation would you suggest? In case you should decide to publish, at what rate of exchange can royalty payments be made to me in the United States?

Sincerely yours,

George B. Cressey

George B. Cressey

Mr. Y. W. Wang
The Commercial Press
Chungking

葛德石致王云五信（1944 年 5 月 22 日）

The Commercial Press, Limited
Chungking, China
May 23, 1944

Professor George B. Cressey
C/O American Embassy
Chungking

Dear Professor Cressey:

As regards the publication of a Chinese version of your "Asia's Lands and Peoples", we should like to accept it on the following conditions: —

First, you are responsible for the preparation of the translation and for any expenses incurred.

Secondly, we shall accept the manuscript only if it is, in our judgment, up to standard.

Thirdly, no other illustrations shall be contained in the manuscript than a few indispensable maps.

Fourthly, the entire manuscript shall have to pass the government censor before it can be sent to press. We shall have the right to omit portions of the manuscript if required by the censor.

Fifthly, when the manuscript has passed the censor, we shall do our best to bring it out in six months from then.

Sixthly, you shall receive a royalty of fifteen per cent (15%) of the selling price, in Chinese national currency, for the copies sold.

Your reply confirming the above-mentioned terms is requested.

Yours truly
The Commercial Press, Limited
Y. W. Wang
Managing director

王云五致葛德石信（1944 年 5 月 23 日）

care American Embassy
May 23, 1944

My dear Mr. Wang,

I enclose a letter to Professor Chang Yin-tang in Kunming which covers the situation to date. When I hear from him I will send you a copy so that you may be fully informed. I now look forward to having your letter ofqagreement concerning publication, royalty, etc. I shall see that you have a copy of the book in the near future, and will plan to call again before I leave for the United States early in June.

It was a great pleasure to see you again, and I sincerely trust that this time we actually come to the point of publication.

Sincerely yours,

George B. Cressey

Mr. Y. W. Wang
The Commercial, Press
Chungking

葛德石致王云五信（1944 年 5 月 23 日）

AIR MAIL

care American Embassy
June 3, 1944

My dear Mr. Wang,

I am glad to acknowledge your letter of May 23 concerning the publication of a Chinese version of "Asia's Lands and Peoples".

I already have the acceptance of Professor Chang Yin-tang, of the Department of Geography at Southwest Associated University, for the translation. I will pay him U.S. $250, in currency, which I will deposit with my cousin, Dr. E. H. Cressy at 10 Dai chia hang, Chungking. He is authorized to pay Professor Chang such amounts and at such times as you direct. Professor Chang proposes to send you the manuscript in three lots, at the end of August, October and December, and would like to receive $150, 100, and 100 at these times. I suspect that you will want to hold out the final payment until proof is accepted. In other words the matter of payment is in your hands.

I have taken great pains with the English, and I hope that you will be equally insistent upon good Chinese.

I accept your six terms, and look forward to actual publication, at an early date.

Is there any way in which you can register your intent to publish with the censor now, to forestallncompetition? I shall see that you have a copy within a few months, and the few others which come to China will be with the restriction that they must not be used for translation purposes.

I expect to be here for a week or two more. After that my address will be Syracuse University, Syracuse, N. Y.

Sincerely yours,

George B. Cressey

Mr. Y. W. Wang
The Commercial Press

copy to Dr. E. H. Cressy

葛德石致王云五信（1944 年 6 月 3 日）

刘大钧

刘大钧（1891–1962），江苏丹徒人，1915年毕业于美国密歇根大学，历任清华大学经济学教授、北洋政府经济讨论处调查主任、国民政府立法院统计局局长、中国经济统计调查所所长。刘大钧利用统计工具，对民国的工业、农业以及人口都有独到的见解，为民国政府所倚重。葛德石与刘大钧曾经同属太平洋学会，而且都在上海，所以两人过往频繁，葛德石的中国经济统计资料主要来自于刘大钧。现存刘大钧致葛德石信函数封。

'm A. (1000)

LE No. P.

QUIRY NO. P-605

SUBJECT Geography of China

DATE Dec. 15, 1926.

BY D. K. L

經濟討論處

REPUBLIC OF CHINA

GOVERNMENT BUREAU OF ECONOMIC INFORMATION

PEKING

NATURAL REGIONS OF CHINA.

1.--No suggestions.

2.--The southern boundary of the Plain of North China seems to have been placed too far south, at 2-2-2. It should be north of the Hwai River along 3-3-, because conditions along the Hwai River are more like those of Lower Yangtse than the plain of North China. South of Sinyangchow at 3 wheat is the principal crop, while north of it millet and corn are more important. South of the Hwai River rice is still the dominant crop, and even some distance north of it. The northernmost boundary of the rice crop in Kiangsu is Tsingkiangpu, which is north of the Lakes and the Hwai River. There are some low mountains north of the Hwai River which may be considered the boundary line of these two regions, although they are not shown in Goode's base map. Yinshang (穎上) is one of the three most important rice-producing centers of Anhwei, and it is a little north of the Hwai River.

3.--The northern limit of the tea crop is also somewhere along the Hwai River, as much tea is produced in the mountains south of it. Bamboo as a dominant vegetation probably does not reach so far north, but at Chinghwa, Honan (along Tao-Ching railway) there is a small region which produces bamboo which is marketed as far north as Peking as as far west as Shensi and Kansu. (See bamboo map in Vol. III, No. 4 of the Chinese Economic Monthly".) Mulberry limit is not quite clear.

4.--We have no knowledge of any percentages of crops in China, nor do we know where anything of the kind may be got. If anything has been published on this point, it must be pure speculation.

刘大钧为葛德石《中国地理》一书所提建议（1926 年 12 月 15 日）

5.--This Bureau has investigation reports on the economic conditions in many districts in the various regions except the southwest, northeast, Outer Mongolia and Tibet. They may be found in every issue of the Monthly and in many issues of the Bulletin.

6.--Population densities must be a matter of speculation. Your opinion on this is just as good as ours.

7.--The northern boundary of the Shantung-Liaotung region should probably be rounded out a little along the line 5-5. The Chang-pei-shan range extends from the Manchurian Highlands down the Liaotung peninsular and across the sea to the Shantung peninsula. A large break is somewhere along the 5-5 line, along the Sungari River. It would appear better to have the boundary line pass through the break rather than cut across the mountains, since there are mountains on both sides of the line.

8--The following references may be of value on the Plateau of Yunnan:

Major Davies book on Yunnan (copy in the Library of the Royal Asiatic Society)
French sources--much information may perhaps be got through the French Consul General.
F. Kingdon Ward may also be a source for certain information. (See enclosed cutting)
Far Eastern Review--Vol. 15, No. 1, pg. 1;, Vol. 15, No. 12, pg. 1 ; Vol. 10, No. 9 ; April, 1921.
Blackburn Chamber of Commerce Report. (If not at the Library of the R.A.S. then at the library of the Far Eastern Review)
Vice Consul Margary's Report. (Probably in the British Blue Book at the Rar Eastern Review office)
Shanghai Mercury Reprint--Journey in North and North West Yunnan by Acting Consul Litton.

9.--Probably the Blackburn Chamber of Commerce Report will give information which will help you to determine this question.

10--Formosa seems to belong to Fukien so far as its products are concerned, and probably in other respects too. The Chekiang-Fukien region however seems to be too large because economic and agricultural conditions of the Tsientang river valley are almost the same as the Yangtse valley, and quite different from southeast Chekiang or Fukien. According to the lecture notes, Ningpo is included in the Lower Yangtse region, and so the line ought to be somewhere along 4-4. ~~xxxxxxxxxxxxxxxxxxxxxxxxxxxx~~(There are higher mountains, the Hsienhsia-ling (仙霞岭) along the 4-4 line than along the coast or the southern part of Anhwei.)

Northwest Chekiang produces silk, rice, tea (different from Fukien tea), and all other dominant crops typical of the Lower Yangtse valley. Description of some typical districts in this region is given on page 327 of the Monthly, Vol. III, No. 8.

11.--Material on this subject has appeared in various issues of our publications; also see "North Manchuria and the Chinese Eastern Railway", published by the railway printing office, Harbin, "Manchuria, Land of Opportunities", published by the South Manchuria Railway, and the "Manchuria Monitor", a publication of the Chinese Eastern Railway.

12.--No.

13.--Cannot answer. No information.

Other Suggestions

1. The Lower Yangtse region should include a little more of northern Kiangsi than indicated in the map. The boundary line should probably be extended to 8-8, along the foot of the mountains, because the districts north of 8-8 are similar in economic conditions to those around the Poyang Lake.

2. The Loess Highlands should extend further north to 6-6-6, because the region north of the yellow river curve, known as Hou-tao, 後套 is very fertile, and also the southern portions of Suiyuan and Chahar. The northern portions beyond Yinshan (陰山 also known as Tatsingshan (大青山) are much poorer. The article on Paotowchen in Vol. III, No. 6 of the Monthly and several reports on Kweisui, Suiyuan, etc. in the Bulletin describe the conditions of that region in great detail. At present the region enclosed by the Yellow river curve and the Great Wall, under the administration of the Ninghsia Resident Commissioner, is barren through neglect of irrigation and cultivation, but about a century ago it was one of the most fertile regions of China, and was known as Ho-tao (   ). Even now it can be reclaimed without much difficulty, if means of communication are improved. Beyond the 6-6 line is the real desert. This line is drawn along the Yinshan on the north and Alshan mountains on the west.

Descriptions of districts more or less typical of the Plain of North

China--Paoting, Shihkiachwang, Hantan and Shunteh--have been published in the Bulletin or will soon be published. A short report on Paoting is found on page 90 of Bulletin 285. See also, report on Nanchang rice on page 290 of Bulletin 275, and report on agriculture in Kiukiang in Bulletin No. 288.

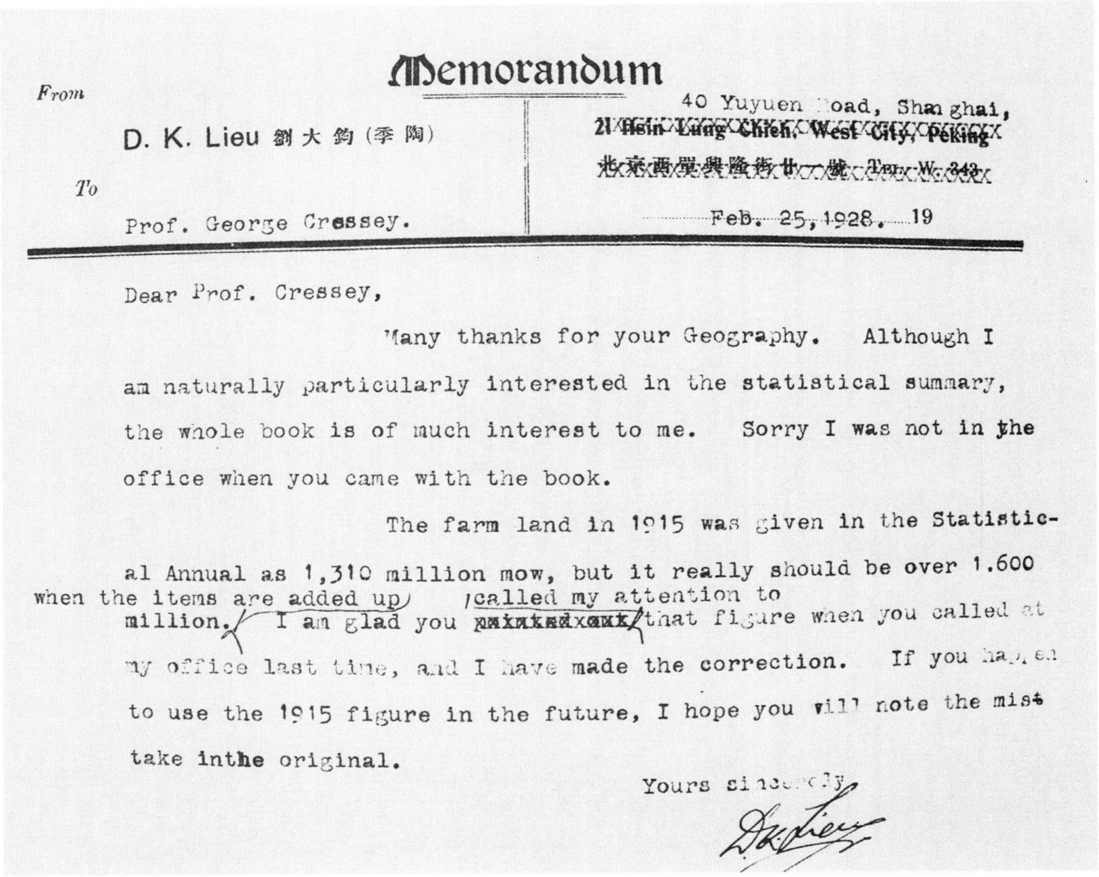

Memorandum

From
D. K. Lieu 劉大鈞(季陶)

40 Yuyuen Road, Shanghai,
~~21 Hsin Lung Chien, West City, Peking~~
~~北京西單興隆街廿一號 Tel. W. 343~~

To
Prof. George Cressey.

Feb. 25, 1928. 19

Dear Prof. Cressey,

Many thanks for your Geography. Although I am naturally particularly interested in the statistical summary, the whole book is of much interest to me. Sorry I was not in the office when you came with the book.

The farm land in 1915 was given in the Statistical Annual as 1,310 million mow, but it really should be over 1,600 million, when the items are added up. I am glad you ~~pointed out~~ called my attention to that figure when you called at my office last time, and I have made the correction. If you happen to use the 1915 figure in the future, I hope you will note the mistake inthe original.

Yours sincerely,
D. K. Lieu

刘大钧致葛德石信（1928 年 2 月 25 日）

Reprinted from the "CHINESE ECONOMIC JOURNAL" March, 1928

To Prof. George B. Cressey

Compliments of
D. K. Lieu

Statistics of Farm Land in China

BY D. K. LIEU AND CHUNG-MIN CHEN

Chinese Government Bureau of Economic Information

Head Office:
1-A Chang Pu Ho, Nan Ho Yen, Peking.

Shanghai Office:
20 Museum Road, Shanghai

附刘大钧赠葛德石《中国农田统计》一文封面

中美文化協會
CHINESE-AMERICAN INSTITUTE OF CULTURAL RELATIONS
CHUNGKING, CHINA

SECRETARY GENERAL'S OFFICE
FAN CHUANG

Dec. 31st, 1943,
Sa-Ping-Pa, Chungking.

Professor George B. Cressey,
Care of Dean Hu,
The Central University.

Dear Prof. Cressey,

Since I came back to Sa Ping Pa, I have been laid up with a pain in the back and the right arm and so I have not been able to see you here, nor arrange for a lecture by you at the Chungking University. As you will probably go back to the city to spend the new year there, I shall have to postpone the pleasure of seeing you again till I am able to go to town.

With best wishes for a happy new year,

Sincerely yours,
D K Lieu
D. K. Lieu.

刘大钧致葛德石信（1943 年 12 月 31 日）

BUREAU/OF/NATIONAL/ECONOMIC/RESEARCH

P.O.Box No.9, Shapingpa,
Chungking, May 20,1944.

Prof. George B. Cressey,
c/o the American Embassy.

My dear Prof. Cressey,

I am glad to receive your letter of the 16th., and learn that you have returned from your last trip to the Northwest and Southwest. As I have not gone to town this week, your letter was forwarded to me from the Central Bank Research Department and did not reach me until Friday afternoon. So I was not able to call on you at the appointed time, or send you a telephone message. Last week, however, I telephoned to the Embassy a couple of times, but was told you had not yet returned.

Thank you for the suggestion of having lunch with you at your office instead of at the Institute. However, since you were away from China many years, and have only returned for a trip, I have wanted very much to invite you to lunch to"express my welcome" . Onle because of my arm trouble and later, your trips to the other cities, it has been postponed so long. As you are leaving again for the States soon, the invitation will become a sort of a farewell party instead.

I will come to town next Wednesday afternoon, and wonder if you can have lunch with me next Friday or Saturday? The place will still be the Chinese-American Institute, but if you prefer Chinese food, we may go to some of the Chinese restaurants in the vicinity of the Embassy. However, this time I will call at your office before 12 and go to the Institute or the restaurant together.

When you receive this letter, kindly send a note telling me if you have time, next Friday or Saturday. I may ring you up too next Thursday, but as/my hearing is defective, I may not be able to do so if I cannot get some one in the Bank to do it for me. I think there should be some people in the Research Department who can speak English well to do the telephoning, but it would be surer if you will send me a reply. Of course if there be any air -raid alarm at the appointed time, all arrangements will have to be called off. Otherwise I will certainly be at your office not later than 12 on that day.

Looking forward to seeing you soon,

Sincerely yours,

D.K. Lieu

P.S. Kindly excuse my failure to call on you yesterday.

刘大钧致葛德石信（1944 年 5 月 20 日）

THE CENTRAL BANK OF CHINA

Research Department,
Szechuen Salt Bank Building,
June 8, 1944.

Prof. George B. Cressey,
c/o the American Embassy,
Tseng Chia Ai.

Dear Prof. Cressey,

It was a great pleasure to have that long talk with you at the Chinese-American Institute the other day. After my discussion with Prof. Staley the next day, I have made plans to revise some chapters of my book, as well as the order of their arrangement, but my plans are not yet definite. As eight chapters have already been written, any thorough-going revision would mean the rewriting of many chapters, which I intend to avoid unless it is absolutely necessary or very desirable. The following is the table of contents which will probably be final.

China & International Economic Cooperation. Post-War

Chap. I. Introduction.
II. The Guiding Principles of International Economic Cooperation.
III. China's Economic Background.
IV. Her Economic Policy & Problems.
V. Balance of International Payments.
VI. Foreign Trade.
VII. The Currency Question.
VIII. Other Problems Involving International Economic Cooperation.
IX. Ditto, continued.
X. Conclusion.

Of the eight chapters already written, two will be thoroughly revised and form a new chapter according to the above plan. I have not yet started to write Chapter VIII of the new plan, but think there will be a number of questions to be discussed besides currency, trade and foreign investments. (The last subject is discussed in Chapter V.) If these questions can be properly grouped into two groups, they will be dealt with in Chapters VIII and IX; otherwise there may be more than two chppters for these problems. The chapter headings will probably be modified when the book is completed. Prof. Staley advises me to put the chapter on Relief and Rehabilitation in my original plan immediately after Chapter IV, but as I am not sure if I can get sufficient material for a separate chapter on that subject, I am afraid it will have to be discussed in connection with other topics in Chapters VIII or IX.

If you have any suggestions about the general contents of the book, I shall be very grateful if you will let me know. As to your question concerning the repayment of foreign loans mentioned at our last meeting, I intend to discuss that in connection with foreign trade. Thanking you in advance,

Sincerely yours,

D.K. Lieu

刘大钧致葛德石信（1944 年 6 月 8 日）

THE CENTRAL BANK OF CHINA

P.S. You expressed your surprise at finding many things in China which are now hard to obtain in America. Among them you mentioned the comparative abundance of iron ware in Chungking, and I suppose it is true also in other parts of China. According to my understanding, there is an excess of iron production over demand, which may appear at first sight to be quite unexpected, when a country has been engaged in a life and death struggle for eight years. The explanation is that the demand for iron for military purposes in China is much smaller than that in any other country, because ~~Chinaxixx~~ the Chinese army is not mechanized, and the Chinese arsenals are unable to produce heavy shells, heavy arms, aerial bombs, etc., which consume a lot of iron and steel. In addition to that, the productive capacity of the steel works in China is exceedingly small, being limited by their equipment. Most of them use electric crucibles, each of which can make only a couple of tons of steel a day. Only a year ago some Bessemer furnaces were set up. On the whole the productive capacity of the iron works is much larger than that of the steel mills, and the latter constitutes a bottle-neck which has now caused many iron mills to close down or suspend operations. The excess iron has been manufactured into iron ware of all sorts, and that is why we are not short of these as we should be.

There are also more leather goods for civilian use in China than probably in America. In England I understand leather goods are strictly rationed, and I think shoes are rationed also in America. Here again the explanation is the limited demand for them in the army. As you know, the Chinese soldiers wear straw sandals, and they have no leather belts or straps. I understand leather is used extensively only in the cavalry.

As to the small things manufactured abroad which are found more readily in China than in America, such as fountain pens, American etc., the explanation is that they are supplied to the Chinese market by the American service men in China. There is also an abundance of these things in India, ~~xhxxxgx~~ the same source. and they come from Apparently some of the service men do not need as many things as are supplied them by the U.S. Army PX stores, and so they either give them away to their Chinese friends, or sell them in order to buy things Chinese ~~xxxx~~, such as embroidery goods. There was a large demand for such goods sometime ago, and their price jumped to unusual heights. The same explanation holds true for American butter, coffee, cigarettes, etc. etc.

Dm

陈裕光

陈裕光（1883–1989），浙江宁波人，教育学家。美国哥伦比亚大学博士，毕生从事教育事业，1927–1950 年，任金陵大学校长。葛德石因金陵大学教授卜凯的关系，结识陈裕光。陈裕光曾邀请葛德石前来金陵大学执教，并为葛德石的中国访问提供帮助，而葛德石也邀请陈裕光访问了雪城大学。现存陈裕光致葛德石信函四封。

UNIVERSITY OF NANKING
OFFICE OF THE PRESIDENT
NANKING, CHINA

January 11, 1929

Dr. George B. Cressey
Shanghai College
Shanghai.

My dear Dr. Cressey:

From Mr. Buck I understand that you are soon leaving China and may come back to Chinese universities for further work on geology and that you are very much interested in the University work in general and the projects of the College of Agriculture and Forestry, in particular. May I request you, on behalf of the University to consider joining our University Faculty as one of our Baptist Board quota, after your return, when you have finished your furlough in America. You would have a broad opportunity to develop the Department of Geology and possibly, Geography, as these two Departments have not been entirely taken care of by our staff in the University and I am sure the land utilization project and other projects proposed by the College of Agriculture and Forestry, would feel very much enlightened by your presence. Both Dean Kuo and Mr. Buck are very anxious to have you give us a favorable reply.

Very sincerely yours,

Y. G. Chen

Y. G. Chen.

YGC/FP

陈裕光致葛德石信（1929 年 1 月 11 日）

Commission of Civil Service
Examination,
Goh-lo Hill, Chungking,
China,
Feb. 17, 1941.

My Dear Mr. Cressey:

Your letter of June 5, last year was duly received, when I was still in Chengku. Since then, I left for Chungking in July and returned to Chengku in October. Not very long ago, I came again to Chungking at the request of the Examination Yuan to participate in the work for the impending Higher Examination. I had asked leave of absence from the University, and would stay at Chungking until July. For all this, I failed to send you a reply in time. Hence I must offer you my very humble apology.

Three years and a half have elapsed since the outbreak of the Sino-Japanese War. The Japanese have certainly fallen into dire straits. In a year or two, we would probably win the day. We will heartily welcome you to come to China again at that time. To be sure, after the war, China, especially her Western part will well worthy visiting.

This is always my utmost pride that I translated your great work "China's Geographic Foundations" into our own language. With the consent of you and the McGraw-Hill book Company, I have asked Mr. Y. W. Wang, Managing Director of the Commercial Press in Hongkong to publish the translation. I appreciated very much all that you pointed out for me for revision. But, allow me to tell you my own ideas. To meet the general demand of the Chinese students, I laid special stress on the study of geographic regions of China. A scientific writing such as yours is greatly needed in China, and hence I concentrated my attention in translating the fifteen geographical regions, and entitled my translation "The Geographical Regions of China" "中國區域地理".

To the translation I wrote a preface, in which I intended to tell the readers how I translated the book; in which I expressed my respect to you on the division of the fifteen geographic regions of China, uniquely well-done as it was. Although there are some preliminary studies on the geographic or natural regions of China, your method is, nevertheless, the most rational and scientific. In the near future, the new political divisions of China will be regulated, based on these geographic units, for I am quite sure that the political division of China after the war must be decided from the geographic point of view, This will be the fundamental problem for the reconstruction of China.

If you would kindly permit me to publish the translation, I hope you will to the following for me as I was promised:

First, please write a preface. Better write it with pen and ink in order to put it in type. My translation of the preface will be appended. This will be an honour to me.

陈裕光致葛德石信（1941 年 2 月 17 日）

- 2 -

Second, please send me a copy of the third edition of your book for reference.

Third, please send me several pages of corrections for mistakes which crept into the first English edition.

Lastly, instead of taking any tax on edition, I should like to receive from you a thousand dollars, Chinese currency once for all.

Besides, pray give the sum of money in advance, soon after your receipt of Mr. Liu's letter.

Meanwhile, please urge the Press to have the book published as soon as possible -- I will, of course, do the same -- after a delay of over four years, I hope for the earliest publication of my translation which was completed at Peiping before the war.

I firmly believe that your great work is not only requisite to the students of geography, but equally helpful to the intellectual class in China as a whole

I was fortunate enough to use your original illustrations gratis. Herewith I express my deep thanks to you.

In publishing the book, I will do what the Press will ask me to, and revise it when necessary.

Hoping for an immdiate rply.

Sincerely Yours,

Y. T. Shen

Y. T. Shen.

Professor Dr. George B. Cressey,
Department of Geology and Geography,
Syracuse, N. Y.,
U. S. A.

cc copy to: Mr. Liu Yu-wan, 10 Peking Road Kowloon, Hongkong

UNIVERSITY OF NANKING

NANKING 5. CHINA

OFFICE OF THE PRESIDENT

October 16, 1948

Dr. George B. Cressey
Dept. of Geography
Syracuse University
Syracuse 10, N. Y., U. S. A.

Dear Dr. Cressey:

We are very much interested in your letter of September 29th telling us of the prospects of having a year in China in 1950-51. We shall welcome you and hope your plans will materialize so you may bring your family to share that year with you in Nanking.

At this particular time we have been studying the situation carefully as there have been several inquiries from professors who hope to spend their sabbatic year in China under the Fulbright Bill. It is our hope to establish a research center on our campus which will enable all scholars to make use of the facilities that we have for the purpose of cementing the relationships between the two countries, and bring better understanding of the cultures of both nations. It may be interesting for you to read a statement that has been prepared recently by Dr. Bates, and we enclose a copy for your information.

We realize that we do not have a department of Geography, and one will not find on our campus any advanced studies in Geography.

I hesitate to make any statement about housing at this time. It is always a very critical problem to find sufficient houses for our own faculty and staff and we are troubled to know how we can serve our friends from other countries who wish to spend a year or more on the campus doing more or less independent research. We have a tentative plan to erect a house which will be reserved for the use of scholars who wish to come to Nanking for research, but inasmuch as we must take capital funds to erect the house, we shall have to charge a rental to reimburse us for the equivalent of interest on that money. The house is not built yet but is under consideration. It is only fair to say that we would naturally give preference to a professor who was interested in a particular subject offered by our institution as we would hope to have some help by lectures or seminars during the year in residence on our campus. However we can hold out to you this small ray of hope that if there were no other applicants for that particular year, that we would gladly give you the chance to rent the house and have the privileges of the campus. I am not sure that this gives you sufficient promise, but is the best we can offer at this particular time. We shall be very glad to help you find a house off the campus if you so desire.

We shall be very glad to hear from you from time to time and to know how your plans progress.

With warm regards to Mrs. Cressey and yourself,

Sincerely yours,

Y. G. Chen

Yu-gwan Chen

陈裕光致葛德石信（1948 年 10 月 16 日）

UNIVERSITY OF NANKING
OFFICE OF THE PRESIDENT
NANKING 5. CHINA

February 11, 1949.

Dr. George B. Cressey,
Department of Geography,
Syracuse University,
Syracuse 10, N. Y.

Dear Dr. Cressey:

In spite of all uncertainties we were able to close our last semester on schedule time with little interruption and no reduction of any curriculum class work, although we had a smaller student body. We are opening next semester on the 14th of this month. We had entrance examinations last week and expect to receive 150 new students, with some make-up classes in addition. This latter work is necessary in order to maintain our quality of work.

For the coming term we are expecting to continue our work, hoping that the political disturbances will not affect our educational enterprises. We are expecting 600 students for the coming term. This is a little more than half of the number of students we ordinarily have.

We are still hoping that you can arrange to come to Nanking under the Fulbright Bill. Although we do not have a Department of Geography which would qualify us as a sponsoring institution I am sure that the Central University and the Institute of Geography in Nanking would be strong sponsors and all the institutions in Nanking would be benefited by your being with us. At present there are political uncertainties in Nanking which might affect this planning, but we hope the situation may clear up soon.

I shall be pleased to write you further when the situation seems to be more favorable for a definite decision. Do let me know when there is anything that I can do to help you.

With best regards to Mrs. Cressy and the rest of your family, I remain

Sincerely yours,

Y. G. Chen

Chen Yu-gwan

YGC:CBS.

陈裕光致葛德石信（1949 年 2 月 11 日）

第四章
葛德石与沪江大学校长的通信

沪江大学（Shanghai College）是1906年由美国南浸信会和北浸礼会在上海联合创办的教会大学，是民国时期中国十三所基督教会大学之一。在1911年至1927年间，来自北浸礼会的传教士魏馥兰担任沪江大学校长。1928年至1938年，刘湛恩担任校长。沪江大学坐落在上海东郊的杨树浦，东滨黄浦江，交通便利，不染繁华，于热闹场得净土，洵一读书佳境也。1924年至1929年，葛德石在沪江大学创建地质地理系，并担任助教授兼系主任。沪江大学是葛德石教书育人之地，也是葛德石考察研究中国之平台。葛德石的沪江大学通信主要是他与前后两任校长魏馥兰和刘湛恩的书信往来。

魏馥兰

魏馥兰（Francis John White，1870—1959），1891年被北浸礼会派遣来华，1906年参与创建沪江大学，并于1911年起担任了十七年校长，为沪江大学历史上任期最长的校长。在任内，魏馥兰将黄浦江畔的一片荒滩建设成为现代大学校园，奠定沪江大学的格局。魏馥兰长袖善舞，坚持学校的中国化。1929年第一任华人校长刘湛恩任职后，他又默默地在宗教系任教六年。魏馥兰的人格与贡献赢得了沪江大学师生的一致尊重。1936年，魏馥兰退休返回美国，沪江大学董事会授予他终身名誉校长，并把学校礼堂命名为“思魏堂”。葛德石与魏馥兰的通信现存四封，涉及葛德石的聘用以及沪江大学地质地理系的办学状况。

校學大江滬

SHANGHAI COLLEGE

PRESIDENT'S OFFICE

SHANGHAI, CHINA

Jan. 14, 1921

Mr. Geo. B. Cressy,
Suite 150, South Divinity Hall,
University of Chicago,
Chicago, Ill.

Dear Mr. Cressy,

Your cousin, E.H., has given me your letter regarding the possibility of a position as teacher of geology. There is no question about the necessity for teachers of geology in China. Our authorities only hesitate because we cannot have all the teachers that we would like to have. I am urging them to ask you to come when your preparation is completed and I firmly believe that there will be a place for you, but of course I cannot promise. It may be that in the near future I will be able to make such a promise but sometimes people move slowly. We have courses in geology and geography and I believe if you were prepared in those subjects that a place would be ready for you by the time you were ready for it.

Regarding the teaching of geography, there are not many colleges in America that teach geography but most universities do. I have long had the conviction that it ought to be taught in college and I am teaching the subject myself. I would be glad to devote my life to such a work but probably cannot do so and would be glad if you came to Shanghai if you could take geography and geology which are so closely allied.

I would be glad to have you write to Dr. J. H. Franklin, 276 Fifth Ave., New York City, our foreign secretary, about the question. It would urge him to decide if you were to write to him.

Yours truly,

F. J. White

魏馥兰致葛德石信（1921 年 1 月 14 日）

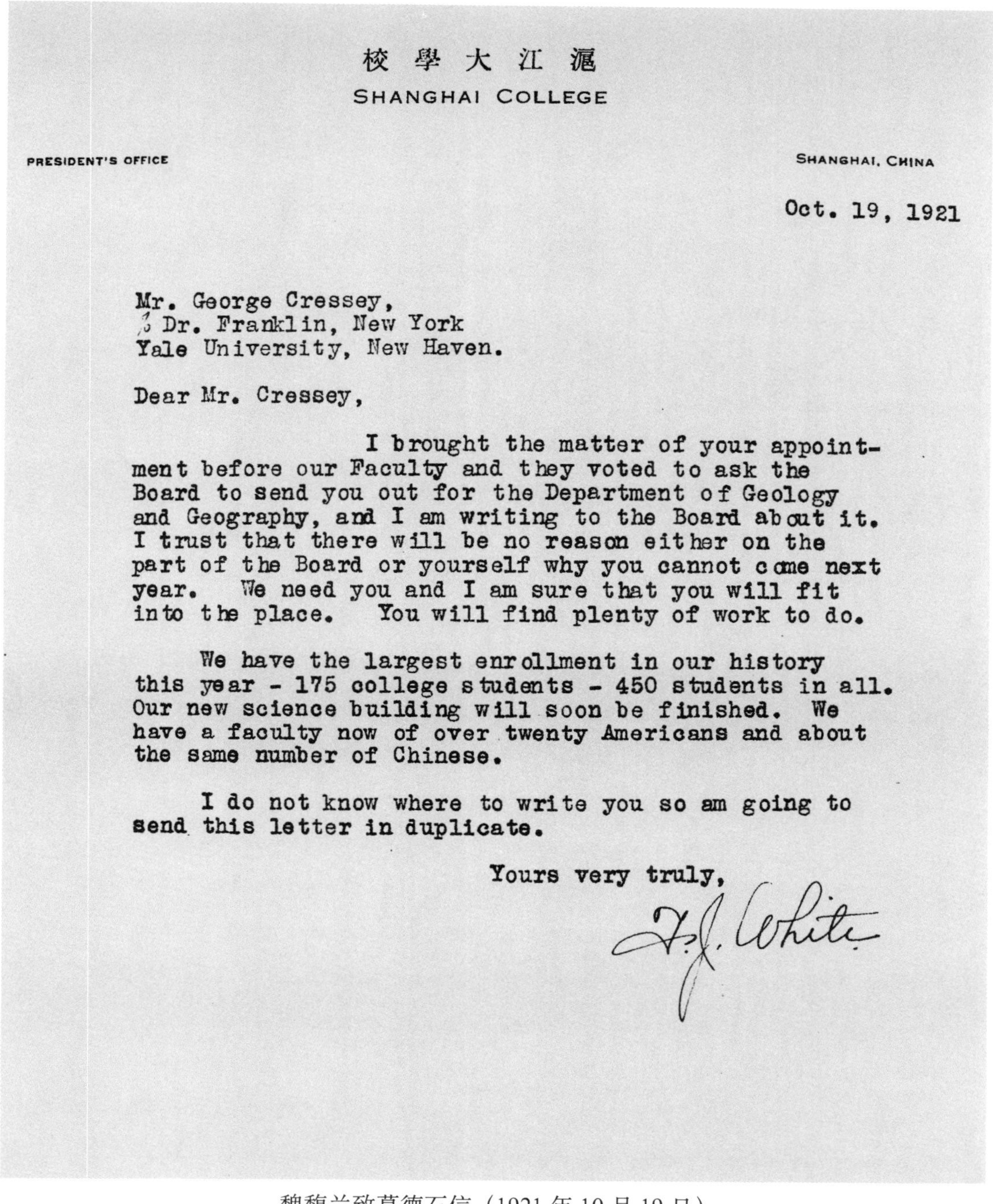

校學大江滬
SHANGHAI COLLEGE

PRESIDENT'S OFFICE

SHANGHAI, CHINA

Oct. 19, 1921

Mr. George Cressey,
℅ Dr. Franklin, New York
Yale University, New Haven.

Dear Mr. Cressey,

I brought the matter of your appointment before our Faculty and they voted to ask the Board to send you out for the Department of Geology and Geography, and I am writing to the Board about it. I trust that there will be no reason either on the part of the Board or yourself why you cannot come next year. We need you and I am sure that you will fit into the place. You will find plenty of work to do.

We have the largest enrollment in our history this year - 175 college students - 450 students in all. Our new science building will soon be finished. We have a faculty now of over twenty Americans and about the same number of Chinese.

I do not know where to write you so am going to send this letter in duplicate.

Yours very truly,

F. J. White

魏馥兰致葛德石信（1921年10月19日）

YALE UNIVERSITY
DEPARTMENT OF
GEOLOGICAL SCIENCES

NEW HAVEN, CONNECTICUT

Box 1121 Yale Station
New Haven Connecticut
Dec. 4, 1921

My dear Dr. White,

Both copies of your letter of October 19th have arrived and I am glad to learn of the status of matters at your end of the line. Things have moved rather slowely here until quite recently so that I have been uncertain as to the possibilities of an opening. I have recently had the opportunity of taking luncheon with Dr. Franklin and he has outlined the matter of relative proportion of Northern and Southern members of the Fauulty; I understand that not until after the next meeting of the Board will the question be settled, if then. While I have not committed myself on the matter, nor in fact have had the opportunity to do so, there are a few things which might now be considered.

When I talked with you in Chicago this past Spring I was uncertain as to finishing up the work on the doctorate before going out. Since then I have decided in the affirmative because I feel that without the work which it entails there will be a bar to the finest sort of work. I am fortunate enough to hold a Dana fellowship here but I shall probably be going back to Chicago next fall to finish up. This will mean 1923 before I will be able to come out, and only then if all goes well! You mention the fact that you would want me to cover both Geology and Geography, which is entirely to my liking. I feel that the two are closely related but it is only fair to say that my major is along the lines of the former. Geology is itself so broad and diverse a field that one finds three years short enough to master

葛德石致魏馥兰信（1921年12月4日）

the technique in even one division. I have had numerous courses in Geography and am now carrying on some research under Dr. Ellsworth Huntington; my interest lies in the field of relationships and influence rather then statistics.

I take it that in setting up a Department of Geology and Geography you have in mind nothing short of the very best so far as circumstances will allow. I do not know what equipment and facilities you have in mind but I am sure that you realize their need in constructive work. Such matters as books, maps, and laboratory equipment may well wait until they are directly needed but there are a few things which should be lookied after in the near future. Much valuable material of general value appears in the state and national geological survey bulletins and these are generally available free of charge or in the case of state documents for the postage. The supply for free distribution is limited and if nothing was done for a year or so, considerable expense would be entailed. Again, much of value may be obtained here at Yale and also in Chicago in the way of duplicate books and equipment for a very nominal sum. I mentioned the matter of slides in our conversation and while I have been too busy to tackle it so far, there are large collections of negatives here and if the materials are available, I shall doubtless be able to make up a number of value. The point is just this. Should the Trustees and the Board act favorably upon my appointment, an advance appropriation can be used to decided advantage. As I understand that the Board meets about the tenth of January and the Trustees before then, this is merely a preliminary suggestion on my part which may be taken up in more detail in the case of favorable action.

Rewritten
plus: research
viewpoint
send catalogue
present equipment

December 12, 1926

My dear President White,

In connection with our conversation of Nov. 29th and at your request, I should like to give you the following memorandum. I have delayed putting it together in order that I might go over the various points in detail. As I explained to you at the time, I am intensely interested in our doing a thoroughly first class piece of work. I trust that after reading over these notes you will not put me altogether in the class with Rodney Gilbert for as I have said on many occasions I marvel at the growth which the College has made. If I were not interested I would not criticise.

May I call your attention to the fact that I have seen eight of the other Christian colleges and visited a very considerable part of real China, as much perhaps as most members of the faculty. What I may say has thus a certain background of observation extending over three years and a half. While this does not give the fullest perspective, the recency of my own academic life in America preserves certain ideals which all too easilly become lost out here.

In our conversation it was not my desire to raise the question of personalities and your doing so, as you will recall, was only over my protest. It is a very real problem, perhaps the most fundamental of all, but since we

葛德石致魏馥兰信（1926 年 12 月 12 日）

- 3 -

flourishing Science Club when inspiration is absent from the classroom and investigation does not feature in the laboratory.

A very unfortunate situation arises from the peculiar relation of Physics, Chemistry and Biology to the College. Elsewhere the Business Manager is in charge of the upkeep of buildings, purchase of supplies, etc. Since these departments each have budgets running into the thousands of dollars, the college has taken advantage of these funds and turned over administration of the building to the several departments, each of which is a little kingdom. Altho the College has dropped supervision of the building, noone has assumed it. As a result the place is very dirty, countless minor repairs go unattended to, and there seems to be no pride in the general appearence of things. With the three janitors as at present the place should look like a palace. I may say frankly that the spirit of the Science Group is most unfortunate, and there is little desire to do anything along this line. Perhaps the Faculty Council should redefine the place of the Science Group in detail.

I take it that the place of Science in our general program is thoroughly agreed upon. We are interested in it for itself, and also for the contribution which it can make philosophically to our Christian purpose and for its emphasis on precision and exactthought. Each of these factors are greatly needed by our students. At present our teaching is mediocre and this contribution largely wanting.

- 5 -

would likewise suggest the consideration of a general survey course without laboratory but with extensive lecture demonstrations for those not majoring in Science. If we are not actually sending students to the P. U. M. C., why sacrifice the whole Science work to that cause. Other subjects are in my mind, but I have already written enough to indicate the exceedingly unfortunate state of affairs. Except for perfunctory recitations and routine laboratory exercises, the major Science departments are almost non-existant.

II. Geology

The Department of Geology and Geography has grown during the past three years from nothing to one of the best in the country. In my annual reports you have had a statement of the material development, and you doubtless know of the work which is being done both in and outside the regular classes. In my reply to your letters of 1921 suggesting that I come to the College, I stated that in coming to Shanghai I was interested in building up the best department possible and nothing less so far as facilities permitted. With this year we are in a position to begin serious work.

Quite naturally I am a strong believer in both Geology and Geography. May I ask seriously, however, why Shanghai College should have such a department? I presume that very few American colleges of 400 have a full-time instructor

- 7 -

may arise in 1929 when I return to America, altho less serious because of the subordinate place of geology. In view of all that I have said above, this may not be the place to raise the question of a second person in geology and geography. In a normal situation, however, I would suggest the advisability of adding a part time instructor next year, perhaps some student who could grow into the work, to serve full time in 1928-9 and during my absence. Such a person might handle a course in the Academy too.

III. The College

The function of Shanghai College as I personally would like to see it is that of a Christian college of liberal arts and sciences doing work of the highest scholarship and culture for a carefully chosen group of serious students. A report of the Harvard Student Council presented this year expresses just about my idea.

> "College education is not simply a matter of attending classes and getting satisfactory grades. The purpose of the college should be to educate cultured men and women who shall be prepared in all the qualities of mind and character and personality to assume positions of active helpful leadership in the world"

This implies that classroom work is only half of a college education, and emphasizes culture as apart from mere knowledge. The college must be concerned not alone with the curriculem but with developing social contacts and leadership. I thus refer to a quality proposition where numbers are secondary.

for our largest tasks. I am not in favor with a "church school". The situation with regard to the Southern Board is a constant irritant. It is true that I have no personal complaint about such matters as creed or evolution, but we have only recently lost Dr. Webster and the agitation is wearing as you best know. In talking with outsiders about the College, one is forced to keep apologizing for the position of the Southern Board. I doubt if we have much of a future if matters continue as they are now.

- - - - - - - - - - -

Having said all this, may I assure you of my sincere interest in the College, and my desire that I may contribute toward making it such an institution as I have described.

Sincerely yours,

George B. Cressey

刘湛恩

刘湛恩（Herman C.E. Liu，1896–1938），出身湖北农家，美国哥伦比亚大学教育学博士，1928 年出任沪江大学首位华人校长。1938 年被日军暗杀于上海，震惊中外。葛德石与刘湛恩的通信现存十四封，主要是关于葛德石在沪江大学地质地理系的续聘问题。

January 26, 1928

My dear President Liu:

I am writing to acknowledge your letters of the 14th and 18th. Mrs. Cressey and I are both deeply grateful for the action of the Executive Committee in inviting us to return to the college for another period of service. We have greatly appreciated the opportunities of these past six years and have found many happy relationships on the campus.

The question of our return to China, however, is quite uncertain. I should thud not want to put myself in the position of making any particular requests of the Board. As matters stand I do not feel that I am able to accept the invitation without more specific statements with regard to our relationships to the college and the future place of the department. I shall be glad if you will bring this letter to the attention of the Executive Committee.

Sincerely yours,

George B. Cressey

President H. C. E. Liu,
Shanghai College.

葛德石致刘湛恩信（1928 年 1 月 26 日）

校學大江滬
SHANGHAI COLLEGE

PRESIDENT'S OFFICE

SHANGHAI, CHINA

March 3, 1928.

My dear Dr. Cressey:

In accordance with your request, I have presented your letter of February 21st to the Board of Directors at their meeting on February 25th. The Resolution adopted by the Board was as follows:

> "In reply to Dr. Cressey's letter, we feel strongly that he should remain in the institution and we urge him to withdraw his resignation."

Now I am taking the liberty of returning your letter of resignation. Let me assure you again of the full confidence of the Board and myself in you and Mrs. Cressey. It is my sincere hope that you will withdraw your resignation and decide to stay with the College permanently. Whenever I can be of any service to you or your Department, please do not hesitate to let me know.

Trusting that you have had a very pleasant visit to Nanking, and with warmest personal regards to your family and your good self, I am

Yours very cordially,

Herman C. E. Liu, President.

Dr. Geo. B. Cressey,
Shanghai College,
Shanghai.

HCEL/D

刘湛恩致葛德石信（1928 年 3 月 3 日）

March 17, 1928

Dear Dr. Liu;

The following information is in response to your request of the 15th.

1.

With regard to the courses to be offered next year I am unable to give this information until the question of the two appropriations from the Institute of Pacific Relations is settled. These projects have been approved by the China Council and Honolulu, and must now go to the Foundations in New York.

The courses which I should like to see the department offer if we can get the right man in geography are as follows. Courses now given are underlined, courses to be possibly omitted next year are in parentheses.

	Geography	Geology
Freshman	101 World Activities	--
	102 Geographic Influences	--
Sophomore	--	101 Physical
	--	102 Historical
Junior	103 China	103 (Petrology)
Senior	104 Rest of Asia	104 (Economic)
	105-106 Subject undetermined	105-106 Principles

2.

Research projects recently completed are as follows:

The Climate of Eastern Asia during the Glacial Period.
The Geology of Shanghai.
The Geography of China.

Research projects still in progress:

Glaciation in Asia during the Pleistocene.
The habitability of central Asia during the time of man's evolution.
The origin and climatic meaning of the loess
sub-project The loess of the Nanking Hills.
Other geologic and geographic problems in Manchuria and Mongolia.

葛德石致刘湛恩信（1928年3月17日）

- 2 -

Research projects proposed for next year:

Field studies in the Ordos and Alashan deserts of Inner Mongolia during June, July and August, dealing with desert processes, climatic changes, geographic influences, and agricultural possibilities.

The preparation of a new base map of China, compiled de novo from original sources. This will form the base for about two dozen maps dealing with climate, topography, agriculture, population and human use. To be published as an atlas of Comparative Geography by the Commercial Press.

Completion of a book on the geography of China, involving studies of natural resources, conditions of life, and regional geography. In cooperation with the Institute of Pacific Relations.

Cooperation with the University of Nanking in an extensive field investigation of Land Utilization.

3. The extension service of the department consists of lectures both on the campus and elsewhere. More than twenty will be given during the present year. It is proposed to continue this next year. As much writing will be done as secretarial assistance may make possible.

4. Requested budget for the coming year.

Present appropriation This includes heat, light, janitor service and upkeep, as well as scientific equipment, operating expenses and travel for visiting speakers.	$ 650.00
Instructor Returned student at $150. per month The Institute of Pacific Relations will probably pay the college $1320, so that the college will need to add $480. This person will teach part time and do research under my direction.	1800.00
Total budget requested	$ 2450.00

Sincerely yours,

George B. Cressey

August 17, 1928

Dear President Liu:

The following memorandum is in reply to your letter concerning the Five Year Policy. I am interpreting this as a statement of the scope and organization of the Department of Geology and Geography as I should like to see it in the near future.

1# Position There should be a recognition of the unique place of geology and geography in Shanghai College. Although normally minor subjects they are offered so rarely in China that if the college desires to mantain a department at all it should be willing to place it fully on a par with the other science work.

2. Staff There should be an Instructor in addition to the head. This additional person should be a returned student with special training in geography. The teaching load should be adjusted to provide time for travel, research, writing and extension.

3. Teaching The emphasis in the elementary courses should continue to be broadly cultural and inspirational. Laboratory work should be added for its training in exactness. As political conditions become more stable, the department should train students for teaching and professional positions.

4. Research There should be official recognition of the opportunity and obligation to contribute to the knowledge of the earth sciences in China. The department should have as one of its definite tasks the discovery and dissemination of information.

5. Finances There should be provision either within the budget or from special funds for travel. Both geology and geography are essentially field subjects, and it is unfair to expect necessary field work to be financed personally.

6. Equipment Our present equipment is one of the best in the country, but needs to be strengthened as regards library facilities, demonstration material, and laboratory equipment. This is particularly true for geography.

7. Relationships Despite several helpful readjustments during the past year by the Dean, the department is still imperfectly adjusted to the registration requirements of the five

葛德石致刘湛恩信（1928 年 8 月 17 日）

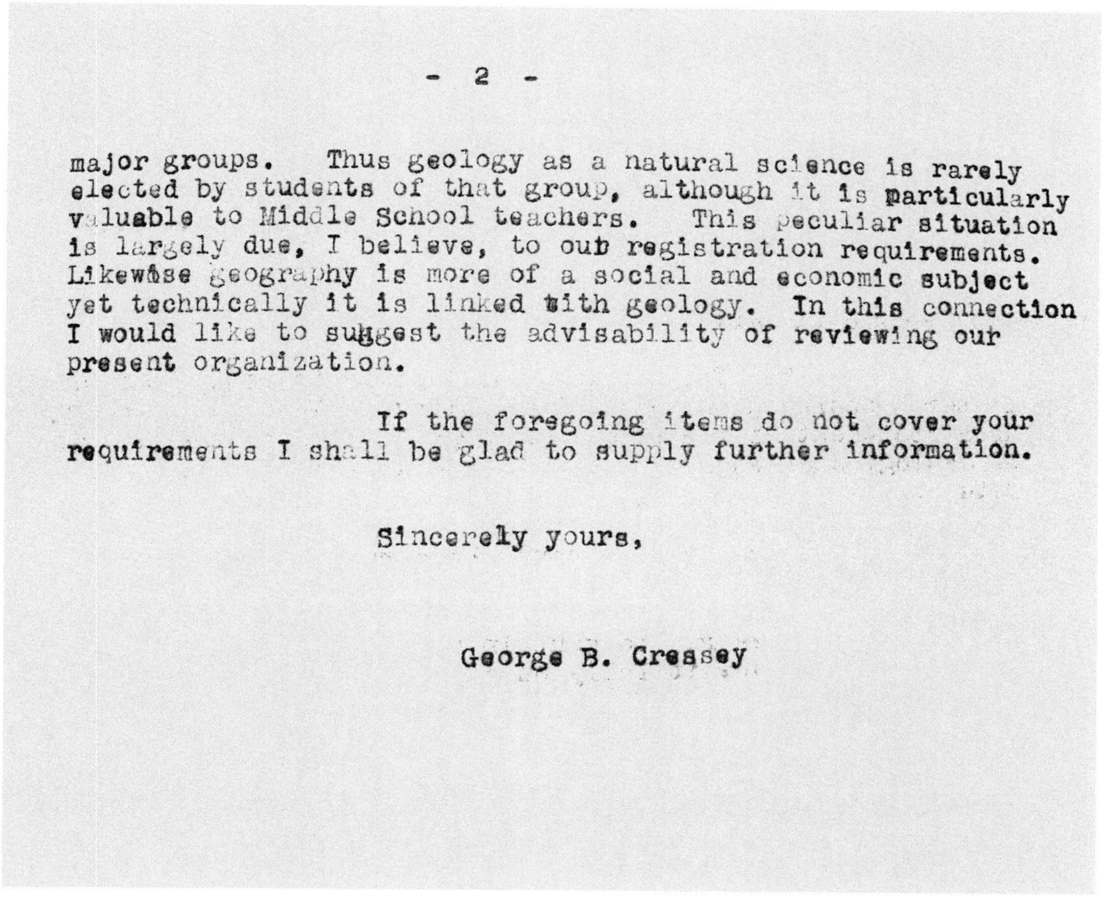

- 2 -

major groups. Thus geology as a natural science is rarely elected by students of that group, although it is particularly valuable to Middle School teachers. This peculiar situation is largely due, I believe, to oub registration requirements. Likewase geography is more of a social and economic subject yet technically it is linked tith geology. In this connection I would like to suggest the advisability of reviewing our present organization.

If the foregoing items do not cover your requirements I shall be glad to supply further information.

Sincerely yours,

George B. Cressey

滬江大學校

SHANGHAI COLLEGE

PRESIDENT'S OFFICE

SHANGHAI, CHINA

January
18 1929

Dr. G. B. Cressey,
Campus.

My dear Dr. Cressey :

A circular vote by the members of the Executive Committee unanimously requests you and Mrs. Cressey to return after furlough to continue work in the Department of Geology and Geography.

I have just received your letter dated this morning. Will you please come to see me at your earliest convenience and talk the matter over?

Yours very cordially,

Herman C.E. Liu,
President.

/Tu

刘湛恩致葛德石信（1929 年 1 月 18 日）

March 27, 1929

My dear President Liu:

I am just sending you a note to wish you "Bon voyage" and to hope that you have a pleasant and profitable visit on the other side of the world. I am sure that you will find a very sympathetic audience both in the Boards and from people in general.

You have been in America quite as recently as I have so that I could not attempt, even if I desired, to interpret America's attitude toward China. My impression, however, is that frank statements of the present situation will be well received.

I am particularly sorry that we have not been able to have more time to discuss the place of the department and our own relationships to the College. I think that my annual report and our earlier correspondence covered the essential points, and I may merely add again that it is not primarily a question of finances. I believe that Mr, Hanson has told you of our conversations on this point, and I am sorry that nothing has been taken up either by the Board of Directors or the Senate. I do not feel that I should want to go ahead on any programme without a complete understanding and full approval of one, or both, of these bodies.

I have already written my parents that you will be passing through Granville, and they have written that they will be very glad to have you stay with them while there. My father's address is:- Dr.F.G. Cressey, Granville, Ohio.

Again wishing you a pleasant voyage and a safe return to Shanghai.

Sincerely yours,

George B. Cressey.

GBC:IN

葛德石致刘湛恩信（1929 年 3 月 27 日）

滬江大學校

SHANGHAI COLLEGE

PRESIDENT'S OFFICE

SHANGHAI, CHINA

March
28 1929

Dr. George B. Cressey,
Campus.

Dear Dr. Cressey:

Just a line concerning your proposition to try to secure funds for the development of your Department. I should like to see you, and talk this matter over, but since that is impossible at this time, because of lack of time, this note will constitute our "official approval," if such you wish to call it.

You may feel that Shanghai College will support you in any efforts you may make to secure additional funds, and to develop your department on a basis that would justify the asking for funds. We shall plan to arrange your teaching hours, during your next term with us, in such a way that you can do the traveling necessary for the development of your department, and make the necessary arrangements as to assistant, etc, if funds and circumstances permit.

I wish you the best of luck in this undertaking. I hope that you will have a splendid furlough, and that you will return to us refreshed, and full of new ideas.

Cordially yours,

Herman C. E. Liu
President

/AR

刘湛恩致葛德石信（1929 年 3 月 28 日）

滬江大學校

SHANGHAI COLLEGE

PRESIDENT'S OFFICE

SHANGHAI, CHINA

September 23, 1929

Dr. George B. Cressey,
Granville, Ohio, U.S.A.

Dear Dr. Cressey:

I have just returned from Europe, via Suez. The Sino-Russian situation has tied up the railroads so that it was impossible for me to return via Siberia, as I had planned. I had a very pleasant time in America and Europe. However, I regret that I could not be here to wish you Godspeed and a pleasant voyage when you left last Summer. I trust that you are having a very pleasant furlough, and that you are getting a good rest. We certainly appreciated having you with us, during the past few years, and we hope you will return, after your furlough period.

Things are going quite well at the College. We have opened with the largest enrollment that we have ever had. There are 503 registered in the College, 388 in the Middle School, 66 in the Kindergarted and Elementary School, and over 600 in the Social Center Schools. While the spirit is fine, and chapel attendance good, we had a Retreat yesterday to discuss ways of making the religious atmosphere even better. We are hoping that this may be a very successful year.

Again assuring you of my appreciation of your services, with kindest personal regards to Mrs. Cressey and your good self, I am,

Cordially yours,

Herman C. E. Liu
President

HCEL:AR

刘湛恩致葛德石信（1929 年 9 月 23 日）

9 Scholary Terrace,
Newton Centre, Mass.
October 24, 1929

President H. C. E. Liu,
Shanghai College,
Shanghai, China

My dear President Liu:

Mrs. Cressey and I were very glad to receive your letter of September 23rd with its news of the opening of the college and the large registration. You may be sure that the campus has been very much in our thoughts, for the years on the campus have made it a very real home to us both.

We are now settled in Newton Centre which is a suburb of Boston, and I am going in to Harvard daily where I have a faculty appointment as Research Associate. Harvard has splendid library facilities and it is very pleasant to work in such a stimulating atmosphere. I am finishing up the last couple of chapters of The Geography of China and expect to do quite a little writing during the winter. I have heard nothing from the Commercial Press since we left Shanghai, but expect to be receiving the proof any day. They seem to be rather slow. In addition to my work at Harvard I am planning on some work in geography at Clark University in Worcester. We are both enjoying the United States tremenduously, but at the same time our hearts are in China. You know we hope to die in Peking!

We have been so busy visiting relatives and getting settled that we are only now begining to think of the future and of the problems which relate to our return to the college. I presume that all in our position find it difficult to make the desision for there are many factors involved. Some of our difficulties are personal and others relate to the place of foreigners in China in general. You will recall that before you left we talked over quite a number of matters relating to the organized place of the department in the curriculum, its standing and size, my own research interests, and the ever present problem of finanses. I still have a very real question as to the wisdom of a department such as mine in a college the size of Shanghai, especially if we are to remain out of the federated university. You know ~~also of o~~

葛德石致刘湛恩信（1929 年 10 月 24 日）

President H. C. E. Liu -2- October 24, 1929

also of our housing experiences; I wonder whether you are able to make us any specific offer in this line?

I hope very much that you will be able to write me definitely on these matters in the near future, including if possible some definite statement by the Administrative Council or the Board of Directors. I am not attempting to outline the questions involved in this letter for I have covered them in detail before, neither do I in any sense want to seek an issue or drive a bargain. I am sure that we will find it difficult to reach our decision, and it will help greatly if we may have some specific statements as to what we may look forward to at the college. Since I hope to reach a decision during the first semester, there will scarcely be time for any correspondence. In any case I shall wait until there is time for your reply to reach us. What the final outcome will be I can scarcely predict, for we are trying to keep a very open mind, but in all frankness I must remind you of what I said while you were in Shanghai, namely that our return is not entirely certain.

With kindest regards to all on the campus, and with best wishes for a splendid year

Sincerely yours,

George B. Cressey

滬江大學
SHANGHAI COLLEGE

PRESIDENT'S OFFICE

SHANGHAI, CHINA

November 21, 1929

Dr. George B. Cressey,
5 Ripley Terrace,
Newton Centre, Mass., U.S.A.

Dear Dr. Cressey:

It gives me great pleasure to inform you that at its meeting on November 2nd the Board of Directors of Shanghai College promoted you from the rank of Assistant Professor to that of Professor. This is done in accordance with the ranking system recently adopted, and to show our appreciation of your good services.

With kindest personal regards, I am,

Cordially yours,

Herman C. E. Liu
President

HCEL:AR

刘湛恩致葛德石信（1929 年 11 月 21 日）

5 Ripley Terrace
Newton Centre, Mass.
January 6, 1930

President H. C. E. Liu,
Shanghai College,
Shanghai, China

My dear Mr. President:

It is with sincere regret that I am writing this letter to present to you, and through you to the Board of Directors, my resignation as Professor of Geology and Geography. These past six years have been a source of genuine satisfaction to Mrs. Cressey and myself, and our decision has been a difficult one to make.

In now closing my official connections with the college I should like to make especial mention of my appreciation of the assistance which has made it possible to build up the department from practically nothing at the begining to its present status which compares favorably with that of any college in China. In view of the distinctive reputation which Shanghai College has established in the field of the earth sciences, I trust that the Board of Directors will take steps to continue and strengthen the standing of the department.

With best wishes for the future of the college, I am

Sincerely yours,

George B. Cressey

Copy to
Dr. J. H. Franklin
Mr. L. C. Hylburt

葛德石致刘湛恩信（1930 年 1 月 4 日）

滬江大學校

SHANGHAI COLLEGE

PRESIDENT'S OFFICE

SHANGHAI, CHINA

February 20, 1930

Dr. George B. Cressey,
5 Ripley Terrace,
Newton Centre, Mass., U.S.A.

Dear Dr. Cressey:

On behalf of the Board of Directors, the faculty, and the student body, we deeply regret that we must accept your resignation. We do not like to consider it as a resignation, but shall consider it as a leave of absence. We hope that you will come back to China and find it possible to return to Shanghai College.

We greatly appreciate the valuable contribution that you have made to Shanghai College in building up the Department of Geology and Geography, and your academic interest and relation to the faculty. We feel that you have made a great contribution to China. Your book will be a permanent contribution.

With kindest personal regards, I am,

Cordially yours,

Herman C. E. Liu
President

HCEL:AR

刘湛恩致葛德石信（1930 年 2 月 20 日）

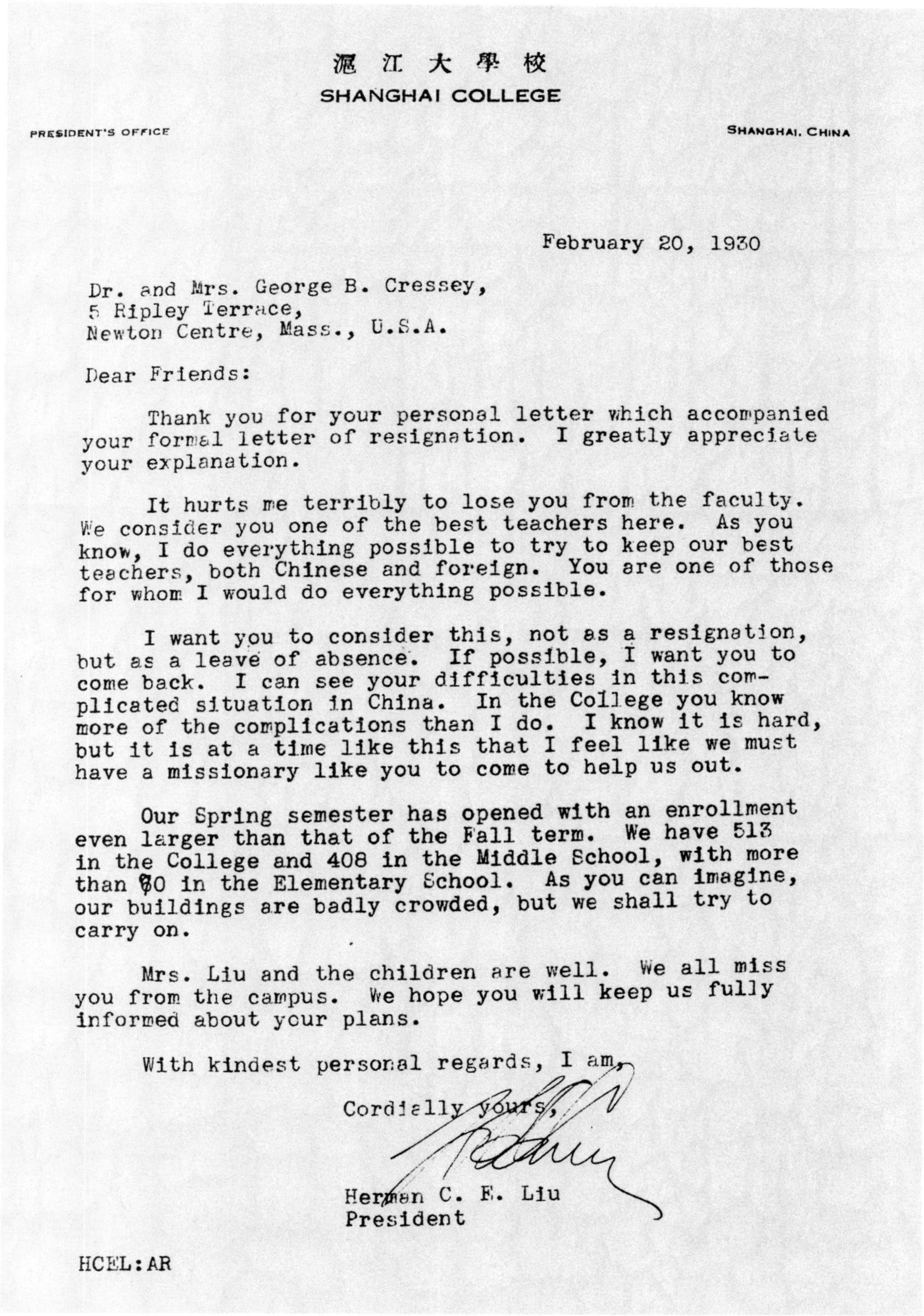

滬江大學校
SHANGHAI COLLEGE

PRESIDENT'S OFFICE

SHANGHAI, CHINA

February 20, 1930

Dr. and Mrs. George B. Cressey,
5 Ripley Terrace,
Newton Centre, Mass., U.S.A.

Dear Friends:

Thank you for your personal letter which accompanied your formal letter of resignation. I greatly appreciate your explanation.

It hurts me terribly to lose you from the faculty. We consider you one of the best teachers here. As you know, I do everything possible to try to keep our best teachers, both Chinese and foreign. You are one of those for whom I would do everything possible.

I want you to consider this, not as a resignation, but as a leave of absence. If possible, I want you to come back. I can see your difficulties in this complicated situation in China. In the College you know more of the complications than I do. I know it is hard, but it is at a time like this that I feel like we must have a missionary like you to come to help us out.

Our Spring semester has opened with an enrollment even larger than that of the Fall term. We have 513 in the College and 408 in the Middle School, with more than 80 in the Elementary School. As you can imagine, our buildings are badly crowded, but we shall try to carry on.

Mrs. Liu and the children are well. We all miss you from the campus. We hope you will keep us fully informed about your plans.

With kindest personal regards, I am,

Cordially yours,

Herman C. E. Liu
President

HCEL:AR

刘湛恩致葛德石信（1930 年 2 月 20 日）

President Herman C. E. Liu, M.A., Ph.D.

SHANGHAI COLLEGE

HISTORY. Shanghai College was founded in 1906 by the American Baptist Foreign Mission Society and the Foreign Mission Board of the Southern Baptist Convention. It was first known as Shanghai Baptist College and Seminary. Dr. R. T. Bryan was the first President of the Theological Seminary, and the late Dr. J. T. Proctor was the first President of the College. After the College and the Seminary had been combined, Dr. F. J White was elected President. Under his careful guidance the institution enjoyed a phenomenal growth. Almost the youngest of the Christian colleges in China, it is among the foremost in faculty, student body, and equipment. In 1928

1

附《沪江大学宣传册》刘湛恩照

滬江大學校

SHANGHAI COLLEGE

PRESIDENT'S OFFICE SHANGHAI, CHINA

February 28, 1931

Dr. George B. Cressey,
School of Geography,
Clark University,
Worcester, Mass., U.S.A.

Dear Dr. Cressey:

Your kind letter of January 9th reached me in due time. I am indeed very sorry that the Commercial Press has not been able to publish your book, "The Geography of China," as soon as we expected. I have taken up this matter with the highest authority of the Commercial Press. They all assure me that they will do their utmost to put it out before the meeting of the Institute of Pacific Relations next Fall. They just sent me a copy of the letter which they wrote to you, dated February 24th. I am enclosing it herewith.

If I can be of any further assistance, please do not hesitate to let me know.

Everything is going on well in the College. The Spring term has opened with our usual large enrollment. We are especially happy to welcome back Mr. and Mrs. Gordon Poteat.

With kindest personal regards, I am,

Cordially yours,

Herman C. E. Liu
President

HCEL:AR

刘湛恩致葛德石信（1931 年 2 月 28 日）

SHANGHAI COLLEGE

Shanghai

September 20, 1926.

To whom it may concern;

This is not a patent medicine ad nor an appeal for money. Neither is it a chain letter. Despite all apprearences it is supposed to be a personal answer to your letter of x months ago. Hence kindly read on. I have always had a low estimate of the fellow who writes to all his friends in wholsale lots, but now here I am. My pile of unanswered letters continues to mount, and without recourse I am driven to this circularizing method. Know ye all, however, that I now propose to revert to my one-time faithfullness in letter writing. Like Monkey Ward, all letters will be answered promptly, satisfaction guaranteed or your postage (five cents, please!) refunded. Try once more and be convinced.

To business. My teaching in Shanghai College continues to provide the wherewithall for three a day. I have four courses a semester totalling eleven hours, and nearly a hundred students sit under my inspiring tuitilage. The geology department is in our fine science building and occupies seven rooms on the top floor. Much of my time the past two years has been taken up with organization and in getting out lectures. From now on I shall be doing more research. All of our work is in English, altho I do jabber a bit of this language if necessary.

The college has just opened with 400 students, mostly men, and there are also 250 in the High School. Shanghai is a great cosmopolitan city of over two million and is now the second port in the world in tonnage cleared. Nearly 4000 Americans live here and one sometimes forgets that he is in China. Movies, traffic cops, more Buicks than Fords, and six daily newspapers in English give quite a foreign touch. Shanghai College has fifty acres along the river just below the harbor and it is a great sight to see the ships of the world going past our door.

Most of you know that I have been doing quite a bit of travelling around this corner of the world. When I first came out to China by way of Europe I came across the Gobi Desert from Siberia, the next summer I got into Tibet and saw some more of Mongolia, and last summer I - rather "we"- honeymooned in Shansi up in the northwest. This season I wanted to do more work out in Inner Mongolia, but it was impossible to get there on account of the fighting. Instead I decided to make a geological study of the Lwan River which flows down from the Mongolian tableland to the sea north of Tientsin. All went well until the night of July 13th (not a Friday) when I was suddenly attacked by a gang of half a dozen brigands. I had a Colt but it was all too sudden to do anything. These brethren were looking for guns and money, but in the process they treated me to a pretty [illegible] ing-up.

附葛德石致沪江大学全校公开信（1926 年 9 月 20 日）

- 2 -

What they didn't steal they broke so that my losses ran to over a thousand dollars (relief checks should have ten cents added for exchange!). That finished this summer in a hurry, but I am all set for another season. Fortunately they didn't carry me off for ransom.

Such is the life of a geological adventurer on this side of the Pacific. For those of you who are rock hounds (that, dear reader, is our term for the gentle geologist) I am working on climatic changes in eastern Asia during and since the ice age. Next month I am expecting to go to Japan to give a paper on said subject at the Pan-Pacific Scientific Congress. Sedimentation and structural problems are other lines on which I have research under way.

China these days is going thru one of the periodic break ups which have characterized the transition from one dynasty to another for forty centuries. It will doubtless be several tens of years before civil peace and prosperity are fully restored. The calmness of the average citizen in the face of the political anarchy and chaos is very difficult for us from the West to understand. There is no active public opinion. At present the central government in Peking is a farce, and the country is broken up into half a dozen groups of provinces under the control of rival militarists. No real issues are involved and the names of the various generals are of no moment. Feng's armies have been chased into the desert west of Peking by Chang, but are intact and will come back some day. Wu is just now being defeated around Hankow on the Yangtze by an expedition from Canton under another Chang. Most of the million and a half soldiers are untrained coolies, but in some of the battles there are aeroplanes, hand grenades, machine guns, and bloody warfare. Much of it, tho, is only talk and treachery. The service of supply is exceedingly weak, and most armies merely live off the country. Woe to the farmer who has available grain or mules for there is no law or justice against the soldiers.

Beneath all the warfare which is ruining the people thru taxation and brigandage, is a more fundamental readjustment. This is especially noticeable in Shanghai where large modern factories and the impact of the West is producing a hybred civilization. In the interior the old family system is intact, but along the railroads and rivers there is a great social upheaval. Generalization is futile and what the product will be no one knows. It will certainly require generations before real democracy and enlightenment as we understand it becomd a fact. But then, how can we from new America say what old China should adopt in government or culture or religion! It is most interesting to see a nation in process of evolution.

With the rush for modern education, a host of pseudo-universities have sprung up where one receives a degree for a short attendance and suitable fee. Much of the widely advertised political activities of the Chinese student may be charged up to institutions of this kind. As a group the student class is full of enthusiastic, ignorant, selfish nationalism and yet lacks the courage to face the great internal problems of the country. Imperialism may be a fact, but one cannot help feeling that China's problems are largely internal.

- 3 -

We have had no student trouble here at Shanghai College during the past year, and expect none. Our people do faithful serious work, but you never can tell. I find on comparion that these students put in more time on their lessons than students in America, but they fall down in reasoning power. Many of them are fine fellows who will be able to make a large contribution to China. I feel that our work out here is thus distinctly worth-while.

What more do you want to know? It looks now as the we shall be coming to the U. S. A. about 1929. That is pretty long to wait to ask your questions, so you'd better obey that impulse NOW. Marion (the wife, you know) joins me in due regards to all. Take what you are entitled to and pass the rest on. I shall be prepared for a flood of letters on the next boat. Come early and avoid the rush.

Sincerely yours,

George B. Cressey

SHANGHAI COLLEGE
SHANGHAI, CHINA

上海滬江大學

DEPARTMENT OF GEOLOGY
GEORGE B. CRESSEY

February 21, 1928

The Board of Directors,
Shanghai College,
Shanghai,

Gentlemen:

I herewith present my resignation as Assistant Professor of Geology in Shanghai College effective June 30th, 1928.

Mrs. Cressey and I have been in China for five years and feel that it is now time that we should return to the United States. We greatly appreciate the privilege of our association with the college but believe that the institution should be made increasingly Chinese.

I am already in correspondence with a well qualified Chinese student of geography who is now in America, Mr. Huang Kuo-Chamg, and if the Board so desires he could doubtless be secured for the department.

With best wishes for the development of the college, I am

Sincerely yours,

George B. Cressey

George B. Cressey

附葛德石致沪江大学董事会信（1928 年 2 月 21 日）

第五章
葛德石其他与中国相关的信件

1935 年，葛德石结束中国考察返回美国，根据他在中国半年的所见所闻，上书总统罗斯福陈述对美国东亚政策的意见。葛德石认为美国在东亚的政策，特别是白银买入政策，在中国产生了严重后果，损害了美国的良好声誉和市场。葛德石建议美国不要冀望以这种方式来解决大萧条问题，相反，美国应该尽一切努力与东亚保持经济和政治上的相互理解，最大限度地避免冲突。

1954 年 2 月，葛德石再次以一个从事了三十年中国研究的地理学家身份上书总统艾森豪威尔，对中美关系提出三点建议，建议尽快承认北京政权。3 月，美国国务院助理国务卿给葛德石回信，申述美国政府的立场：美国毫无选择地制裁中国的共产党政权，限制他们与自由世界的贸易，在政治上孤立他们，葛德石对此立场无可奈何。

March 19, 1935

The Honorable Franklin D. Roosevelt
The White House
Washington, D. C.

My dear Mr. President:

I am deeply concerned with the increase of international tension, especially in the Far East. I particularly regret the action of this country in holding provocative naval maneuvers in the mid-Pacific at this time; together with our silver buying policy which is having such serious internal consequences in China and endangering our good will as well as market in that country. The effect of this latter policy may be to drive China into the financial arms of Japan and thus strengthen the country against whom we presumably seek to prepare in our naval operations.

I have recently returned from the Orient in connection with work for the National Research Council and have thus been able to view the effects of our actions as they appear from Asia. I regard both naval operations and the silver policy as dangerously imperiling our attitude of the good neighbor.

War must be averted at all costs. If some measure of our present economic ills are due to the World War, further conflict will but intensify them. I see no necessity for conflict with the Orient but I am deeply concerned over the possibility that we may inadvertently turn in that direction as a way out of our momentary financial dilemma. The depression creates a despair where the apparent prosperity of war times may seem an easy solution.

I would urge that the United States make every effort to insure harmonious understanding, economic and political, in order to avert any likelihood of war, and that we give testimony of our pacific sincerity by avoiding inflammatory gestures. We are particularly fitted to take the lead in creating good will around the Pacific.

Specifically, I express the hope: (1) that the naval maneuvers will not extend beyond the longitude of Hawaii and Unalaska (Dutch Harbor), (2) that we demonstrate our neighborliness to China by a revised silver policy or other economic assistance, and (3) that we withdraw completely from the Philippines within a decade and disavow all military aspirations west of Hawaii, including any support of the open door policy by armed force except by united international action.

葛德石致罗斯福总统信（1935 年 3 月 19 日）

February 15, 1954

Dear Mr. President:

I should like to comment on our China relations. I write as a geographer who has devoted three decades to Asiatic problems.

1. I see no prospect that the Nationalist government can return to the mainland; we must therefore live with Communist China for many years. Our best long range strategy is to separate Peking and Moscow, hoping later to modify policies within China. This means building up Peking economically so that it becomes less dependent on Moscow. I regard this separation as a desirable and feasible goal.

2. I strongly oppose recognition of Peking at the moment, but we may be wise to do so a year or more hence. Recognition should not imply approval, any more than we approve of Moscow or Madrid. I dislike all totalitarian states, but it is impossible to dictate their internal operations. Quite obviously, we should extend no recognition unless the Peking government will reciprocate, and will conform to minimum diplomatic courtesies and treaty provisions. For political reasons this recognition may need to wait until after our own elections. As a feasible beginning, we might first permit Japan to expand her trade with China, and later gradually enlarge our own direct trade with the Chinese mainland. We should next agree not to use our own veto in China's possible admission to the United Nations, and finally extend formal recognition. American public opinion must be educated along these lines.

3. The most difficult problem concerns Taiwan. The island holds a great number of refugees, many of them American trained, who would be liquidated if Taiwan were turned over to the Communists. No solution is possible so long as Taipei and Peking both claim to speak for all China. Could the United Nations guarantee neutralization, or would the respective governments accept the status quo as the price of dual recognition, pending a plebiscite a decade hence? Here is a major task for diplomacy; everything else waits on its solution. //While we continue to support Chiang Kai-shek, we must make it clear that readjustments must follow./

Sincerely yours,

George B. Cressey

President Dwight Eisenhower
The White House
Washington, D. C.

gbc:mep

葛德石致艾森豪威尔总统信（1954 年 2 月 15 日）

ADDRESS OFFICIAL COMMUNICATIONS TO
THE SECRETARY OF STATE
WASHINGTON 25, D. C.

DEPARTMENT OF STATE
WASHINGTON

March 12 1954

Dear Dr. Cressey:

The President has referred to me your letter of February 15th, of which you were thoughtful enough to send me a copy, outlining your views on U.S. policy with respect to China. I assure you that those views will receive from all of us in the Department of State concerned with Chinese affairs the full consideration they deserve on the basis of your long and distinguished career in the field of Asian studies.

I am sure I am speaking for the Administration, however, as well as putting forth my own strong convictions, when I take exception to the conclusions you have reached. On two scores it seems to me that we have no choice but to continue maintaining present sanctions against the Chinese Communist regime and, to the full extent consistent with our other responsibilities, to stimulate the maximum international support for those sanctions. These sanctions include restrictions on Communist China's commerce with the free world, the denial to the Communists of Formosa, political isolation of Communist China, and recognition of the Republic of China in Formosa as the rightful government of China and as the only Chinese government entitled to represent China in the United Nations.

The reasons, as I say, seem to me to be of two kinds. On the one side there is the character of the regime. Its record, both domestically and internationally, could hardly be worse. It has, with full intent, by direct or indirect means, caused the death of millions of Chinese. It has invaded every sphere of Chinese life in fastening its tyranny and its alien-inspired ideology, physically and morally, upon Chinese society. At the same time, it has invaded and tried to take over the whole of Korea and is now apparently engaged in incorporating North Korea into the Chinese territories it controls. It is heavily supplying the Vietminh in Indochina and is giving guidance and doubtless other forms of assistance to Communist organizations seeking the overthrow of the legitimate governments of the other Southeast Asian states. I cannot think what we would stand to gain by seeking to come to terms with such a regime in any way that could be interpreted as our condoning its actions. That any relaxation of our opposition to the Chinese Communist regime would be so interpreted and would

persuade

Dr. George B. Cressey
Maxwell Professor of Geography
Syracuse University
Syracuse 10, New York

美国国务院回葛德石信（1954 年 3 月 12 日）

- 2 -

persuade the Chinese Communist regime itself that its course of conduct was proving profitable, I have little doubt.

On the second score, a relaxation of the embargo on strategic shipments to Communist China, or any relaxation of controls on other commodities that would strengthen the economic base of China's military potential, would augment the capability of that regime to intimidate or successfully attack its neighbors. Any move on our part toward recognition of the regime or toward accepting it as a power with a legitimate voice in the affairs of the international community, would inevitably enhance its prestige. Owing to the bonds of ideology and common interest between them, we do not see any possibility of a divergence between the Soviet Union and Communist China while the latter is under its present leadership. Any gains we might help Communist China make while that partnership is in existence would unquestionably be regarded by it as demonstrating the value of that partnership. We feel that our policy of forcing Communist China to look to the Soviet Union for help which the Soviet Union is ill equipped to provide offers the most promising means of subjecting the relationship between them to strain. If the relationship is such that it cannot be strained to any effect, we may still expect the policies we are following to confine to a minimum Communist China's ability to do mischief. Accordingly, from either point of view, these policies would appear to be the correct ones.

Another factor that enters into our reasoning is the situation of the Chinese minorities, numbering some ten million, in Southeast Asia. To the extent that these minorities regard themselves as primarily Chinese, they will be oriented either to Taipei or to Peiping. The latter has, by promises and threats, been actively engaged in trying to bring them to heel. We consider it of great importance that the National Government continue to serve as a focal point of Chinese loyalties and as the representative - recognized as such by a majority of the nations of the world - of Chinese nationality. We believe it has deserved the increasing support it is receiving from the overseas Chinese.

I cannot help believing that if those opposing our present policy toward China were subjected, as we are daily in the Department of State, to the spectacle of the Peiping regime's calculated cruelty to the Chinese people and to the nationals of our own country and of other countries, and to the arrogance of that regime and its unremitting excoriation of everything we stand for, they would come to agree with us that for the United States to take a less firm line toward the Chinese Communists would merely move them to contempt.

Sincerely yours,

Walter S. Robertson

Walter S. Robertson
Assistant Secretary

总统办公室回信

March 17, 1954

Dear Mr. Robertson:

I am indeed indebted to you for your thoughtful letter of March 16 replying to my own letter of February 15 addressed to the President.

I am sure that we are in full agreement as to the inhuman character of the present Communist regime in China and elsewhere. I hold no brief for any totalitarian governments, either of the left or of the right. I obviously agree with you that recognition under the present conditions would be most unwise. My letter to the President, however, looked forward to a time when international tensions might be eased and considered the possibility that the People's Republic of China, like the Communist governments of Yugoslavia and the Soviet Union, might be willing to enter into minimum diplomatic relations. If there is a reasonable possibility that this situation might develop, we should be prepared for it. I wish that we might change the internal operations of many foreign governments, but this is obviously inappropriate for a democratic democracy. In other words, the time may well come within a few years when the international activities of the Peking government are such that we should appropriately exchange recognition.

I approach the problem from two points of view--my concern that we do not abandon the many friends of democracy on Taiwan and, second, that we endeavor to separate Peking from Moscow. The latter I regard as a desirable and feasible operation. The realistic problem in all this is that while competent students may reach wise decisions, we must at the same time carry public opinion with us. It is unfortunate that this is currently so volatile.

Sincerely yours,

George B. Cressey

Mr. Walter Robertson
Department of State
Washington, D. C.

gbc:mep

葛德石致美国国务院信（1954 年 3 月 17 日）